THE LAST VETERAN

Also by Peter Parker

THE LAST VETERAN
Harry Patch and the Legacy of War

———∞∞∞———

PETER PARKER

FOURTH ESTATE · *London*

First published in Great Britain in 2009 by
Fourth Estate
An imprint of HarperCollins*Publishers*
77–85 Fulham Palace Road
London W6 8JB
www.4thestate.co.uk

Visit our authors' blog: www.fifthestate.co.uk

3

A catalogue record for this book is available from the British Library

ISBN 978-0-00-726550-3

Typeset in Adobe Garamond by Birdy Book Design

Printed in Great Britain by Clays Ltd, St Ives plc

For
my godson
Julius Lunn

– next generation –

CONTENTS

Armistice
1918

Breathless they paused. Out there men raised their glance
To where had stood those poplars lank and lopped,
As they had raised it through the four years' dance
Of Death in the now familiar flats of France;
And murmured, 'Strange, this! How? All firing stopped?'

THOMAS HARDY, 'And There Was a Great Calm'

News that the Great War for Civilisation had finally come to an end was greeted by noisy rejoicing on the streets of London and other cities around the world, but what struck most people on the battlefields of France and Belgium was the silence. At 11 a.m. on Monday, 11 November 1918, after four and a quarter years in which howitzers boomed, shells screamed, machine guns rattled, rifles cracked, and the cries of the wounded and dying echoed in no man's land, everything suddenly fell quiet. Across parts of Belgium a thick fog had descended that morning, with visibility down to ten yards. In the muffled landscape the stillness seemed almost palpable. Since for most soldiers news of the approaching armistice did not reach them until an hour or less before it was implemented, it is extraordinary that the guns really did fall silent at exactly the planned time. In one part of the line near Le Cateau a German machine gun was firing at the British troops in the opposite trench until the very last minute. 'At precisely eleven o'clock an officer stepped out of their position, stood up, lifted his helmet and bowed to the British troops. He then fell in all his men in the front of the trench and marched them off.'

Of those who survived, Air Mechanic Henry Allingham of the Royal Air Force was still in Belgium on the morning of 11 November. Ninety years later he recalled that his fellow servicemen 'grabbed hold of anything that would make a lot of noise – to celebrate, you see. They let off stray shells, Very lights and whatnot. A lot of men, some who'd been right through the war, didn't make it through the night.' Others merely got very drunk, while Allingham himself went to bed and enjoyed the unaccustomed luxury of a good night's sleep. The revelling of his fellows took its toll and the following morning few of the ranks were ready to move out at 8 a.m. as planned. It was therefore not until three hours later that they began their long route march through Belgium to Cologne, where the defeated German people surprised Allingham by their friendliness. They may have lost the war, but they were presumably as relieved as the victors that it had finally ended. It was 'a cheerless, dismal, cold misty day' in the Forêt de Mormal on the Franco-Belgian border, Gunner B.O. Stokes of the New Zealand Field Artillery recalled. 'There was no cheering or demonstration. We were all tired in body and mind, fresh from the tragic fields of battle, and this momentous announcement was too vast in its consequences to be appreciated or accepted with wild excitement. We trekked out of the wood on this dreary day in silence.' Captain Guy Chapman of the Royal Fusiliers had a similar experience, marching back through the fog to Béthencourt: 'The band played but there was very little singing,' he recalled in his war memoir, *A Passionate Prodigality*. 'We took over our billets and listlessly devoured a meal. In an effort to cure our apathy, the little American doctor from Vermont who had joined us a fortnight earlier broke his invincible teetotalism, drank half a bottle of whisky, and danced a cachucha. We looked at his antics with dull eyes and at last put him to bed.'

Others were rather more ebullient. Gunner G. Worsley of the Royal Field Artillery received the news of the Armistice while serving in France and remembered doing a cartwheel when a trumpeter sounded the ceasefire. He visited the house of a local woman who was inclined to think the war should continue until Berlin was taken. When Worsley complained that this might result in him getting killed, the woman replied, 'Sanfairyann' (the British soldiers' approximation of the French expression *ça ne fait rien* – that doesn't matter). 'Sanfairyann be buggered!' Worsley retorted. '*I'm alive*. The war's over. That's good enough for me!' It was not merely French civilians who thought that the end may have come rather too soon. Even some British troops, embittered by their experience and worried that the ceasefire might prove only temporary, felt that the war should carry on 'until Germany's armies are really beaten in the field, her line broken and if possible her country invaded'. Private Albert Marshall recalled that when an officer told soldiers in the Essex Yeomanry advancing on Lille that there was to be an armistice, 'You never heard so much grumbling and swearing in all your life, because we'd got them on the run.

We wanted to drive them back to Berlin.' Percy Wilson, who had been told by a recruiting officer that the war would be over by Christmas 1914, was still in uniform in November 1918, serving close to the German border. When an officer announced that the Armistice was to be signed, several soldiers were annoyed that they would not be allowed, as they saw it, to finish the job. 'I don't *want* a bloody armistice,' one soldier complained; instead he 'wanted to get over that border [and] show them what the war's been like'. Eighty-six years later, the 105-year-old Wilson still believed that had the soldiers been allowed to pursue the Germans back over the border there would have been no Second World War: 'They would absolutely have pounded the Germans to bits.' There were similar reactions among some airmen. 'I confess to a feeling of anticlimax, even to a momentary sense of regret,' Cecil Lewis recalled in *Sagittarius Rising*, his classic memoir of life with the Royal Flying Corps. 'We were a new squadron, fresh overseas, we wanted – particularly the new pilots – to justify our existence, to carry out in action the thing we had been training for.'

Not everyone who wanted to celebrate could always find the means to do so. Lewis was in a small and remote village just north of the Ypres Salient in Belgium when news of the Armistice reached him: 'There was nothing to drink in the whole village and nowhere to go to. All we could find was a dump of Hun Very Lights, of all colours, left behind in their retreat. This pyrotechnical display was all we could contribute to the gaiety of Armistice night.' At the RFC aerodrome in France, recalled Sergeant Charles Watson of 11 Squadron, a celebratory bonfire got out of hand when people began throwing full cans of aviation fuel on to it: 'They went up with such a bang that troops nearby thought the war had started again.'

Elsewhere even worse behaviour prevailed. Private Eric Hiscock, a boy soldier who at the age of seventy-six published a resonantly titled survivor's memoir, *The Bells of Hell Go Ting-a-Ling-a-Ling*, recalled drunken Australian soldiers going on the rampage in the red-light district of Boulogne, demanding that the local prostitutes should give their services free by way of celebration. At sea, meanwhile, there were no women with whom to celebrate, and sailors had to improvise. An order to splice the mainbrace was issued aboard HMS *Revenge*, remembered a former Royal Naval Seaman, 106-year-old Claude Choules, in 2005, and everyone received an extra tot of rum. The ship's company was invited by the officers to join them in a celebratory dance on the quarterdeck, which they did to the accompaniment of the ship's band.

Some of those who had been at the front were back in Britain when the Armistice was declared. Two of the war's best-known poets, Robert Graves and Siegfried Sassoon, saw the Armistice being celebrated there. Graves was stationed near Rhyl with an Officer Cadet Battalion. 'Things were very quiet up here on the 11th,' he told his fellow poet Robert Nichols. 'London was full of buck of course but in North Wales a foreign war or a victory more or less are not considered much. Little boys banged biscuit tins and a Very light or two went up at the camp but for the rest not much. A perfunctory thanksgiving service with nothing more cheerful in it than a Last Post for the dead; and then grouses about demobilization.' In his celebrated memoir *Goodbye to All That*, however, Graves records: 'The news sent me out walking alone along the dyke above the marshes of Rhuddlan (an ancient battlefield, the Flodden of Wales), cursing and sobbing and thinking of the dead.' Sassoon, meanwhile, was in Oxfordshire on indefinite sick leave after being wounded in the head in July. 'I was walking in the water-meadows by the river below Cuddesdon this morning – a quiet grey day,' he wrote in his diary. 'A jolly peal of bells was ringing from the village church, and the villagers were hanging little flags out of the windows of their thatched houses. The war is ended. It is impossible to realise.' That evening he travelled to London, where he was unimpressed by the capital's 'buck': 'masses of people in streets and congested Tubes, all waving flags and making fools of themselves – an outburst of mob patriotism. It was a wretched wet night, and very mild. It is a loathsome ending to the loathsome tragedy of the last four years.'

Other soldiers may have been in Blighty for the Armistice, but they were still on active duty. Private Harry Patch of the 7th Duke of Cornwall's Light Infantry was on an exercise on the Isle of Wight. He had been invalided home in September 1917 with wounds incurred when a shell had exploded above his Lewis-gun team in Belgium. He had spent ten months convalescing, but was eventually passed A1 and placed on a draft to return to the front. Rumours that a ceasefire might be declared had reached Golden Hill Fort, the hexagonal Victorian barracks at Freshwater in which Patch and his fellow soldiers were billeted, on the morning of 11 November. They were practising on a rifle range that day and had been told that if an armistice was signed a rocket would be sent up. When this happened everyone cheered and the officer in charge ordered them to get rid of their spare ammunition by firing out to sea so they wouldn't have to carry it back to the stores. For Patch, the Armistice meant he would not have to return to Belgium as planned, and eighty-eight years later he remembered his feelings of joy and relief.

Some felt that the ceasefire had not come soon enough. Twenty-one-year-old Lieutenant Norman Collins of the Seaforth Highlanders, who had been twice wounded, was on leave when the Armistice was announced. 'I was up a bit late that morning, I was shaving, and the sirens went. My first feeling was "It's too late – all my friends are gone – it's too late. It's no use having an Armistice now."' For others the ceasefire really was too late. One of the most famous stories about the end of the war describes a telegram delivered to a house in Shrewsbury at noon on 11 November. With the church bells 'still ringing, the bands playing and the jubilant crowds surging together', the family of the poet Wilfred Owen learned that he had been killed in action on 4 November. Even the morning of 11 November itself was not without its casualties, including Private George Edwin Ellison of the 5th Royal Irish Lancers, who is thought to be the last British soldier to be killed in action in the war. Evidence that the fighting went on up until the very last moment is provided by a plaque on the wall of a house at 71 rue de Mons in Ville-sur-Haine, where a hapless Canadian soldier, Private George Lawrence Price of the 28th Northwest Infantry, was shot dead by a sniper on 11 November at 10.58 a.m.

For most of those left alive at the front, a desolate landscape in which once bustling towns and villages had been reduced to piles of smoking rubble and acre upon acre of woodland reduced to splintered and blackened stumps, there was little enough cause for rejoicing. The longed-for day had finally arrived but the majority of combatants were too physically exhausted and emotionally depleted to enjoy it. Most of them simply felt relief that the war was finally over. In the great silence, men were able to reflect on what they had been through and remember the comrades they had lost. After years crouching in the front line, it was hard to imagine that snipers were no longer training their rifles on your trench. 'You were so dazed you just didn't realize that you could stand up straight and not be shot,' one soldier remembered in the 1960s. 'My first thought was "So I'm going to live",' another recalled almost three-quarters of a century after the Armistice. 'I was stunned, total disbelief, and at the same time a secret and selfish joy that I was going to have a life.' Others simply felt lost. The war had swallowed them up and occupied their every waking moment as it was to haunt their dreams in the future: it was hard to imagine what life would be like now that it was over. Some had joined up or been conscripted so young that they could remember no other kind of adult life. 'Straightaway we felt we had nothing to live for,' Sapper Arthur Halestrap of the Royal Engineers recalled. 'There was nothing in front of us, no objective. Everything you had been working for, for years, had suddenly disappeared. What am I going to do next? What is my future?'

Halestrap's future stretched farther ahead than he could possibly have imagined that November morning. Eighty-five years later to the day he would lead a service of remembrance at the Menin Gate at Ypres, rising from his wheelchair to recite lines from Laurence Binyon's poem 'For the Fallen':

> They shall grow not old, as we that are left grow old:
> Age shall not weary them, nor the years condemn.
> At the going down of the sun and in the morning
> We will remember them.

First published in *The Times* on 21 September 1914, and intoned at countless Armistice Day services since, Binyon's lines have become almost too familiar, but were given a new immediacy when spoken by a 105-year-old who by November 2003 was one of a handful of men still alive to have served in what, with good reason, is still sometimes called the Great War. Given the appallingly high casualty rates, few of those who fought on the Western Front had any realistic expectations of growing old or being wearied by age. Some who survived, however, attained very great ages indeed, achieving the rare distinction of having lived in three centuries.

Born on 8 September 1898, Arthur Halestrap could remember his parents receiving letters from relatives serving in the Boer War. He also remembered the death of Queen Victoria and the coronation of Edward VII. His father worked in Southampton for the White Star shipping line, and as a boy Halestrap had walked on the decks of the *Titanic* while it was in dock there. He had tried to enlist two months after the outbreak of war on 4 August 1914, but at the age of sixteen was rejected as too young. He worked instead as a post office telegraphist, excellent training for someone who in September 1916 finally joined up as a signaller with the Royal Engineers.

It was not until January 1918 that Halestrap got to France, and his first experience of being shelled occurred when he was part of a convoy marching up to Brigade HQ in the dark. The horses that were pulling the wagon he was accompanying got stuck in the mud and panicked as the shells started falling, but to his surprise Halestrap did not really experience fear. His months of training had instilled in him a rigid discipline that ensured he got on with the job in hand whatever the circumstances, and he managed to get the wagon moving again across a landscape illuminated by Very lights and shell-bursts. He subsequently took part in the attack in which the British successfully breached the supposedly impregnable Hindenburg Line in September 1918. His job was to set up transmitter-receivers, which meant carrying cumbersome equipment up the line, then going over the top in order to erect radio masts in places that would not attract enemy fire. Although he was not always in the front line, he spent enough time in the trenches to become accustomed to lice, keeping his head down to avoid snipers, advancing under shellfire, and muttering apologies when obliged to walk across the battlefields' litter of dead bodies.

In sum, his experiences, which may strike us today as extraordinary, were little different from those of millions of combatants. What made Halestrap unusual was that he was still alive to recall them all those years later. Like many combatants, he had survived a number of close encounters with the enemy. While he and a group of soldiers were taking pot shots at a low-flying German observation plane, the pilot responded in kind with a revolver. One bullet slammed into the table beside which Halestrap was standing, missing him by an inch. On another occasion a shell hit an old brewery where Halestrap and his fellow signallers had set up a radio station. Fortunately they had barricaded the windows with sandbags and were protected from the blast. Even when the Armistice had been declared, Halestrap, still in France, managed to outwit death. He caught Spanish flu, a global pandemic that between 1918 and 1919 killed more people than the war did: in Britain alone some 250,000 died. When Halestrap first showed symptoms, a senior officer reckoned that there would be little chance of him surviving the long and gruelling journey to a medical station and so decided to fill him up with rum, wrap him in a blanket and let him take his chances. Halestrap could remember nothing between being given the rum and waking up three days later apparently restored to health. In later years he made some thirty pilgrimages to the battlefields and cemeteries of France and Belgium in order to pay his respects to those who were less fortunate in their close encounters with death. He outlived both his wife and his two children and eventually died in his sleep, aged 105, on 1 April 2004.

Unusual as Halestrap's story is, it is far from unique. Most of those whose experience of the Armistice I have described lived on into their nineties and beyond, becoming a select band who could recall for much later generations a war that scarred a century. The year Halestrap led the ceremony at the Menin Gate, it was reckoned that he was one of twenty-seven surviving British veterans of the First World War, the youngest of whom was 103. Thereafter the numbers steadily dwindled. Thirteen men (including Halestrap) and two women were interviewed for a two-part BBC television documentary, *The Last Tommy*, but seven of them had died by the time the programme was broadcast in 2005. A year later, the official count stood at nine, not all of whom had seen active service. Numbers were continually being readjusted – and not always downwards. There have been occasional discoveries of 'new' veterans, who had not previously identified themselves – though in Britain, apart from a man whose claim could not be verified because crucial documents were missing, none of these had seen action. Unlike their great-grandchildren's generation, for many of whom celebrity at any price has become a major ambition, these veterans did not want fame or court publicity. They understood, however, that people were bound to be interested in them and they remained gracious when calls were made on their rapidly dwindling time and energy. Most of them were perfectly ordinary people who after the war continued to lead perfectly ordinary lives until longevity forced them into the limelight.

As increasing attention was drawn to this small group of men and women, it became clear that eventually it would soon diminish until only one member was left: the Last Veteran. To be the last of anything is an achievement of sorts, but on the whole it is a melancholy and potentially lonely one, as much about extinction as survival. It makes us think of the threatened species with whom we share the planet, as the writer J.R. Ackerley did in 1964. Ackerley suggested a parallel between a death in the animal kingdom and the death of a generation:

> In 1914 a tragedy occurred, so shocking, so awe-inspiring, so poignant and so irreparable that if all mankind had put on sackcloth and ashes it would scarcely have seemed an adequate expression of their shame and repentance. Doubtless the First World War springs to your self-important minds. Let it spring off again. [...] It was the death of a pigeon. She was female, and she died of old age on September 1, 1914, at one o'clock in the afternoon.

This solitary bird was in fact a passenger pigeon called Martha, living in Cincinnati Zoo, and the last of her once abundant species. One of the final great hunts of the passenger pigeon, which was killed for its meat, took place over five months with a casualty rate of some 50,000 every day. No wonder Ackerley saw a parallel between this mass slaughter and what had happened on the Western Front – particularly since he was writing in 1964 when the fiftieth anniversary of the outbreak of the war was being widely marked. He had himself been wounded in action on the Somme on 1 July 1916 and therefore became one of the 60,000 casualties suffered by the British that terrible day.

The chances were always that the Last Veteran would in some ways be no more distinctive of his kind than Martha was of hers. After leading a life for the most part no different from that of many of his contemporaries, he would nevertheless achieve the signal distinction of being the last Briton to have fought in the Great War. The significance of this did not escape politicians, and there were suggestions that this man, whoever he might turn out to be, should be given a state funeral. This was put before the House of Commons by a former leader of the Conservative Party, Iain Duncan Smith, on 18 April 2006. The idea had been around for some time before this, and Duncan Smith had been prompted to propose it formally after being approached by one of his constituents. Duncan Smith had wondered whether such an event might be considered invidious since there were still many people alive who had fought just as bravely and honourably in the Second World War. The constituent immediately replied that 'the first world war was different, and that everyone who fought in the second world war recognised that. There was something peculiar about the conditions and nature of that conflict.' Duncan Smith went on to outline what it was about the First World War that set it apart from other conflicts: the huge casualty figures (one million dead and two million wounded in the British Empire alone); the fact that the bodies of almost half those killed on the Western Front were never found; the appalling conditions in the trenches. Duncan Smith also quoted two examples from the 'flood of letters' he had received on this subject, both from nine-year-old schoolgirls who supported the idea of a state funeral. He concluded:

> A society that forgets its past and is embarrassed about remembering the sacrifice of those who have gone before is one that loses its past and, with that, loses its future. As those young people I referred to were able to remind me and many of my colleagues, there is something special about pausing to remember. We are not dwelling on or glorifying war, but remembering the sacrifice of those whose sole responsibility was to aid and abet their colleagues and to protect and defend the society in which they lived, and which nurtured them.

A short debate followed in which Duncan Smith's proposal was broadly welcomed, although everyone agreed that nothing could be done without first ascertaining the wishes of the family of the last veteran to die. If for any reason the family did not want a state funeral, it was suggested, a national service of commemoration should be held instead. Don Touhig, then Parliamentary Under-Secretary of State for Defence, cautioned that however appropriate a state funeral might seem, and whatever popular support there was for it, there might be logistical difficulties in ascertaining who really was the last veteran. More than half the service records of the period had been destroyed during the Blitz, and so reliance was put upon those veterans who had identified themselves. No one was under any obligation to identify themselves and there might be veterans who preferred anonymity or had either by choice or oversight not made themselves known: as recently as March of that year two new French veterans had been 'discovered'. To further complicate matters, Touhig stated that the government's definition of a last veteran was rather more flexible than the generally agreed one. He argued that anyone who had served during the war, and even those who had not finished their training and were still in Britain when the Armistice was declared, should be recognised as veterans. It became clear that some sort of service of commemoration might be a more workable arrangement than a state funeral, and this was what the government eventually decided upon. On 27 June 2006 the Defence Secretary, Des Browne, announced that: 'A National Memorial Service will allow the whole nation to honour the valour and spirit shown by the veterans of WW1 and will commemorate an entire generation.' This would take place in Westminster Abbey within about twelve weeks of the death of 'the last known World War One veteran'. As with Duncan Smith's original proposal, the ceremony would be modelled on the one that took place on 11 November 1920 when Britain's Unknown Warrior was laid to rest in the Abbey 'among the most illustrious of the land'.

A state funeral for the Last Veteran would undoubtedly have provided a neater symmetry than a mere service of commemoration, since it would have marked the end of a prolonged period of national mourning which started with the state funeral of the Unknown Warrior. Not only was the Unknown Warrior, like the Last Veteran, an individual representative of all those who served in the First World War, he was also an individual chosen at random, or at any rate by chance, just as the Last Veteran achieved that status by an accident of longevity.

Ever since the Armistice there have been arguments, not all of them seemly, about how the First World War should be remembered, commemorated and represented. In all this the veterans have played a significant and sometimes controversial role. Veterans were not always seen as remarkable, fêted and honoured because they provided a link with a particularly poignant piece of our history. Over the years they had been treated with a great deal less deference and consideration, had been obliged to fight for their rights, had been involved in later battles in which the weapons were bricks and batons and the enemy was the forces of law and order in their own country. They had been both the centrepiece of our national acts of commemoration, and dismissed as increasingly irrelevant, standing in the way of liturgical reform. Above all, they had remained a constant reminder of a major historical event that in all sorts of ways, not least the psychological, shaped the twentieth century.

In Britain the international catastrophe that was the First World War has been adopted as a peculiarly national trauma, one that has cast its shadow down the years and haunts us still. There have been other wars since 1918, and in all of them combatants have had to endure privation, discomfort, misery, the loss of comrades and appalling injuries. Even so, the First World War continues to exert a hold upon the collective imagination in Britain in a way it does not in, say, the USA. The statistics are, of course, extraordinary. On the First Day of the Somme 20,000 British soldiers were killed, the equal of the entire sum of casualties of the Boer War. The number of British service personnel killed in the Second World War was less than half the number killed in 1914–18. Even when you add in the many more civilian casualties Britain suffered during the Second World War – some 60,000 – the overall number of deaths is still smaller than the dreadful tally of the Great War. Over 30 per cent of British men who were aged between twenty and twenty-four in 1914 were killed in action or died of wounds; of those aged between thirteen and nineteen the figure is more than 28 per cent; some 200,000 women were left widows and 350,000 children left without fathers.

Bad as this was, it was not unique to Britain. France, Germany and Austria each not only lost more combatants than Britain, but also lost a higher proportion of their overall population: France lost 1 in 28, Germany 1 in 35, Austria 1 in 50, Britain 1 in 66, Italy 1 in 79, the USA 1 in 2,000. Furthermore, although the mass slaughter on the Western Front was indisputably awful, for all the talk of 'mechanised killing' it does not compare with the industrialised murder carried out by the Nazis during the Holocaust. It remains a grim statistic that of the six million British who fought in the First World War roughly one in eight were killed, but they were at least killed fighting in defence of their country or for some sort of patriotic principle rather than simply rounded up for liquidation. It is not even a question of numbers. The long lists of names on First World War memorials, many of them from the same family, tell of the losses sustained by individual villages, towns or cities, but none of them speaks so eloquently of communities destroyed as, for example, the interior walls of the Pinkas Synagogue in Prague, where the names of some 80,000 Jewish victims of the Holocaust from Bohemia and Moravia are inscribed, arranged by where they once lived: men, women and children, street after street after street. The bomb that fell on Hiroshima in 1945 eclipsed anything produced by even the greatest bombardment of the trenches, resulting in between 100,000 and 200,000 deaths in an instant.

Regardless of the historical and demographic facts, when remembering the First World War the British continue to talk about a lost generation. There is a sense that as a nation we have never quite recovered from this loss, that the flower of British youth was cut down in Picardy and Flanders, that an irreplaceable wealth of talent and an almost prelapsarian state of innocence were destroyed for ever between the years 1914 and 1918. Cast out of the Edwardian Eden, where it was somehow always perfect summer weather, we have ever after tended to look yearningly back rather than expectantly forward.

The war has become part of who we are. It occupies a disproportionately large place in our sense of the world and its history and remains a seemingly endless resource not only for historians, but for novelists, poets, dramatists and composers, for cinema and television. The sounds and images of the war are so imprinted on the national consciousness that we recognise them instantly: the foreign place names such as Mons, Ypres, Loos, Passchendaele and the Somme, which retain a familiarity even for those who could not point to them on a map; the lines of men at the recruiting offices on 4 August 1914 and the rows of crosses (now replaced by rounded headstones) that marked where those bank-holiday crowds ended up; the scarlet poppies blowing in a landscape rendered unrecognisable by shellfire; the mud and the blood, and the big guns in France that could be heard this side of the Channel. When in 1980 Kenneth Macmillan created a ballet using Poulenc's *Gloria*, all he had to do was place tin helmets on the dancers' heads to make this joyous piece of music into a requiem. Indeed, the war is constantly used – some might say dragged in – as a reference point in the arts: Andrew Davies's television adaptation of *A Room with a View* (2007) dispensed with E.M. Forster's happy ending and had George Emerson killed in the trenches, while Kenneth Branagh's film of Mozart's *The Magic Flute* (2006) sent Tamino off to the Somme. The complex philosophical ideas, with their Masonic elements, that characterise the struggle between Sarastro and the Queen of the Night in *The Magic Flute* could, Branagh felt, be presented to a wider audience if the action was moved to the Western Front. 'By giving each an army and presenting visually the landscape of the First World War, there is a sense of import and scale about the actions of these characters,' he said. 'The Great War provides a territory both literal and metaphoric that is as emotive and complex as the opera itself.'

This territory is a disputed one. Our popular notion of the war – formed largely by what was written about it by those who fought in the front line, and by later artistic reimaginings of it – is that it was indeed uniquely horrible; that it was conducted by an incompetent High Command that repeatedly sacrificed thousands of men in order to gain a few yards of churned earth; that it was characterised by 'mud, blood and futility'. There is, however, another view of the conflict, one argued by such leading military historians as Correlli Barnett, John Terraine, Huw Strachan, Brian Bond, Nigel Cave, Gordon Corrigan, Trevor Wilson and Robin Prior, and supported by a generation of younger so-called 'revisionist' historians such as Gary Sheffield. These historians point out that not all the generals were callous incompetents, nor all rankers hapless and unwilling victims; they insist that some of the battles were brilliantly planned and fought; they remind us that we did after all win the war. They are exasperated by the Anglocentric attitude to the war that prevails in Britain, pointing out not only the war's international dimensions but also the even larger losses sustained by other combatant countries. The British tendency to think of the war only in terms of the Western Front, they argue, gives us a hopelessly skewed impression both of its conduct and of its wider significance. They dismiss the War Poets as unrepresentative, complain about the way the war is taught in schools where literature is given precedence over history, and retain a particular loathing for two of the most enduringly popular representations of the war, the play *Oh What a Lovely War!* and the television tragicomedy *Blackadder Goes Forth*. In short they feel that the British are obsessed with the 'tragedy' of the war and are incapable of seeing the bigger picture. Their view of popular representations of the war can be summed up by the title of Gordon Corrigan's 2003 study: *Mud, Blood and Poppycock*.

The impact of such books on interpreting the war in universities is considerable, and there is no doubt that many of them are meticulously researched and cogently argued. Their impact on the public at large, however, is as yet limited. As Gary Sheffield comments in the introduction to *The Forgotten Victory* (2001), which is one of the best, most approachable and most persuasive of these 'revisionist' histories: 'For the last decade and a half I have sat in academic seminars in which historians have complained about the difficulty of shifting public opinion on these issues. It seems that every time an important new book comes out, another popular book or television programme appears repeating the same old tired myths.' The two sides in this argument have become – to use an appropriate verb – entrenched, and it seems unlikely that either will yield in the foreseeable future.

It is no part of this book's aim to take up this quarrel, but in tracing the way in which the First World War has been remembered and commemorated, and by looking at the way in which the experiences of those who fought in it on the front line have shaped this process, the many corrective 'facts' adduced by military historians are less relevant than what the majority of people in Britain have believed and continue to believe about the war. We do not define ourselves as a people by facts, but by received ideas – ideas that have a symbolic rather than a literal truth. Among the long-cherished ideas that the British have about themselves is that they believe in fair play and favour the underdog, they are phlegmatic and always see the funny side of any given situation, and they are among the most tolerant people in the world. All these notions could be 'disproved' by citing examples of contrary behaviour, but they persist as a generally accepted truth. As far as the war is concerned, we may no longer believe that angels appeared to protect the British at the Battle of Mons in 1914, that a Canadian serviceman was 'crucified' on a barn door near Ypres, or that Germans bayoneted babies and boiled down corpses in order to produce soap, but we still believe – with considerable justification – that the First World War was a great national tragedy and that an entire generation was profligately and unnecessarily sacrificed.

By giving a scholarly overview of campaigns and strategy

military historians can usefully and instructively tell us what the war was about; but what really interests us is what it was *like*. For that we have always turned to those who were there, notably the poets and memoirists, but latterly to those more ordinary people, the diminishing band of living witnesses whose voices had yet to be stilled. As one schoolchild who met 110-year-old Henry Allingham in 2007 remarked: 'The books tell us about the battles but they don't tell you what people who were there thought about them.' The gulf between military history and personal experience was demonstrated by the man who did indeed become Britain's Last Veteran, Harry Patch, when talking about Passchendaele: 'I'm told we attacked on 16 August, but the date doesn't mean much to me. I know it was about six weeks before I was wounded, so I suppose the middle of August is about right. I remember the names – Pilckem Ridge was one and the other was Langemarck – but it is such a long time ago that I can't quite connect them up in my head.' Patch may have forgotten the exact dates and places, but he knew what a battlefield was like – not from the maps that were studied at GHQ, but because in 1917 he was stumbling over one.

For Patch, the First World War was not about military intelligence, the deployment of battalions or the plan of attack. It was about wading around in filth with no opportunity to bathe or change your lice-ridden clothes for the whole four months you were at the front. It was about discomfort and fear and exhaustion and having your best friends quite literally 'blown to pieces'. As the last British Tommy to revisit the battlefields over which he and so many other men had fought ninety years before, Patch commented in 2007:

Some of the boys buried here are the same age as me, killed on the same day I was fighting. Any one of them could have been me. Millions of men came to fight in this war and I find it incredible that I am now the only one left. Just like them, when I went over the top, I didn't know whether I would last longer than five minutes. We were the PBI – the Poor Bloody Infantry – and we were expendable. What a waste. What a terrible waste.

It is the living witness of the men on the front line that we have lost now that the Last Veteran has died.

ONE
The Unknown Warrior
1919–1921

The tomb and the Cenotaph bear witness to the greatest emotion
this nation has ever felt. Children are brought here every year; and
so the memory, without the sharpness, perhaps, felt by us who lived
through it, goes on with another generation. In this way a nation
keeps alive its holy places.

H.V. MORTON, *The Spell of London* (1926)

In the immediate post-war period a number of large, well-
orchestrated public events – culminating in the funeral of the
Unknown Warrior on 11 November 1920 – showed a nation
drawn together in grief. It would be hard not to be moved by the
sense of national unity that these occasions suggested, but they
took place against a background of considerable unrest in Britain.
The country had not only been involved in four long and costly
years of war but had endured numerous social and economic
problems on the home front. Even before the war, the long
Edwardian summer of myth had in reality been disrupted by
serious industrial disputes. To the increasing alarm of employers,

trade unions had grown in power since the beginning of the century and Britain had begun to be dogged by strikes which were largely the result of wages failing to keep pace with inflation. It was not at all clear that the wave of popular patriotism that appeared to overwhelm the country when war was declared would sweep away the widespread differences between employers and workers. A joint meeting between the Labour Party, the Trades Union Congress and the General Federation of Trade Unions was convened towards the end of August 1914 with the intention of urging employers and workers in key industries to pull together for the duration of the war. A great many workers, some of them in industries vital to the war effort, had already abandoned their jobs in order to join up, and serious labour shortages were soon apparent in engineering, munitions and mining. For some people, working and living conditions were such that a spell in the army seemed to offer a lucky escape from poverty and drudgery into a life that provided a secure wage, free food and clothing, and the possibility of adventure overseas.

Those who stayed behind soon realised that their value to the country had increased, and they not unnaturally felt that their working conditions should reflect this. Rumours and even evidence that some manufacturers were making huge profits from war production and not passing anything on to their employees fuelled anger and led to a series of strikes. The first serious one occurred in Glasgow in February 1915 when 5,000 engineers, whose union had been asking for a rise of twopence an hour since the previous June, laid down their tools. The dispute spread until some 10,000 members of the Amalgamated Society of Engineers at eight engineering plants were on strike, but it lasted only a little under three weeks. Dissatisfaction with the settlement of the strike led to the forming of the Clyde Workers' Committee. In particular, the CWC challenged the 1915 Munitions of War Act, which had been passed in order to ensure the uninterrupted production of weapons and ammunition. Although agreed by trade union leaders, the Act was seen by many as an opportunistic erosion of workers' rights, including the right to strike.

Meanwhile a rent strike had also broken out in Glasgow, where landlords had attempted to raise rents and evict tenants who could not or would not pay. Many of the tenants were women whose husbands were at the front and who had entered the workforce, finding employment in munitions factories. The refusal of some 20,000 of them to pay rent gained support among other industrial workers, who threatened to come out on strike in sympathy. In order to prevent the disruption of war production, the government was obliged to introduce new legislation protecting tenants' rights. The government also had to accede to the demands of miners in South Wales who came out on strike in July 1915 in a dispute with mine-owners. There was little else it could do since a prolonged stoppage of coal production would have been disastrous.

Back on Clydeside the 'dilution' of the munitions industry by allowing unskilled men and women to fill the large gaps left by those who had enlisted – by this time about a quarter of the workforce – was causing further unrest. A refusal in March 1916 to allow one of the leaders of the CWC to investigate the conditions under which such people were employed in one factory was seen as an affront to the rights of shop stewards and led to more strikes in 1916. Opposition to the Military Services Act, which introduced conscription at the beginning of March, fuelled additional protests in Glasgow and led to the arrest and imprisonment of several activists under the deeply unpopular and draconian Defence of the Realm Act, which had been passed without debate four days after war was declared in August 1914. The Act restricted trade union activity (strikes and lockouts had been outlawed in the munitions factories), regulated – which is to say decreased – pub opening hours, and generally cracked down on dissent and any other behaviour thought to be unpatriotic or unhelpful to the conduct of the war.

In 1918 even the police went on strike. Prevented by the Crime Act of 1885 from belonging to any sort of union, many police had nevertheless responded to an anonymous letter published in the September 1913 issue of the *Police Review* announcing that just such an organisation was being formed. Throughout the war many policemen secretly became members of the unrecognised and technically illegal National Union of Police and Prison Officers, which was established to address their grievances over pay and conditions. The 1918 strike was triggered by the sacking of a police captain who had been active in this union, which by then claimed to have 10,000 members and was demanding proper recognition. The entire Metropolitan Police Force of London, numbering 12,000 members, went on strike on 30 August, and the Prime Minister, David Lloyd George, while refusing to recognise the NUPPO on the grounds that such an organisation could not be contemplated while the country was at war, nevertheless met with its representatives and agreed to many of their other demands. The union's membership subsequently saw a rapid growth, reaching some 50,000 by the time of the Armistice.

The British people were suffering in their homes as well as in the workplace. German submarine raids caused massive losses among the merchant marine, which meant that there was a lack of imported goods, so food prices soared. Coal rationing was introduced in October 1916, and in December of that year a Food Controller was appointed as part of the newly formed Ministry of Food. People were encouraged to monitor their own consumption, but rumours in 1917 that Britain's food supply was all but exhausted led to panic buying, after which rationing was introduced: sugar in December, followed by butter, meat, jam and tea.

It was one thing to eat less for your country in times of war, but rationing was no more over by Christmas 1918 than the war had been in 1914, and its continuation long after the Armistice caused considerable resentment. Victory may have been greeted with jubilation, but it did little to calm the industrial and social unrest that pervaded the country. A more general imbalance between supply and demand in goods was not much helped by the fact that there was no immediate return to peacetime conditions in factories either. The Munitions of War Act had obliged many manufacturers to adapt their factories for the production of vital armaments, and it would take time to reconvert production lines so that they could return to making the goods they produced before the war. The Defence of the Realm Act remained in place, and the gulf that had opened up during the war between the Western and Home Fronts, fuelled by mutual incomprehension and, on the part of the serving men, a degree of hostility towards those who for whatever reason had not joined up, was not healed by peace. Soldiers at the front had resented the fact that the jobs from which they were absent had been taken over by those who had stayed at home rather than join them on the battlefields. It was not only 'shirkers' who had usurped them in the workplace: women had been absorbed into the overall workforce in huge numbers and, newly emancipated, could hardly be expected to return to hearth and home the minute the war was over – although many of them did.

'The unity of the nation which has been the great secret of our strength in war must not be relaxed if the many anxious problems which the war has bequeathed to us are to be handled with the insight, courage, and promptitude which the times demand,' Lloyd George declared, and he decided to call a general election for 14 December. He felt that a new parliament 'possessed of the authority which a General Election alone can give it' would be needed 'to make the peace of Europe and to deal with the difficult transitional period which will follow the cessation of hostilities'. Just how difficult that transitional period would be soon became apparent.

Often referred to as a 'khaki election' because it took place immediately after a war, the 1918 general election might equally have been dubbed a 'petticoat' one, since it was the first in which women – at any rate, women property-owners over thirty – had the vote. With the massive losses suffered in the war, the women's vote was more significant than its legislators might have envisaged. Given that many of those in khaki were still on active service abroad and that many women were in mourning for a husband, son, father, brother or fiancé, it must have looked like a 'black' election as much as a khaki one at the polling booths. The shadow of the war certainly loomed over the election in Nottingham, where now redundant shell cases were used to make up the shortfall in ballot boxes. It was also the first election in which men who were not property-owners were allowed to vote, but they had to be twenty-one. Many former servicemen like Harry Patch, who was twenty when the election took place, discovered that while they were deemed old enough to be sent off to fight for their country, they were still considered too young to vote. The result of the election was an overwhelming victory for a coalition chiefly composed of Liberal and Conservative members under the renewed premiership of Lloyd George.

It was all very well to win a general election, but Lloyd George now needed to lead the country into a post-war future with all its attendant problems. Making the peace in Europe would prove to be a great deal easier than maintaining it at home. In his Special Order of the Day for 12 November 1918, the Commander-in-Chief General Haig had assured his victorious but exhausted troops that 'Generations of free peoples, both of your own race and of all countries, will thank you for what you have done'. Similarly, the Liberal Party's election manifesto had promised: 'In the field of creative reform at home, social and industrial – our first duty is owed to those who have won us the victory and to the dependants of the fallen. In the priorities of reconstruction they have the first claim, and every facility should be given them not only for reinstatement, and for protection against want and unemployment, but for such training and equipment as will open out for them fresh avenues and new careers.' Unsurprisingly after such promises, those returning to Britain from the battlefields expected to find it the 'fit country for heroes to live in' that Lloyd George's government had pledged.

Getting back to Britain in the first place was often difficult: one of the principal complaints among the armed forces was the slow pace of demobilisation. An end to hostilities did not mean an immediate end to war service, and even soldiers who had been in Britain on 11 November 1918 often had a long and frustrating wait before they returned to Civvy Street. The army had been very quick to recruit soldiers but less swift to let them go. 'It had taken three days to get me into uniform,' Harry Patch recalled, 'but it would be five months before I got out of khaki and out of the army.' The government's decision to give priority to men whose particular skills were required to get the wheels of industry turning once more was particularly unpopular, chiefly because many of these so-called 'key men' had been considered too important to send to France and had been allowed to enlist only when the fighting forces had been seriously depleted. This meant that those who were last in were often first out – a policy that did not find favour among those who had been serving for much longer periods. Guy Chapman remembered the anger caused when the first person from his battalion to be demobbed was a man who had seen only fourteen weeks' service: he was a miner and therefore needed back in England. This demobilisation by individual rather than by battalion was logistically complex and destroyed the sense of group loyalty that had kept men going during the war. Under pressure, the scheme was eventually abandoned, but while in force it led to mass discontent.

The discipline that had carried many of the soldiers through almost unimaginable hardships at the front seemed merely irksome now that the war was over, and it began to break down. On the Isle of Wight Harry Patch's company particularly resented being ordered about on parade and taken for route marches by a peacetime officer who had risen from the ranks. The men finally refused to turn out for this officer, even when he challenged them with a revolver. They subsequently returned to talk to him with loaded weapons, and when he cocked the trigger of his revolver, the men responded by pulling back the bolts of their rifles. 'Now, you shoot, you bugger, if you dare,' one of the men shouted, and the officer very sensibly backed down. A brigadier was sent to Freshwater to sort out what had in effect been a mutiny. He listened to both the officer's account and the men's grievances. One man complained that they had joined up for the duration but were still waiting to be demobilised and return to their jobs three months after hostilities ceased. The brigadier, perhaps fearing that disaffection among the ranks would spread, gave orders that the company be excused parades. Thereafter they only did fatigues – little more than keeping the camp tidy – until they were demobbed. 'We had decided ourselves that we were more or less civilians, and that army rules no longer applied to us,' Patch recalled.

A small mutiny at Golden Hill Fort was easy enough to deal with, but by January 1919 much more worrying instances of military insubordination were occurring elsewhere. Fears of the sort of mass revolt that had occurred in Russia led to a misguided decision to keep British forces hard at it in order to distract them from any revolutionary ideas they might be entertaining now that they no longer had a war to fight and were anxious to leave the army as soon as possible. It was one thing to have demob delayed, quite another to be subjected to increased military discipline without any particular purpose in view.

The worst, most prolonged mutiny took place at Calais in January 1919 and was a direct result of the men's impatience at the slow pace of demobilisation. Private John Pantling of the

Royal Army Ordnance Corps (RAOC) stationed at the Val de Lièvre camp had been arrested and imprisoned for making a seditious speech to his fellow soldiers, some of whom subsequently broke into the jail in which he was being held and helped him escape. The sergeant who was guarding Pantling was then arrested, but released when the mood of the men was felt to be growing ever more dangerous. As on the Isle of Wight, a senior officer listened to the men's grievances and agreed to some concessions and an improvement in conditions, but the subsequent setting up of so-called Soldiers' Councils in the various army camps at Calais smacked too much of Soviet practices for the military authorities, and it was decided that Pantling should be found and rearrested. When he was, not a single one of the 2,000 men at Val de Lièvre answered the reveille. An equal number of men from a neighbouring camp joined the Val de Lièvre contingent in marching on GHQ to demand the release of the troublesome private. This was granted, but by now the mutiny had spread, with some 20,000 men involved. General Byng, a seasoned soldier who had led the Third Army to victory the previous year, was sent to Calais to put an end to the disturbances, but his troops simply joined the mutineers. Eventually a further meeting was organised at which further concessions were granted, and on 31 January the mutiny came to an end.

Such behaviour was not confined to troops still serving abroad, and January 1919 proved a testing time for Lloyd George's coalition government, which – apparently without consulting the army – had promised rapid demobilisation. While General Byng was dealing with the RAOC in Calais, General Trenchard of the RAF had been sent to quell a disturbance at Southampton, where

20,000 soldiers had mutinied and taken over the docks. To his considerable surprise, Trenchard was manhandled by the troops he had come to address and was obliged to summon armed troops from Portsmouth together with a detachment of military police. These men surrounded the unarmed mutineers, who, perhaps aware of Trenchard's reputation for ruthlessness, called off their action.

Mutinies were not simply confined to the army. Five hundred members of Trenchard's RAF stationed in squalid conditions at Biggin Hill in Kent reacted to a particularly disgusting supper one evening by convening a meeting at which 'The Red Flag' was sung and a decision was taken to disobey orders. The following morning, as at Val de Lièvre, reveille was ignored and a deputation was sent to the commanding officer with a long list of demands. The authorities agreed to inspect the camp and capitulated almost at once, sending the men on leave while the whole place was overhauled. Meanwhile, there were small individual mutinies in the navy. The red flag was hoisted on a patrol boat at Milford Haven, while, encouraged by dockers and 'agitators', the crew of a large cruiser at Rosyth refused to sail to Russia. Further mutinies and demonstrations by soldiers awaiting demobilisation took place at Shoreham, Dover, Folkestone, Bristol, Sydenham, Aldershot and at Osterley, where in January 1919 some 1,500 members of the Army Service Corps, who had learned that they would be the last troops to be demobilised, commandeered lorries and drove them to Whitehall, where they obstructed the entrance to the War Office. The following month, finding food and transport entirely inadequate for their needs, 3,000 fully armed soldiers setting off back to France from Victoria Station decided instead to march on Horse Guards Parade. A nervous Winston Churchill, then Secretary of State for War, receiving assurances that he could rely upon the loyalty of a reserve battalion of Grenadiers and two troops of the Household Cavalry, gave orders for the demonstrators to be surrounded and disarmed. Threatened with machine guns and fixed bayonets, the protesters surrendered, and like all the mutinies mentioned, this one ended without bloodshed.

Once demobbed, men still faced problems returning to civilian life. The thousands of servicemen who had been severely wounded in the war had to readjust to a drastically circumscribed world. Over 41,000 of those injured had lost one or more limbs, while a further 272,000 had suffered other sorts of incapacitating wounds. Others, who showed no visible signs of injury, were suffering from shell shock, 'neurasthenia', or other forms of battle trauma which made them unsuited to an immediate return to work: some 65,000 of them were awarded disability pensions. Even those who had emerged from the war able bodied and sound of mind often found themselves out of work. Andrew Bowie, who had served with the 1st Queen's Own Cameron Highlanders and would live to the age of 104, was just twenty-one when the war ended. 'I was happy to get out of the army and to return home,' he recalled, 'but the prospects were very bad.' Before the war he had worked in accountancy, but his small firm could not afford to re-employ him when he was demobbed. 'You go away as a boy and come back as a man. What are you going to do? There were so many people like that. There seemed to be no future for you.'

Luckier veterans, mostly those who had been self-employed or in work as skilled craftsmen, found their jobs still waiting for them – though they were often expected to take a cut in wages. Many of the younger men had been apprentices before the war. This system, which stretched back to the Middle Ages, allowed youths to be taken on by a master craftsman who would teach them a trade in exchange for a guarantee that the apprentice would continue working for a set period after he had become skilled. A small wage would be paid while the apprentice learned his craft and the contract between him and his employer would be recorded in a document called an indenture, which would be cancelled at the end of the set term. Corporal John Oborne of the 4th Dorsetshires had been an apprentice joiner in Bath since the age of fourteen, and when the war started was put to work making boxes for shells and torpedoes while waiting to come of military age. After the war ended he stayed on in the army until the beginning of 1920 in order to save up the £50 he would need to buy a set of tools when he returned to his peacetime profession. His old firm was prepared to take him back to complete his apprenticeship, but the pay offered was less than what he would receive if he stayed in the army. He nevertheless completed his apprenticeship and remained with the firm until he retired in 1975, living on to the age of 104.

Harry Patch, on the other hand, refused to accept the terms offered by his old company, also in Bath. He had served three years of his apprenticeship as a plumber, from the age of fifteen, before being called up, and was expected to complete a further two years, at the same paltry wage of ten shillings a week, when he returned. 'I was effectively being penalised for serving my country,' he said. He was now twenty-one and about to be married and so refused the offer, doing odd jobs and private work instead. The problem for him now was that his old firm would not sign his indentures. He consulted his father's solicitor, who offered the opinion that the war had rendered such contracts invalid. Even if Patch's contract with his employer had not effectively been broken when Patch was called up, it was certainly broken by delayed demobilisation. Those who volunteered or had been conscripted had signed up only 'for the duration': by failing to release Patch from the army as soon as the war was over, the government had broken the contract once more. Patch nevertheless felt, as a matter of pride, that he was entitled to have his indentures signed. After a great deal of wrangling, and after he had accepted a job with another company, his employers eventually agreed. He remained in the plumbing trade for the rest of his working life.

Some veterans had gone to the war straight from school without ever being trained for any sort of job other than fighting, and had no experience of the workplace. Others had spent so long in the services that through lack of practice they had almost forgotten the skills they once had, or had missed out on the technical advances that had been made in their absence. Employers were reluctant to take such men on, and this bred even more resentment among the veterans towards those who had stayed behind and were preferred as employees. It was reckoned that around one million men returned from the war to find they had no job. The government provided those who had served in the ranks with unemployment benefit, but former officers were supposed to have sufficient private means to keep them going and were left to fend for themselves. While still in France awaiting demob, Guy Chapman's battalion was visited by representatives of the commission for the employment of ex-servicemen. Chapman was told that at twenty-eight he was 'far too old' and that consequently nothing could be done for him. A fellow officer was told that 'military distinction was a quite useless recommendation for civil life'. The writer Gilbert Frankau, who had joined up immediately at the outbreak of war and served as an officer at Loos, Ypres and on the Somme, spoke for many in his poem 'Only an Officer':

> Only an officer! Only a chap
> Who carried on till the final scrap,
> Only a fellow who didn't shirk –
> *Homeless, penniless, out of work,*
> Asking only a start in life,
> A job that will keep himself and his wife,
> 'And thank the Lord that we haven't a kid.'
> *Thus men pay for the deeds men did!*

Unemployment among all classes would remain a major problem in the immediate post-war period, and veterans sporting medals reduced to playing barrel-organs in the streets or peddling matches, shoelaces and other small items became a common and shaming sight. A poignant postcard of the period, on which a poem about the sacrifices made in France and the broken promises about employment back home was printed, came with the following message:

PLEASE READ THIS. Can you help this Ex-service Man by buying this Poetry. PRICE TWOPENCE. So please patronise an Ex-Soldier, Out of Work. NO PENSION. NO DOLE. I am a Genuine Discharged Soldier NOT AN IMPOSTER. I am compelled to sell these to keep myself, wife and children.

Sold entirely by unemployed Ex-service men.

Even those in employment were often dissatisfied with wages and working conditions. In Glasgow in January 1919 an agreement negotiated on behalf of engineers and shipbuilders between the trade unions and employers for a forty-seven-hour working week was rejected by the Clyde Workers' Committee on the grounds that a forty-hour week was preferable because more people – in particular discharged servicemen – would be needed for jobs. Accustomed to the 'red' reputation of the Clyde, the employers and government did not take too much notice of the strike called by the CWC at the end of January. After four days, however, 40,000 men had laid down their tools and were joined not only by Glasgow's electrical workers but by 36,000 Scottish miners. Ex-servicemen were used as pickets, naturally arousing public sympathy, and on 29 January some 60,000 people attended a demonstration in George Square, Glasgow, while a delegation was granted an audience with the Lord Provost. A vain attempt to disperse the crowd by mounted police led to a pitched battle not only in the square but in other parts of the city, and many were injured. Fearful that Scottish troops might side with the strikers, the government sent massed English troops to Glasgow, some of them in tanks. Peace was restored and on 10 February the strike was called off, its aim unrealised. Politicians nevertheless feared that without the war effort to hold the nation together, discontent and dissension would spread throughout society.

In the immediate aftermath of war, the interests and aims of workers often coincided with those of former servicemen. Indeed, the earliest associations of veterans had a strong political dimension, and the British Legion – associated latterly with garden fêtes and genteel volunteers selling poppies – grew out of surprisingly radical beginnings. The Legion itself did not come into existence until 1921, but a number of other veterans' associations were founded while the war was still being fought. There had long been charitable organisations set up on behalf of British war veterans, ensuring that old soldiers did not simply fade away in penury. The professional soldiers who fought in the First World War, however, were outnumbered by civilians who, in the language of the times, had answered the nation's call, either by volunteering or because they had been conscripted. In return, it seemed only right that they should be entitled to benefits provided by the state rather than having to rely upon handouts from charities. Veterans who had left the service began organising themselves into associations that would lobby for pensions and for disability and unemployment allowances.

The earliest grouping, formed in September 1916, was the National Association of Discharged Sailors and Soldiers, which had strong links to both the Labour and Trades Union movements. The similarly named National Federation of Discharged and Demobilised Sailors and Soldiers, formed in April 1917, was sponsored by a Liberal MP and held its inaugural meeting at the

National Liberal Club. It was open only to those who had served in, or risen from, the ranks, presumably because the Federation felt, as the government did, that former commissioned officers could look after themselves. The Comrades of the Great War was proposed in August 1917 by Lieutenant Colonel Sir John Norton-Griffiths, a Conservative MP (supported by Lord Derby, the then Secretary of State for War), with the express intention of providing an organisation without what he considered the radical, even revolutionary, affiliations of the other associations. The most radical of them all was the short-lived National Union of Ex-Servicemen (NUX). This was founded in 1918 by John Beckett, a former soldier and a member of the International Labour Party who believed that ex-servicemen's associations could flourish only if they maintained links with other workers' organisations whose aims were deemed more or less identical. Workers' organisations often agreed, as may be judged by the pronouncements of Wal Hannington, a trade union official and founder member of the Communist Party of Great Britain. He regarded the unemployed former servicemen 'who had come from the bloody battlefields only to be cast on to the industrial scrap-heap of capitalism' as key components in the political struggles of the post-war period. There was a great deal of unseemly infighting among the disparate ex-servicemen's groups, but by the end of the war they had become a force to be reckoned with.

By the summer of 1919, the Federation was rumoured to have two million members and was described in the House of Commons as 'a huge shapeless, and menacing mass, on the verge of collapse into anarchy'. Evidence of this had been seen a few days earlier when the Federation organised a demonstration in

Hyde Park to protest about the lack of employment opportunities for discharged and disabled servicemen. Having listened to speeches in the Park, and passed a resolution that 'unemployed ex-servicemen shall immediately be found work at trade union rate of wages' or, failing that, an increased unemployment benefit of £1 8s (rising to £2 for those with children), the 10,000 or so protesters declared their intention of marching on Buckingham Palace and the Houses of Parliament. Prevented by a police cordon at the top of Constitution Hill from approaching the Palace by the most direct route, the demonstrators took another, where their way was once again barred. In Victoria Street the road was being dug up, and this provided the protesters with wood blocks and chunks of concrete, which they hurled at the police, and scaffolding poles, which they used to trip up the horses of the mounted division. Having abandoned their attempt to storm the Palace, they headed for the House of Commons, where they 'swept away a line of mounted policemen' in Parliament Square and 'surged forward alongside St Margaret's Church, throwing missiles at the flying line of police'. Mounted police reinforcements that had been held in reserve then charged the crowd, 'drew their truncheons and used them freely'. Numerous people on both sides ended up in hospital. It took almost an hour to disperse the rioters, who departed only after they were addressed by James Hogge, the Liberal whip who had formerly been the Federation's president and was still lobbying on their behalf in Parliament.

It was against this background of military and civil unrest that plans were made to celebrate the peace, and Virginia Woolf was not merely voicing the cynicism of pacifist Bloomsbury when she wrote that there was 'something calculated & politic & insincere' about the first of these great public events, the Peace Day celebrations in July 1919. In observing that they were 'some thing got up to pacify & placate "the people"', she had a point. Although the Armistice had been declared on 11 November 1918, the Treaty of Versailles, which marked the official end of the war, was not signed until 28 June 1919. Peace Day in Britain, which was to be celebrated somewhat paradoxically by a military parade, was originally set for early August to coincide with the anniversary of the outbreak of war. At the suggestion of the King, who wanted this Victory Parade of all the Allies to take place as soon as possible after the signing of the treaty – and possibly did not want to be seen to be lagging too far behind the French, who would celebrate their own victory on Bastille Day, 14 July – the government subsequently moved the date forward to 19 July. Recognising that jubilation would need to be tempered by some acknowledgement of the massive losses Britain suffered in gaining that victory and securing the peace, Lloyd George proposed at a very late stage that a monumental catafalque should be placed on the parade route so that the passing columns of soldiers could salute their dead comrades. Something similar had been planned by the French for their celebrations. Lord Curzon, who headed the Peace Celebrations Committee, declared that a catafalque – technically a raised platform on which a body rests temporarily before a funeral – might do for papist Continentals but would be regarded by the British population as wholly alien. A huge cross at Admiralty Arch was suggested as an unimaginative and some-what crass alternative, but fortunately someone had the sense to consult Sir Edwin Lutyens, who had been advising on the layout of military cemeteries in France and Belgium.

It was lucky that Lutyens was a quick worker. He produced a design almost immediately – supposedly within ten minutes of the idea being put to him on behalf of Sir Alfred Mond, who, as the First Commissioner of Works, was the government minister responsible for overseeing public buildings and statues. Lutyens' design was of a symbolically empty sarcophagus on top of a pylon, a rectangular truncated pyramidal tower of the sort often used to flank temples in Egypt. Lutyens thereby transformed a catafalque (on top of which an effigy would logically rest) into a cenotaph, which, he explained, was 'a monument to a deceased person whose body is buried elsewhere' and was thus wholly appropriate to the circumstances. He understood that as a focus of national mourning for the whole Empire, with its many races and creeds, the Cenotaph had to be non-denominational. It therefore lacked any Christian symbolism or inscription, much to the displeasure of many in the Church. Its decorations were restricted to religiously neutral wreaths, ribbons and flags and the all-embracing words 'The Glorious Dead'. Resembling solid stone but in fact constructed from wood and plaster, the Cenotaph was reasonably easy to erect in Whitehall during the fortnight left before the Victory Parade took place. No sooner had it been erected than people began to lay wreaths against it. These piled up to such a degree that they had to be cleared away in order to make room for the troops to march past on Peace Day.

It was originally proposed that the march should pass through the East End, but the Peace Celebrations Committee decided that the residents of Vauxhall, Kennington and Lambeth should be favoured instead on the grounds that they 'were much more British on the whole than the East End which was largely composed of foreigners' – in other words Jewish and other immigrants who had settled there and were clearly regarded as insufficiently assimilated, even though many of them had fought in the war. As a consequence, the route was redirected south of the river and would extend no farther east than St George's Fields in Lambeth. On the morning of Wednesday, 19 July, some 15,000 servicemen from most of the Allied countries, arranged alphabetically (starting with the Americans) and led by the British, French and American commanders-in-chief, Field Marshals Haig, Foch and Pershing, set out from Albert Gate at the south end of Hyde Park, where many of the participants had bivouacked overnight. (Haig was evidently in a better mood than he had been at the Armistice when he refused a summons from Lloyd George to take part in a ceremonial drive through the capital with the French C-i-C and the Prime Ministers of France and Italy, declaring in his diary that he had 'no intention of taking part in any triumphal ride with Foch, or with any pack of foreigners'.) Missing from this parade of the Allies were troops from the Indian subcontinent, whose contribution to the war had been considerable: some 1.27 million men, 827,000 of them combatants, among whom 49,000 sepoys (infantrymen) were killed in action. When bringing forward the date of the parade at such a late stage, the government had failed to take into consideration how this might affect those who had farthest to come. Working to the original timetable, 1,500 Indian troops had set sail from Bombay on 29 June; on 19 July they were still at sea.

Marching four abreast, the rest of the Allied representatives passed through Belgravia, heading south to cross the river over Vauxhall Bridge, through Kennington and Lambeth and the park where the Imperial War Museum would later stand. From there, they marched back north over the river via Westminster Bridge, past the Houses of Parliament, turning up Whitehall and saluting the Cenotaph as they passed. They then wheeled left through the south-west corner of a packed Trafalgar Square to go down the Mall to salute the King at Buckingham Palace. After this, the column marched along Constitution Hill to Hyde Park Corner, then along the south side of Hyde Park, ending up at Kensington Gardens, where everyone dispersed. As impressive as this parade of living soldiers was, it was as nothing compared with what might have been seen if the dead of the Empire had been able to march past the Cenotaph in their place. Someone made the calculation that if the dead were lined up four abreast in a continuous column, it would take them three and a half days to pass by. If they had set out from the north of England, the first of these ghosts would have reached the Cenotaph just as the last of them was leaving Durham.

The Victory Parade was followed by all manner of public entertainments in the London parks; including open-air concerts and theatrical performances, the climax of which was a massive firework display in which likenesses of the Royal Family, the Prime Minister and British military leaders were pyrotechnically created. In spite of some complaints that the money squandered on celebrating the peace would be better spent on alleviating the problems of unemployed former soldiers, similar peace celebrations took place all over the country, with parades passing through bunting-draped streets lined with cheering crowds.

Not that such events always went off smoothly. When mean-spirited local authorities in Luton refused to allow a group of ex-servicemen to hold a memorial service in a municipal park, the town clerk's office was torched and firemen were forcibly prevented by incensed veterans from approaching the town hall as it was gutted. The army had to be called in to restore order, the entire town was placed under military occupation for four days, and the bill for damages was reckoned at some £200,000. Hopes that a Peace Day would pacify disgruntled former servicemen were further dashed at Chertsey, where several hundred of them refused to take part in the celebrations because they hadn't yet secured their pension rights. Similar discontent was felt in Wales, where at Merthyr Tydfil jubilant celebrations were replaced by a sombre service of thanksgiving attended by 22,000 people, followed by a meeting at which a resolution was passed calling for higher pensions for former servicemen and their dependants. In Manchester unemployed servicemen held their own parade, carrying placards demanding better treatment. Elsewhere former soldiers boycotted the celebrations. They felt they had done quite enough marching during their war service and certainly weren't going to turn out on parade for what they regarded as a display of militarism.

Whatever the veterans' feelings may have been, those who had come to mourn their dead evidently regarded Peace Day as worthwhile. The Victory March had no sooner passed the Cenotaph than crowds of the bereaved surged back and began laying flowers and wreaths once more. This may have been a civic nuisance, and may have aroused the fury of the *Church Times*, which declared that ecclesiastical buildings rather than this gimcrack secular shrine were the proper places for worship and commemoration, but the people appeared to have spoken. Because it was in essence a stage prop, the Cenotaph had not been designed to last more than a couple of weeks, but the original plan to dismantle it after ten days had to be abandoned because of public sentiment. A similar stay of execution had been granted an earlier memorial erected in Hyde Park in August 1918 to commemorate the fourth anniversary of the outbreak of war. Whatever the original intention, this huge, flag-draped Maltese Cross had become a focus for national grief, and the bereaved had made a habit of laying wreaths at its foot. Indeed, in a photograph published in the *Illustrated London News* of the shrine being blessed by Arthur Winnington-Ingram, the Bishop of London, it is hard to make out the shrine at all beneath the mounds of flowers. When, the following year, it was announced that the shrine would have to be demolished because of its decayed condition, there had been an outcry, even though Lutyens had been commissioned to design a more permanent replacement. Plans for a new monument had, however, been shelved when the war ended. The temporary Cenotaph now fulfilled a similar public function and the cheers had scarcely died away after Peace Day than there were calls to replace it with a permanent one made of Portland stone. The cabinet had agreed to these demands by the end of July.

None of this meant that the temporary Cenotaph could be swept away there and then, inconveniently sited though it was in the middle of a major London thoroughfare, and it would remain in place until building work began on its more solid replacement. Throughout the rest of July, people continued to lay flowers, much to the annoyance of the Board of Works, who felt that this practice should be discouraged. All men who walked past it automatically doffed their caps, and representatives of numerous organisations – including some 15,000 members of the Federation of Discharged and Demobilised Sailors and Soldiers en route to a rather more peaceful rally in Hyde Park than their previous one – continued to visit the monument and lay wreaths. There always seemed to be someone standing before it, head bowed in remembrance or recollection.

The Cenotaph also became the focus of the first anniversary of the Armistice, which attracted even larger crowds than those attending Peace Day. This was something of a surprise to the government, which, it seems, originally had no particular plan to observe the occasion. The notion of marking it with a two minutes' silence in which the whole country would pause to remember the dead was put before the War Cabinet only on 4 November. The idea came from Sir Percy FitzPatrick, a South African author and politician, one of whose sons had been killed in action in 1917. Throughout the war a silence had been observed in South Africa at noon every day so that people could think about the sacrifices being made, and Sir Percy suggested to Viscount Milner, the Secretary of State for War, that a similar observance once a year in the mother country would be an appropriate way of ensuring that the Empire's dead were not forgotten. The cabinet agreed, but this last-minute decision meant that the idea needed to be announced to the people quickly and forcibly. A personal request from the King that at 'the eleventh hour of the eleventh day of the eleventh month, there may be for the brief space of two minutes a complete suspension of all our normal activities' was placed in all the newspapers on 7 November. Most papers followed this up with a reminder to the nation on 11 November itself, which fell on a Tuesday. Ensuring that everyone stopped what they were doing at the correct and same moment was complicated, but church and other bells, factory sirens, exploding maroons and artillery fire were all used to mark the moment. Given the very short notice people had been given, and the practical difficulties of stopping industry, commerce and even traffic in their daily round, it is remarkable how widely the silence was observed. There was no service at the Cenotaph, as there is today, but the King and Queen had sent wreaths and the British and French Prime Ministers arrived shortly before 11 a.m. to lay their own tributes. Equally, there was no parade or march-past by veterans: unlike on Peace Day, the focus of the first anniversary of the Armistice was bereaved civilians. As the maroons went off, silence fell over the vast crowd of men, women and children. Men removed their hats, women bowed their heads, soldiers stood to attention and saluted. As *The Times* eloquently put it: 'the very pulse of time stood still'.

A national day of mourning seemed appropriate: there were, after all, a great many people to mourn. British Empire losses – those who were killed or missing, presumed dead – stood at a staggering 1,104,890. Frustrating as it must have been for those still in uniform long after the end of hostilities, there were many soldiers who never came back at all, since the government had decreed that the bodies of those killed in action would not be returned to Britain for burial. This would have been impractical while the war was still being fought, but the real reason behind the decision was that in the interests of national unity it was important that all the dead should be treated equally. The practice that had obtained after Waterloo, when officers' bodies were shipped home while other ranks were shovelled into unmarked mass graves, clearly wouldn't do in the present circumstances. While wealthier families might have been able to make private arrangements for their dead to be brought home, many of those whose husbands, fathers, brothers and sons had been killed would have been hard pushed to find the money for a funeral in peacetime, let alone to pay for a body to be transported across the Channel or from other even more distant theatres of war. Soldiers would therefore lie with their comrades where they had died.

This noble-sounding idea was not always matched by the circumstances in which 'the Fallen' were dealt with during the war. Some of the dead, uncoffined and with blankets serving as shrouds, were buried in civilian cemeteries, but by early 1915 it was already clear that the scale of the casualties was such that land would have to be acquired to create new military cemeteries. In the meantime, burials took place where possible behind the lines. These may often have lacked individuality, with several bodies laid together in specially dug trenches, but they were dignified affairs with a proper religious service conducted by a padre and attended by soldiers from the same company of the deceased. Given the chaos of battle, however, and the difficulty of bringing in the dead under fire, many soldiers were quite literally buried where they fell. Even when a soldier was identifiable, and had died recently and comparatively 'cleanly', burials in the field could be hurried and basic affairs, with bodies tipped into convenient shell holes and covered with a few shovelfuls of earth or mud while someone said a brief prayer. Personal effects would be placed in marked bags to be returned in due course to relatives, and the man's tin helmet would be hung on a bayonet or on a rifle thrust into the ground, barrel first. Where there was no rifle or bayonet, a bottle containing a piece of paper inscribed with identifying details of the dead soldier would be stuck in the ground. In some places burial parties had time to use bits of wood and wire to fashion crude crosses.

Elsewhere it was a matter of gathering up remains that had been lying around for some time or had been scattered by shell-fire, and doing the best you could. Even when people had been given a decent burial, the ground in which they lay was often later fought over as opposing armies advanced and retreated. The most careful burial could prove very temporary indeed as high-explosive shells churned up the earth once more, destroying graves and redistributing the dead piecemeal. Given these conditions, it is perhaps not so surprising that over 300,000 of the 750,000 British and Empire troops killed in action on the Western Front still have no known grave.

One of the jobs undertaken by the British Red Cross was to ascertain what had happened to those who were listed as 'missing in action'. This term was not always a euphemism, and the Red Cross was occasionally able to bring good news to distraught relatives. Soldiers unaccounted for may have been lying unidentified in hospitals, or been taken prisoner. Stories abounded of soldiers separated from the regiment during battle and found wandering behind the lines wholly disoriented, or perhaps suffering the effects of shell shock. Mostly, however, the missing were rightly presumed dead. The Red Cross's job was hampered by the fact that at the beginning of the war no system of recording burials had been organised, so that even when a soldier was known to have died and had been given a proper burial, it was not always easy to find the site. The careless practices of Waterloo had long since been abandoned, but marking and maintaining soldiers' graves in distant engagements such as the Boer War in South Africa remained a fairly haphazard affair. This may have been deemed acceptable for Tommy Atkins, the professional soldier, but many of the dead of the First World War were civilian volunteers and conscripts and their families expected them to be treated accordingly.

It was while working with the Mobile Unit of the British Red Cross Society based at Lille that Fabian Ware, a former editor of the *Morning Post*, took it upon himself to begin making a note of British graves and their locations. The Unit had been formed in September 1914 after the Secretary of State for War, Lord Kitchener, had asked for volunteers to go in search of soldiers who had gone missing and might well be wandering lost in the chaos that often prevailed in the aftermath of battle. It was a curiously amateur yet effective organisation, made up of people in civilian vehicles who not only drove around looking for lost soldiers but also collected the wounded and transported them to hospitals. Ware subsequently persuaded the Adjutant-General of the British Expeditionary Force that his project to record burial sites should receive official War Office backing, and in March 1915 a Graves Registration Commission was created. Ware himself was given the rank of major and by October the Commission had registered over 31,000 graves, all of which had their temporary markers replaced by wooden crosses on which details were indelibly recorded. Lists of names and locations were drawn up and Ware entered negotiations with the French authorities to acquire land in perpetuity for the construction of British war cemeteries.

Once created, cemeteries required considerable effort to maintain, and so in January 1916 Ware set up the National Committee for the Care of Soldiers' Graves. News of this organisation's work had reached Britain, and relatives of the dead began to direct their enquiries to this new body as well as to the Red Cross. In order to answer these enquiries, the Graves Registration Commission was reorganised in the spring of 1916 into the Directorate of Graves Registration and Enquiries (DGRE), supplying relatives with information about and even photographs of burial sites. The intention was that after the war was over people would be able to visit these graves, but at the time such pilgrimages must have seemed a very long way off.

In May 1917, the National Committee for the Care of Soldiers' Graves became the Imperial War Graves Commission, constituted under royal charter and with the Prince of Wales as its president. The Commission undertook the daunting task of providing a marked grave for every corpse, even those whose headstones would merely read 'A Soldier of the Great War: Known Unto God', a designation for the unidentified chosen by Rudyard Kipling, who had been appointed literary adviser to the Commission, and whose own son, killed at the Battle of Loos in 1915, was among those with no known grave.

Someone who conducted many burial services at the front, both of the known and unknown, was an army chaplain called David Railton. The son of a leading figure in the Salvation Army,

Railton served on the front line as a padre throughout the war and had been awarded an MC in 1916 for tending the wounded under fire. It was Railton who came up with the idea after the war that a single unidentified serviceman should be brought home to Britain as a representative not only of those whose bodies had never been found or identified, but of all those who had been killed in action. In August 1920 he sent this proposal to the Dean of Westminster, Herbert Ryle, who, in passing it on first to George V and then to Lloyd George, shamelessly claimed it as his own. The King rejected the idea as in poor taste, and there was some worry that such a gesture might reopen wounds that were in the process of healing, but it won acceptance when placed before a cabinet meeting in October. Once again, preparations had to be made hastily since it was decided that a state funeral of this representative of all the dead should take place on Armistice Day, 11 November, followed by burial in Westminster Abbey.

By making the funeral of an unidentified soldier brought back from the battlefields the focus of the second anniversary of the Armistice, the Church had a chance to reassert itself at the centre of the commemoration. At the insistence of the Archbishop of Canterbury, Randall Thomas Davidson, there had in fact been a short service of dedication when the temporary Cenotaph was unveiled (Lloyd George had favoured an entirely secular event), but Lutyens' empty tomb still seemed to the Church distressingly pagan. Now, however, there was an opportunity to reclaim Armistice Day for God.

Selecting the soldier who would become known as the Unknown Warrior was made into an elaborate procedure, and there are several different versions of what happened. The most reliable account is that provided by Brigadier-General L.J. Wyatt, GOC the British troops still based in France and Flanders, who took part and provided a written account in a letter published in the *Daily Telegraph* in November 1939. In conditions of strictest secrecy, four unidentified British bodies were exhumed from temporary battlefield cemeteries at Ypres, Arras, the Aisne and the Somme on the night of 7 November 1920. These exhumations were carried out by four carefully selected teams made up of an officer and two other ranks. Presumably the rankers were handed the shovels and sacks, while the officer was there to direct operations, but none of the men was told why the bodies were being dug up and brought back by field ambulance to GHQ at St-Pol-sur-Ternoise. The men were further instructed that if they discovered anything that revealed the rank or regiment of the soldier they had exhumed they should immediately rebury the remains and select another grave. The intention was that any of the relatives of the 517,773 combatants whose bodies had not been identified could believe that the Unknown Warrior might be their lost husband, father, brother or son; but on the advice of the Abbey, which was nervous about the possibility of receiving more recent and potentially noisome remains, it is probable that instructions had been given that the four disinterred soldiers should have died early in the war on the grounds that such bodies would have been reduced to mere bones.

The four sets of remains were placed in the corrugated-iron chapel at the cemetery of St-Pol-sur-Ternoise and each draped with the Union flag. Sentries were posted at the chapel doors and Brigadier-General Wyatt, accompanied by one of his staff, a Colonel Gell, selected one of the bodies at random. One story that had wide circulation was that the Brigadier-General was blindfolded, but this would have been both unnecessary and unbecoming to his exalted rank. Once the body had been chosen, it was placed in a plain coffin and, after an ecumenical (though Christian) service the following morning, was taken by field ambulance to Boulogne to lie in the *chapelle ardente* of the castle there. A French guard of honour stood beside the coffin that night, and the following morning a pair of British undertakers arrived, bringing with them a specially designed casket made of oak that had grown in the grounds of Hampton Court. It was bound with bands of studded wrought iron made in the foundries of Wales, and a crusader's sword donated from the royal collection at Windsor was held in place on the lid by an iron shield on which was inscribed:

A British Warrior who
fell in the Great War
1914–1918
for King and Country

The plain coffin was placed inside this elaborate box, which on the morning of 9 November was taken by horse-drawn hearse, through guards of honour and to the sound of tolling bells and bugle calls, to the quayside. There, saluted by Maréchal Foch, it was loaded on to the destroyer HMS *Verdun*, which would carry it across the Channel to Dover. The coffin stood on the deck, covered in wreaths and surrounded by a French guard of honour, as the ship moved slowly out of the harbour.

The sight of HMS *Verdun* emerging from the heavy fog that

hung over the Channel as it reached Dover inspired one musical student to compose a tone poem on the subject. Lilian Elkington's atmospheric *Out of the Mist* received its first performance at a student concert in Birmingham later that year. 'The opening is quiet, with muted lower strings, as the ship feels her way through the murk,' the composer wrote in a programme note. 'After a pause mutes are removed, the air grows brighter, and the deep gloom upon men's spirits is somewhat relieved … Gradually the style enlarges and becomes more elevated as larger views of the meaning of sacrifice calm the spirit.' The final section of the work is marked double-forte 'as with a burst of sad exultation the representative of the nameless thousands who have died in the common cause is brought out of the darkness to his own'. This description exactly captures the mood of the country when the Unknown Warrior came home. He was greeted at Dover with the nineteen-gun salute usually reserved for field marshals and then handed over by the French to a British honour guard, which accompanied the coffin to the railway station to complete the journey to London by special train. All along the route people gathered to watch the train pass, and assorted uniformed groups stood on station platforms to salute its by now famous, though of course still anonymous, passenger. Even larger crowds, many of them women in mourning, greeted the train when it arrived at Victoria Station, where the Unknown Warrior remained overnight.

Many of these people followed the coffin to Westminster Abbey on the morning of 11 November, tagging along behind the official escort. Draped with a Union flag that had been used by David Railton as an altar cloth at the front, on top of which were placed an infantryman's helmet, belt and bayonet, the coffin had been loaded on to a gun carriage pulled by six black horses. Marching in front of the carriage were a firing party, and massed bands playing Chopin's funeral march. Immediately behind came the twelve pall-bearers, selected from among the highest-ranking officers in the land: Earl Haig, Earl Beatty and Air Marshal Sir Hugh Trenchard representing the army, navy and air force respectively, along with three other Admirals of the Fleet, three more generals and three more field marshals, including Sir John French who had commanded the British Expeditionary Force until relieved of his position in December 1915. These men were followed by representatives of the army, navy and air force, selected from all ranks, marching six abreast and all wearing black-crêpe armbands; then former servicemen, in mufti, marching four abreast. The procession made its slow way through the streets of the capital, which were lined with troops posted to hold back the mourners who, dressed in black, thronged the pavements and fell silent as the gun carriage passed.

Eventually the procession turned into Whitehall, where the new Cenotaph was concealed under huge Union flags. Although the proceedings had a more military flavour than those on Armistice Day the previous year, the focus remained on those who mourned rather than on those who had fought and survived. A group of unemployed ex-servicemen had even been denied permission to join the funeral procession, perhaps as a result of the various demonstrations, some of them violent, in which many out-of-work veterans had participated during the two years since the war ended. Apart from a specially allocated block where 130 'Distinguished Personages' waited, the pavements of Whitehall nearest the Cenotaph had been reserved for the 'Bereaved', selected by ballot and guarded by a line of servicemen from all three forces. With ten minutes to go to the eleventh hour, the gun carriage stopped beside Lutyens' shrouded monument so that the King, in military uniform, could place a wreath upon the coffin, salute and retire. A choir arrayed on either side of the entrance to the Home Office building directly opposite the Cenotaph sang the hymn 'Oh God, Our Help in Ages Past', then the Archbishop of Canterbury said the Lord's Prayer. On the first stroke of eleven, the King stepped forward again to unveil the Cenotaph. There followed a two minutes' silence that was supposedly observed throughout the entire British Empire – though it seems unlikely that those tilling fields or hawking goods under a hot afternoon sun in some of the remoter corners of the Empire could even have known what was taking place in the tiny island kingdom that ruled them, let alone participated in this arcane ceremony. In most countries that had fought in the war, however, silence was observed. A notable exception was the United States, where Armistice Day was largely ignored. A year later the Americans would exhume and bury their own Unknown Soldier and mark 11 November as Veterans Day, but in 1920 people went about their normal business without interruption. Throughout Britain, however, the silence that reigned was as remarkable in its way as the one that fell across the battlefields of France and Belgium exactly two years earlier. At the Cenotaph, the end of the two minutes was signalled by eight buglers playing the Last Post, after which the King and other dignitaries placed wreaths at the foot of Lutyens' empty tomb, then followed the gun carriage to Westminster Abbey, from the tower of which a single bell tolled.

The nave of the Abbey was lined by 100 men who had been awarded the VC and other high military honours, but following a press campaign and a personal plea from Queen Mary the majority of the public invited to attend the service were bereaved women who had lost either a husband or a son, or (as was all too often the case) both. The Dean of Westminster conducted the brief service, during which the casket of the Unknown Warrior was lowered into the tomb excavated for it in the floor of the nave just inside the West Door. Like the Cenotaph, the grave had been sited where people were obliged to take notice of it, in the middle of a thoroughfare: anyone entering the Abbey would have to step round it. In a reversal of Rupert Brooke's famous notion of 'some corner of a foreign field/That is for ever England' because a British soldier was buried there, quantities of earth had been imported from the battlefields so that the Unknown Warrior would lie in the French and Belgian soil over which he had fought.

Once the service was over and the congregation had stepped out into the late morning, the filled grave was covered with Railton's flag and surrounded by Flanders poppies and wooden railings to protect it from the thousands of people who would visit the Abbey to pay their respects. Here, at last, veterans were given or had somehow achieved priority, and the first people to enter the Abbey after the service had ended were disabled former servicemen, along with their unemployed comrades who had been denied a place in the funeral procession. By 11 p.m., when, an hour later than originally planned, the Abbey doors were closed for the night, some 40,000 people had filed past the grave, round which a guard of honour with bowed heads and reversed rifles kept constant vigil. It was clear that the three days originally allotted for the people to pay their respects before the tomb was properly sealed would be entirely inadequate. Huge queues formed long before the Abbey opened again the following morning, and there were similarly long lines of people at the Cenotaph, where it was estimated that 100,000 wreaths were laid within three days of its unveiling. From Trafalgar Square to Parliament Square, people in their thousands waited patiently and moved slowly forward, their places immediately filled as others joined the queues. They came from all over the country, and the queues grew even longer as the time approached for the Abbey to be closed so that a temporary slab could be placed over the tomb. Even the Dean's revised timetable could not accommodate those taking part in what had been dubbed 'the Great Pilgrimage', and it was not until 4 p.m. on Thursday, 18 November, a week after the funeral, that the doors of the Abbey were finally closed so that the tomb could be properly sealed. Once this was done, the pilgrimage continued: when the Abbey opened again the queues were almost as long as they had been in the week following Armistice Day.

'Wonderful to think of this unknown boy, or man, lying here with our kings, our captains, our prophets, and our priests,' one commentator wrote. 'His fame is greater, too; he is Everyman who died in the war. No matter how many mothers believe that he is theirs, they are right; they are all of them right – for he is every mother's son who did not come home from France.' This may have been the intention, but everyone knew that the body was not that of any of the thousands who had been lost at sea or in theatres of war other than the Western Front. Even those who were not privy to the negotiations that took place between the military and ecclesiastical authorities about selecting the Unknown Warrior must have realised that the chances that the person they had lost was now lying among the most illustrious of the land were slender. There was also the question of just how representative of the Empire's million dead the Warrior really was. Although no one actually quite voiced it, the general assumption was that this 'British Warrior' was of pure Christian descent. Some idea of the sort of person many imagined he might be was given by Arthur Machen (the creator of the 'Angels of Mons' myth) writing in the London *Evening News* on the day of the funeral. In an article he fancifully called 'Vision in the Abbey: The Little Boy Who Came to the King by Way of Great Tribulation', Machen imagined a boy playing in an idealised English countryside. 'I see the little child quite clearly,' he insisted, 'and yet I cannot make out how he is dressed. For all I can see he may be the squire's boy, or the parson's, or the cottager's son from that old whitewashed, sixteenth-century cottage which shines so in the sunlight. Or I am not quite sure that he is not a town-lad come to stay with relations in the country, so that he might know how sweet the air may be.' What this little boy was clearly not was a member of the teeming immigrant communities of the poor inner cities, many of whom fought and died for their country. He nevertheless grows up, goes to war, is killed, and becomes the Unknown Warrior.

A suspicion that the authorities at any rate did not really believe that the person they had buried in Westminster Abbey, that Christian repository of the great and the good of the land, could be anything other than a son of the Church of England was confirmed when the following year S.I. Levy, Principal of the Liverpool Hebrew Schools, wrote a letter to Dean Ryle pointing out that the tombstone had carved on it the line 'In Christ shall all be made alive'. As Mr Levy politely pointed out, the religion of the Unknown Warrior was as much a mystery as his identity. Many Jews, he reminded the Dean, had fought and died in the war and were being mourned in Jewish homes across the land. 'Among the unbounded wealth of biblical inspiration a line could have been selected which would not have offended the living religious susceptibilities of the unknown warrior, whatever his faith may have been,' Mr Levy suggested, whereas the chosen line did 'not meet the spiritual destinies of both Jew and Gentile'. Dean Ryle was not accustomed to being challenged and replied testily that given that the Unknown Warrior was lying in a Christian church it seemed only reasonable that one of the five texts selected for his tombstone should carry a Christian message. For all he knew, the Dean added, the Unknown Warrior might even have been a Muslim: 'We cannot hope to please everyone.'

Exactly who was lying in Westminster Abbey did not in the end greatly matter. The Unknown Warrior was intended as a symbol and largely accepted as one. The element of uncertainty over his identity may, however, explain the otherwise odd circumstance that even after all the pomp and ceremony that surrounded the Unknown Warrior's burial, it was an empty tomb which remained the main focus of a grieving nation. People continued to lay huge numbers of wreaths at the Cenotaph every week throughout the twelve months following the funeral. These numbers swelled at Christmas, which was unseasonably mild in 1920, and *The Times* reported that on Boxing Day 'There were more people there [...] than on any day since the Great Pilgrimage came to an end. The base was nearly surrounded by wreaths of evergreen and holly, and the pile reached nearly to the top of the pedestal.' Even a year later on 11 November 1921, when the Unknown Warrior's temporary grave slab was replaced by a permanent one of Belgian marble inlaid with brass lettering made from melted-down bullet casings gathered from the battlefields, *The Times* insisted that 'It was surely at the Cenotaph that the nation's undying gratitude to its glorious dead found [...] its fullest and most complete expression'. The heavens appeared to agree. Although a mist 'obscured the vista' on this 'perfect November morning', 'immediately over the Cenotaph the sky was pure pale blue'.

The commemoration of the dead had certainly gripped the country's collective imagination, but many of those who had survived the war felt themselves forgotten. Among those laying wreaths that November morning was a delegation of ex-servicemen and their families from Poplar in the East End of London. Some of these wreaths bore inscriptions which 'the police were obliged to censor as being likely to be objectionable to those who mourned at the shrine'. Among the inscriptions deemed offensive were 'To the dead victims of Capitalism from the living victims of Capitalism' and 'To the dead not forgotten from the living forgotten'. While some of the veterans wore their war decorations, one had pinned to his coat the pawn ticket for which he had exchanged his medals.

TWO

A Nation Remembers?
1921–1939

Have you forgotten yet? …
For the world's events have rumbled on since those
gagged days …

SIEGFRIED SASSOON, 'Aftermath'

While veterans who faced poverty and unemployment often complained that they had been forgotten, Britain continued to lavish money and attention upon preserving the memory of those who had died. Many felt that in commemorating the dead the nation was neglecting to fulfil its promises and obligations to those who had survived. By the time the Unknown Warrior had been laid to rest in Westminster Abbey, the Imperial War Graves Commission had made considerable progress in the enormous job of providing permanent burial sites for his comrades left behind in Flanders and even farther afield. Most countries in which the war had been fought had followed France's generous lead in handing over land in perpetuity to the IWGC, which meant that cemeteries could now be constructed in Belgium,

Italy, Greece, Iraq, Palestine and Egypt. Similar arrangements would be made with Germany and Turkey.

Once the land was acquired, it was necessary to come to some decision about how the dead should be commemorated. At the invitation of Fabian Ware, Edwin Lutyens and Herbert Baker (with whom Lutyens had designed a new capital of British India in Delhi before the war) had visited the battlefields in July 1917. Lutyens left a wonderfully touching account of what he found in France:

> The grave-yards, haphazard from the needs of so much to do and so little time for thought. And then a ribbon of isolated graves like a milky way across miles of country where men were tucked in where they fell. Ribbons of little crosses each touching each across a cemetery, set in a wilderness of annuals and where one sort of flower is grown the effect is charming, easy and oh so pathetic. One thinks for the moment no other monument is needed. Evanescent but for the moment almost perfect and how misleading to surmise in this emotion and how some love to sermonise. But the only monument can be one in which the endeavour is sincere to make such a monument permanent – a solid ball of bronze!

Bronze balls were not what Ware had in mind. He subsequently asked Sir Frederick Kenyon, Director of the British Museum, to become an adviser to the Commission. After visiting France and Belgium himself, Kenyon submitted a report laying out the principles upon which he believed the cemeteries should be created. They should be surrounded by low walls, within which uniform headstones would mark individual graves arranged without regard for rank or status. In death all men would be equal, officers and their men lying as they had fought, side by side, the headstones merely recording rank, name, regiment, date of death, and age if known. The details, however, were left to Lutyens and Baker, who did not always agree about the design of the cemeteries. Lutyens wanted to avoid all religious symbolism and so came up with the Stone of Remembrance, a sort of non-denominational altar, or (as he described it) a 'great fair stone of fine proportions', raised on a shallow flight of broad steps. Inscribed on the stone were some biblically derived but religiously neutral words chosen by Kipling: 'Their Name Liveth For Evermore'. The more traditionally inclined Baker felt that something specifically Christian and military was called for and designed a huge stone Cross of Sacrifice standing on an octagonal base and faced with a downward-pointing bronze sword. In the event, both designs were used, the Stone featuring in every cemetery containing over four hundred graves, the Cross in all but the smallest plots. In most cases the headstones would be set into concrete beams, buried invisibly beneath the earth, which would keep them both upright and aligned in proper military order.

Appointed alongside Lutyens and Baker for the work in France and Belgium were Reginald Blomfield, who was both a distinguished architect and a garden designer, and Charles Holden, who had served in the war both with the London Ambulance Column and the Directorate of Graves Registration and Enquiries, and would go on to design many buildings for the London Underground. These four men allotted work on individual cemeteries to young British architects, with priority given to those who had served in the war. Elsewhere, John Burnet, who had worked for Kenyon at the British Museum, was given responsibility for cemeteries in Gallipoli, Syria and Palestine; Sir Robert Lorimer, who was best known for redesigning large country houses in Scotland, would work in Italy, Greece, Egypt and Germany; and Edward Warren, who designed numerous buildings for Oxford University, was allotted Iraq. The Director of the Royal Botanical Gardens at Kew was appointed horticultural adviser to the Commission, and Lutyens asked his old associate Gertrude Jekyll, doyenne of the Edwardian country garden, to provide planting plans for a number of cemeteries.

It would naturally be some time before the uniform designs could be put into practice, and 'until such time as they could be handed over to the Imperial War Graves Commission for permanent construction', the cemeteries were the responsibility of the Directorate of Graves Registration and Enquiries, which both organised and maintained them, assisted by such bodies as the Women's Army Auxiliary Corps. The Directorate also remained responsible for searching the battlefields for bodies once the war was over. The vast area to be covered was systematically divided up and allotted to individual 'Graves Concentration Units' consisting of twelve soldiers under a senior NCO, who went back and forth looking for corpses and for isolated graves, the occupants of which they exhumed and transferred to recognised cemeteries. Some 8,000 men were employed in this task, and by the time they had finished in September 1921, 204,650 bodies had been removed from the battlefields and reburied in these cemeteries.

Many relatives of the dead expressed a wish to visit graves as soon as possible after the Armistice, and so a number of religious organisations began conducting groups of the bereaved to France and Belgium. The best known of these was the St Barnabas Society, named after the patron saint of consolation, founded by a clergyman in 1919 in order to subsidise the travel of those who could not afford trips offered by commercial travel companies. Such pilgrimages proved popular. In the seven months between November 1919 and June 1920, for example, the Church Army arranged for 5,000 people to travel to the places where their men lay buried. During this period such places must often have seemed all too redolent of the circumstances in which such men had died. For all the good work carried out by the DGRE, most of the cemeteries were little more than a neat array of wooden crosses standing on bare earth in a bleak landscape where very little was growing. To reach them, mourners would have had to travel through villages that had been reduced to piles of rubble, along rutted roads lined with splintered trees, across ground still churned up by high explosives and littered with barbed wire, burned-out vehicles, abandoned weaponry and all the pitiful detritus of recent warfare. For those who had been unable to attend any sort of funeral for their husbands, sons, fathers and brothers, visiting graves even in these conditions seems to have provided comfort, and by 1923 some 78,500 of them had taken advantage of travelling facilities offered by the Salvation Army and the YMCA. In time these cemeteries would be tidied up considerably and landscaped with shrubs and flower beds. 'The concept was to create a sentimental association between the gardens of home and the foreign fields where the soldier lies', and these particular corners of France and Belgium did indeed begin to look as if they were forever England.

Elsewhere on the Western Front, a tourist industry rapidly developed independently of the pilgrimages conducted for the bereaved. While many people were content to learn about the actual circumstances of the war at the Imperial War Museum, which had been founded at Crystal Palace in 1917 and recorded over three million visitors between 1920 and 1923, others took advantage of the opportunities offered to visit Flanders and Picardy to see where the war had been fought. A number of unemployed veterans of the officer class took out advertisements in the press offering to conduct small groups of visitors round the battlefields by car, their recent first-hand knowledge of France and Belgium a guarantee of authenticity. As early as 1919, tourists could buy books such as A.T. Fleming's *How to See the Battlefields*, but the most popular guides were the illustrated series to most of the major battle sites published by the Michelin tyre company, fifteen of which had been published in English editions by 1921. Prefaced with an overview of the military objectives and brief accounts of the individual attacks, complete with maps, the guides provided a detailed itinerary for the visitor. They also contained before-and-after photographs of devastated buildings and villages and recent photographs of the temporary cemeteries. These photos perhaps tell their own story – as well they might, since one would have no idea reading the Michelin guide to the Somme, for example, that 1 July 1916 was (and still is) the worst day in the history of the British army. Euphemistic phrases such as 'came into contact with the second German positions' abound, and the emphasis is firmly upon what few successes the Allies achieved, with figures given for numbers of Germans taken prisoner but none whatever for the 60,000 British casualties. 'The first assaults on July 1 gave the British Montauban and Mametz, while Fricourt and La Boisselle were encircled and carried on July 3,' we read. 'Coltmaison and Mametz Wood, reached on the 5th, were carried on the 11th.' The cost of all this is not mentioned: you would not know from this book that at Mametz Wood on 7 July alone the Welsh Division lost over 4,000 men. Estimates vary as to the overall casualties for the Battle of the Somme, which dragged on until mid-November, but after 140 days the British had lost some 400,000 men and advanced 6 miles. It was not, perhaps, a statistic anyone wanted to read in the immediate aftermath of the war. The Michelin guides contained enough information to be of interest even to those who did not want to make the journey across the Channel, and by January 1922 sales figures for the guides in Britain, France and America had reached 1,432,000. Later that year George V made a tour of the battle-fields and cemeteries both to pay his respects to those of his subjects who had died and to inspect the work of the Imperial War Graves Commission, of which his eldest son continued to serve as president. A heavily illustrated book about the royal tour, emotively titled *The King's Pilgrimage*, became a bestseller when it was published in 1922.

Others who visited the battlefields had been there not long before. While it is easy to see why veterans might wish to visit the battlefields and cemeteries many years later, the notion of them returning to places where they had so recently endured appalling conditions, and which nature had yet to heal, may strike us as odd. Many veterans were haunted by their experiences at the front, experiences they would be unable to forget however long they lived. These were not experiences that were easy to talk about or share with civilians, even if they were friends or family. Siegfried Sassoon made his notorious public protest against the political conduct of the war in 1917 on behalf of his suffering fellow soldiers partly in the belief that 'it may help to destroy the callous complacence with which the majority of those at home regard the continuance of agonies which they do not share, and which they have not sufficient imagination to realise'. Now that the war was over, veterans were naturally wary of harrowing their families and friends, or worse still boring them, with stories from the trenches. 'There was nobody interested anyway,' George Louth recalled, 'so it was useless telling them and if you did they would only laugh at you, say it wasn't true. It wasn't a conscious thing, nobody talked about the First War in those days, even my wife, even she never heard my story and we were married seventy years.' Louth had joined up in 1915 at the age of eighteen and survived the first day on the Somme in 1916, but was invalided out in December of that year. He would live to celebrate his 103rd birthday in 2000, but 'only once spoke about [the war] from 1918 until 1990'. This was to a woman enquiring after her husband, who had been 'blown to pieces' but was officially listed as 'wounded and missing'. Harry Patch too never spoke about the war. He married happily in 1919, but not once in fifty-seven years of wedded life did he mention the war to his wife. 'I don't think she had any idea about my service, and never brought it up.'

Many veterans felt as if they had been set apart from civilian life altogether, and that the only people with whom they could truly share their feelings were those they had served alongside. The veterans' organisations not only campaigned for the rights of ex-servicemen, they also provided former soldiers with a community and would organise visits to France and Belgium. Ex-servicemen had been among both cemetery pilgrims and battlefield tourists from the very outset, paying their respects to friends who had been buried in haste and without pause for mourning, or visiting places where they had undergone what was fast beginning to seem the defining experience of their lives.

For some, the Western Front had proved so overwhelming that it became the only place they felt they belonged. The Imperial War Graves Commission needed hundreds of gardeners to tend the cemeteries it was building, and it recruited these from among former servicemen. By 1921, 1,326 veterans were employed by the Commission, and they had not only planted over 15 miles of hedges and 75 miles of borders, but had also seeded some 200 acres of bare earth with grass. Many of them spent the rest of their lives in France and Belgium, often marrying local women. Captain Frederick Osborne of the Royal Fusiliers, for example, joined up in 1914 with five friends and fought throughout the war, at the end of which he was the only survivor of the original group. After being demobilised, he returned to the Ploegsteert region and took a job looking after cemeteries. He married a Flemish woman, learned the language, and made his life in Belgium, staying on there after his retirement in 1962.

Britain itself continued to be something of a battlefield during the early 1920s with Armistice Day becoming a focus not only of national mourning but of protests intended to remind everyone that those who *had* returned from the war were still awaiting a home fit for heroes. In October 1920, disturbed by the continuing rise in unemployment (which still included a large number of ex-servicemen), a group of London mayors headed by the Mayor of London and future leader of the Labour Party, George Lansbury, requested an interview with Lloyd George at Downing Street. In support of this deputation, large numbers of the unemployed, many of them wearing their combat medals, descended upon Whitehall. According to Wal Hannington, the trade union official who was leading a North London contingent that day, the crowd was orderly, doing little more than cheering and singing. Nevertheless, Whitehall became severely congested and in order to clear the street mounted policemen charged the crowds, who were packed in so tightly on all sides that they could not retreat and 'were compelled to fight back at the police or simply stand still and be clubbed down'. Eventually, the police were beaten back and the crowd surged up towards Trafalgar Square, but were stopped by reinforcements who struck the workers down as they tried to escape. Hannington recalled that 'dozens of men lay in the roads and on the side-walks groaning with pain as the blood gushed out from wounds inflicted by police batons'. Then a policeman was dragged off his horse, which was commandeered and mounted by an unidentified worker who broke through police lines at a gallop, while men on foot followed in his wake. He managed to reach Downing Street before being 'clubbed down'. The police eventually restored order and the crowd dispersed.

Wal Hannington's *Unemployed Struggles 1919–1936*, from which this account is taken, may be one of the great classics of the British working-class movement, but it is a work of polemic and not always accurate. Hannington's version of events, recalled some fifteen years later, is at odds with the contemporary reports of this incident in *The Times*, for example. The newspaper agreed that the crowd was 'fairly orderly, though noisy', and that the mounted police used newly introduced 'long staves' to belabour the protesters, between thirty and forty of whom suffered injuries, mostly to the head. The newspaper reported, however, that police had been obliged to intervene because a group of the unemployed decided to go to Downing Street to protest rather than, as had been originally planned, wait on Victoria Embankment for the deputation of mayors to report back on their interview with Lloyd George. These protesters 'were heavily reinforced by many hundreds of irresponsible young hooligans who took a leading part in the afternoon's disorders'. These young men apparently threw bottles, stones and brickbats at the police and caused considerable damage to government buildings: the stone balustrade of the Privy Council Office was demolished, several windows were broken at the Treasury and every single window was smashed on the ground floor of the War Office.

Hannington's claim that 'The mayors had not been received by Mr Lloyd George. He was not apparently interested in hearing about the plight of the workless and had conveniently left London' was untrue. Indeed, Lansbury emerged from Number 10 after a meeting with the Prime Minister and attempted to restore order among his supporters. Furthermore, Hannington's 'unknown hero on the white horse' was neither an 'ex-cavalry man' nor even a member of the unemployed, but a nineteen-year-old packing-case maker from Hoxton called Edward Cannadine, who had been exercising a horse and had 'turned into Whitehall to see the demonstration'. At Bow Street Magistrates' Court the following morning, he claimed that 'Someone struck the horse, which got out of control, and he was unable to prevent it charging the police'. Quite what someone from Hoxton was doing exercising a horse in the middle of London was not divulged, but the horse clearly hadn't been taken from the police since it had no saddle. Nevertheless, the court declined to believe that Cannadine was an innocent passer-by caught up in events beyond his control and fined him 40 shillings for 'insulting behaviour'. A number of other protesters were charged with a variety of offences, including three men who had taken the opportunity to break into a jeweller's and make off with £3,000 worth of diamond rings.

Whatever the detailed facts of the case, the protest had forcibly brought the problem of unemployed war veterans into the public eye. According to Hannington, the behaviour of the police 'caused a wave of bitter feeling to sweep throughout London and the provinces'. He claimed – apparently unaware of the clashes between the police and unemployed in Westminster in May 1919 – that

It was the first episode of its kind since the war ended. It came as a shock to many who hesitated to believe that such treatment would be meted out to men who had only recently returned from the battlefields after four years of warfare in which they had been made to believe that 'their grateful country would never forget them'. The 'comradeship of the trenches' was over. Ex-soldiers in blue uniforms were now ready to club down ex-soldiers in rags at the bidding of the only class which had profited by the war.

Questions were asked in Parliament, and there were demands that the left-wing *Daily Herald* (of which Lansbury was both proprietor and editor) should be prosecuted for its comments on the action of the police.

Matters had not improved a year later: the number of unemployed continued to rise inexorably, passing the one million mark by February 1921. While at the Cenotaph on 11 November that year protests were largely confined to the wording on wreaths, elsewhere in the country several violent episodes took place. The two minutes' silence in Liverpool was disturbed by some two hundred men 'purporting to represent the unemployed of the city' (as an unsympathetic *Yorkshire Post* put it), who pushed their way through the silent crowd amid cries of 'What we need is food not prayers' and 'Anyone want a medal?' Worse was to happen in Dundee, where a 'Communist crew, who have labelled themselves, on what justification they would find it hard to explain, the "organised unemployed"' (the *Dundee Advertiser*) sang 'The Red Flag' during the two minutes' silence. After the Last Post sounded, the crowd of mourners turned on the protesters, snatching and destroying their banners and dragging those who were seated on lorries to the ground. It took some time for the police to gain control. Several arrests were made – but only, it seems, of the protesters. The general view of such incidents may be judged by the wife of a veteran lucky enough to be in employment who wrote to the papers suggesting the protesters should be whipped with the cat-o'-nine-tails, or by a former soldier who stated that any ex-servicemen among them must be those who 'were dragged into the army by the conscription net [and whose] names are writ large in the "crime sheets" and sick lists of the unfortunate unit to which they were drafted'.

By January 1922 the number of unemployed had passed two million, among whom were some 50,000 to 60,000 former servicemen. Morale among unemployed veterans was very low indeed. As a former sergeant wrote to the *Daily Express*:

> Life has reached the stage when it is an overwhelming burden. Those for whom we fought in the War have taken from us our means of existence. We are informed that we are not wanted. Industry can carry on quite nicely without us.
>
> This, then, is our reward: to exist on a pauper's pittance, helped out by what we can borrow from a lean and uncertain future.
>
> I look at the wording on my Victory medal.* I think of my hopeless present and my doubly hopeless future, and I curse the system under which I must deny my children and myself even the bare necessities of existence, until, worn out, my mortgage perhaps still unpaid, I sink with a sigh of relief to the grave.

In the run-up to 11 November that year so many ex-service-men found themselves in a similar state that the London District Council of Unemployed decided to join in the Armistice Day ceremony and organise 'a big procession of a fitting character to march past the Cenotaph'. They wrote to the police to inform

---

* The Victory Medal was awarded in 1919 to everyone who had served in the war. On the one side was the winged figure of Victory, while on the reverse was the legend 'The Great War For Civilization 1914–1919' surrounded by a wreath.

them of this plan and were told that although they could not join the main procession they would be permitted to march past the Cenotaph and lay a wreath once the official ceremony had finished.

Some 25,000 of the unemployed assembled on the Embankment on the morning of 11 November, then lined up in Northumberland Avenue awaiting a signal from the police that their march could commence. The large crowd that had gathered to witness the official observance had yet to disperse and had not expected this addition to the day's events. And it must have been an impressive sight, not least because each contingent marched under a banner on which hundreds of medals had been pinned.

Out of the grey mist came the wail of the fifes from the unemployed bands and the measured tread of tramping men. Into Whitehall came the long trail of drab humanity, with their medals hanging from the red banners and the pawn tickets pinned on their coats, as an indictment against the system which praises the dead and condemns the living to starvation. On they came, steady and inevitable. Bemedalled and bearing obvious signs of poverty they stirred the dense throng of sightseers to a sense of deep emotion and a realisation of the injustice which was being meted out by man to man.

'Who are these people?' asked one young woman to another on the sidewalk. 'Why – they're the unemployed.' 'Then good luck to them,' said the first girl bitterly, almost savagely. 'Disgraceful,' snorted a red-faced old man, with a fur-clad young creature on his arm. 'Those men are Bolsheviks,' he said. 'But look at their medals,' said the girl. A woman in a black shawl turned on the old man. 'Shut up your bloody gap! If you'd been out of work as long as my old man, you'd be a Bolshevik.' A murmur of approval went through the crowd.

Wal Hannington, from whose book this colourful description is taken, does not say whether the murmur of approval continued when, after laying a wreath bearing the inscription 'From the living victims – the unemployed – to our dead comrades, who died in vain', the ex-servicemen passed out of Whitehall to the strains of 'The Red Flag' and 'The Internationale'. The march undoubtedly did, however, make people realise that many of these men who had fought in the war being commemorated that November day were returning to 'cold hungry homes'. That said, this impressive and moving demonstration went unreported in *The Times*' account of the day's proceedings.

Groups of unemployed ex-servicemen could still be found marching through the streets collecting money to relieve financial hardship. 'In the main,' Hannington wrote sniffily, these 'Local Unemployed Ex-service Men's Organisations' 'had no clear working-class policy and they appeared to be formed purely for charity-mongering purposes'. By now, however, these numerous groups had been organised into one representative body. In June 1919 the National Federation of Discharged and Demobilised Sailors and Soldiers decided to open its membership to commissioned as well as non-commissioned officers, while the National Association of Discharged Sailors and Soldiers began to shed its links to the Trades Union and Labour movements. An attempt to bring these two organisations together with the

Comrades of the Great War under the umbrella of the Empire Services League had earlier failed because there was a general feeling that this idea had been sponsored by the government for its own ends. The League had in fact been set up partly to oversee the distribution of the residual funds of the Expeditionary Force Canteens and the Navy and Army Canteen Board. During the war these two bodies had provided canteens run by the Army Service Corps, where men on overseas duty or on leave back in Blighty could buy food and drink to supplement the rations they received at the front. Considerable profits had accumulated, and it had been decided that these should be used to help former servicemen. Eventually the Admiralty set up its own Royal Naval Benevolent Trust, leaving the army and air force's share to be administered by the United Services Fund (USF), overseen by the same General Byng who had been dispatched to quell the mutiny at Calais in 1919.

While the USF did much to bring the various veterans' groups together, it was another controversial military figure, General Haig, who was largely responsible for the eventual founding of one organisation: the British Legion. Whatever veterans may have thought of his conduct of the war, Haig won widespread favour after the Armistice by refusing a viscountcy and the substantial pension that went with it until the government had sorted out the payments due to ordinary servicemen. A Joint Conference on Unity was held in August 1920 at which delegates from the five major veterans' organisations (the Federation, the Association, the Comrades, the National Union of Ex-Servicemen and the recently formed Officers' Association) came together under the chairmanship of the Federation's T.F. Lister, who had served in the war as a gunner. One of the principal stumbling blocks for unity was the various political affiliations of these groups, which Lister insisted had to be abandoned in favour of a non-party approach to the lobbying of Parliament. The least amenable to such a suggestion was the NUX, which had been excluded from the United Services Fund and whose members were described in the official history of the British Legion – not entirely objectively, one senses – as 'militants and, perhaps, Marxists, lacerated by their experiences into a bitter, brooding group'. Also suspicious of the proposed coming together of these disparate organisations was the Officers' Association, which had successfully raised funds for itself, including a hefty £637,000 from public donations, and did not wish to see this hard-won money disbursed among other veterans. Indeed, it had already set about applying for a royal charter in order to safeguard these funds. In spite of the very different concerns of these two organisations, and the objections of a loyally leftist senior representative of the Federation, the decision to amalgamate the veterans' associations went through. The troublesome NUX subsequently withdrew from discussions, and shortly thereafter ceased to exist, but over the next few months a draft constitution for what became the British Legion was drawn up and approved at a further conference in December.

Choosing a name for this new body took a great deal of further discussion. Among the suggestions was the Imperial Federation of Comrades and the Warriors' Guild, the latter scotched when some dissident at a conference responded audibly: 'The Warriors *Gulled*!' The less imperialist and militarist 'British Legion' was eventually agreed upon and formalised at a three-day conference at the Queen's Hall in London in May 1921, at which its principles and policy were formulated and its officers elected. Haig became the Legion's president, and the Prince of Wales its first patron. The conference had begun with a silence honouring the dead, and it ended with a Sunday morning ceremony at the Cenotaph, where four representatives of the participating veterans' associations, their rivalries now behind them, laid a laurel wreath.

The fundamental differences that had set the former associations against each other were dealt with in the first principle of the Legion, which was that it 'shall be democratic non-sectarian and not affiliated to or connected directly or indirectly with any political party or political organisations'. Rather than tugging in different political directions, they now all pulled together for the greater good, while in the regions by the end of 1921 small and rivalrous groups had come together with varying degrees of enthusiasm and reluctance to form 1,478 local branches. Individual members each paid an annual subscription of half a crown. According to its 'principles and policies', the Legion had been 'created to inaugurate and maintain in a strong stimulating united and democratic comradeship all those who have served in His Majesty's Navy Army Air Force or any Auxiliary Forces so that neither their efforts nor their interests shall be forgotten that their welfare and that of the dependants of the fallen may be safeguarded and that just and equitable treatment shall be secured to them in respect of the difficulties caused in their lives as a result of their services'. An initial membership of 18,106 in 1921 had leapt to 116,426 by the end of the following year, and to 312,506 by the end of the decade. A sense of comradeship, particularly in small communities, was perhaps what appealed most to former servicemen, the opportunity to get together with those who had undergone similar experiences. There remained some veterans, however, who simply wanted to put the war behind them. Some never joined the Legion at all: Harry Patch had nothing to do with the organisation until very late in his long life, and was not enrolled as a member until 2008.

In the 1920s, however, the Legion was mainly concerned with improving the material circumstances of veterans. While the National Constructive Programme decided upon in 1921 had international objectives, including working for peace 'while taking care that the defence of the Empire is adequately provided for', its principal national objective was to persuade 'Government, Municipal, and Local Authorities, and other employers of labour [to] give preference in employment to ex-service men and women seeking employment'. The Legion even wanted to ensure that women who had taken jobs during the war and were 'not dependants of service men or actual bread-winners' surrendered their jobs to those who had served at the front – though quite how this was to be achieved was not explained. Provision should be made for the retraining of those who had lost their jobs and a guarantee should be given that they would subsequently return to the workforce. Financial and other encouragement should also be given to people starting up their own businesses. Meanwhile, the government should provide 'reasonable maintenance' for those who remained out of work until such time that they secured employment. Particular facilities should be made available to the disabled who wished to work; they should be given 'special preference [...] as regards travelling and admission to places of recreation and entertainment'; and their pensions, and those of war widows and other dependants, should be guarded 'jealously'.

Given that such things would take some time, and much lobbying, to secure, the Legion needed to take the lead in providing money to ease hardship. Consequently it took over assorted funds for disbursement, including £157,000 collected by the National Relief Fund, which had been set up by the Prince of Wales at the beginning of the war. The Legion's core income derived from annual subscriptions, but at first these were slow to come in. The organisation derived much-needed additional income from fund-raising events such as Warriors' Day in March 1921, when various entertainments in theatres and cinemas brought in some £70,000. The seventh anniversary of the outbreak of the war was used to mount a newspaper appeal which raised £10,400. The biggest fund-raising initiative, however, and the one for which the Legion is still best known, was the Poppy Appeal.

One of the most memorable sights on those parts of the Western Front that had not been turned into a quagmire was scarlet sheets of what came to be known as Flanders poppies. The Flanders poppy is in fact the common field poppy (*Papaver rhoeas*), then an equally familiar sight in English cornfields. The seeds of this plant can lie dormant for years but germinate when soil has been turned over, either by the plough or – as at the front – by high explosives. The fragile appearance of the blood-red petals belies this plant's essential toughness, and this, along with the sense it gave of life emerging triumphantly from utter devastation, made it a potent symbol for the soldiers. In one of the war's great poems, 'Break of Day in the Trenches', Isaac

Rosenberg conjures up both the bloody colour and fragility of the poppies, 'whose roots are in man's veins' and whose petals 'drop' everywhere. The sense of wonder caused by glimpsing poppies growing amid chaos and carnage is best caught in a passage from Cecil Lewis's *Sagittarius Rising*. Trudging along roads of splintered trees, past ruined farms, Lewis witnessed 'a desolation, unimaginable from the air':

> Yet (Oh, the catch at the heart!), among the devastated cottages, the tumbled, twisted trees, the desecrated cemeteries, opening, candid, to the blue heaven, the poppies were growing! Clumps of crimson poppies, thrusting out from the lips of craters, straggling in drifts between the hummocks, undaunted by the desolation, heedless of human fury and stupidity, Flanders poppies, basking in the sun!

The Flanders poppy also inspired one of the most popular poems of the war, written at an Ypres dressing station in April 1915 by a Canadian doctor called John McCrae. 'In Flanders Fields' was published in *Punch* the following December, and its picture of the poppies that 'blow/Between the crosses, row on row', followed by an exhortation from the dead who lie there to continue the fight, gained immediate and enduring popularity. It also prompted a reply, endorsing McCrae's sentiments, from a patriotic American called Moina Michael, who was serving in New York with the Overseas YMCA War Workers. After the war she led a campaign for US veterans to adopt the poppy as an emblem. These artificial poppies were made in France and exported to the States, all proceeds going to French children who had been affected by the war. In August 1921, the general secretary of the British Legion was shown some samples and told that the French manufacturers could supply his organisation with similar ones. Keen to find ways to raise funds, the Legion was nevertheless wary of what sounded like a small operation with no apparent credentials. A representative of the Legion was sent to France to investigate. After he came back reassured, a decision was taken to place a large order for paper poppies that could be sold to the public. By wearing the flowers on Armistice Day people would demonstrate that they were keeping faith with the Empire's million dead.

The demand for poppies exceeded all expectations, and hastily improvised additional ones, using somewhat bloodless pink blotting paper, had to be made up at the Legion's headquarters. It is thought that some eight million people sported a poppy on 11 November 1921. Sales raised £106,000, which in terms of spending power is today roughly the equivalent of £1.3 million, and the poppy would become a feature of Armistice Days and Remembrance Sundays thereafter. The Legion decided that rather than leave the manufacture of poppies to a French company they would set up their own small workshop in rented premises on the Old Kent Road, staffed by five severely disabled former servicemen. The British version of the poppy was far more stylised than those made in France, which had multiple petals and stamens. Two versions were made: cotton ones retailing at threepence and larger silk ones, which sold for a shilling – though it was naturally hoped that people would give more than the basic price. The black central boss bore the legend 'Haig Fund', a shortened form of the Earl Haig Appeal, which became the organisation that distributed profits raised by the sale of the flowers.

The demand grew year by year, with gross receipts increasing on average by some £50,000 a year, and the workshop was subsequently moved to much larger premises in Richmond, where it employed 191 former servicemen. Poppies had rapidly achieved official status, and indeed royal patronage in 1924, when the factory first supplied poppy wreaths for the Royal Family to lay at the Cenotaph on Armistice Day. Since the wreaths were more or less imperishable, and all proceeds from their sale went to help disabled servicemen, people began to follow the royal lead, and wreaths made at the Poppy Factory in Richmond gradually superseded the fresh flowers that had hitherto been laid at war memorials. In 1928 an Empire Field of Remembrance was instituted outside Westminster Abbey, in which people 'planted' artificial poppies. This was an immediate success, and was made more practical when it was suggested that the poppies should be attached to small wooden crosses, which people could buy and embed in the sward in neat rows, replicating in miniature the war cemeteries of France and Belgium. Latterly, these crosses would be burned after use and the ashes taken to be scattered on the battlefields.

At the 1922 general election, prompted by the Conservative Party's withdrawal from the coalition government, the British Legion circulated its members with a list of thirteen questions for political candidates to answer. Most of the questions related to employment, pensions and disability allowances, but candidates were also asked: 'Do you support the League of Nation's policy that November 11th should be instituted as a National Day of Commemoration and as a National Holiday?' This fulfilled the Legion's pledge upon its formation 'to institute throughout the Empire a National Day of Commemoration for those who fell in the Great War, and to press upon the Governments concerned the desirability of instituting such a day as a General Holiday'. Although no government agreed to this, Armistice Day was often celebrated in some style once the solemnities at the Cenotaph had been observed, with the evening devoted to balls and dinners. The Legion's proposal highlighted a difficulty felt by Lloyd George when contemplating the Peace Day in 1919: there was a desire to commemorate the dead and at the same time to mark the joyful anniversary of the war's successful conclusion. It might well have been a good idea to have had two separate days, since those who attended balls on the night of 11 November were sometimes virtually accused of dancing on the graves of the fallen, even though the proceeds of such events invariably went to charity. Most of these complaints came from people who had not actually endured the trenches; veterans who recalled their feelings of joy and relief when they realised that the war was over and that they had survived were less inclined to criticise. Haig spoke for many when he publicly declared that there was nothing wrong with people, having taken part in ceremonies at war memorials, to indulge themselves in 'afternoon games suited to the climate', and in the evening 'rejoice according to their taste'.

From 1923, those who nevertheless felt that charity balls were somehow not the right way to spend Armistice night could repair to the Albert Hall, where for four years John Foulds' *World Requiem* was performed annually in aid of the British Legion. A massive work in twenty movements for some 1,250 singers and instrumentalists, the *World Requiem* was a lament for the dead of all nations who had participated in the First World War, its all-embracing nature exemplified by the texts it set, which ranged from the Latin mass and John Bunyan to the medieval Indian mystic Kabir. It was first performed on 11 November 1923 and described nonsensically as 'A Cenotaph of Sound'. The massed chorus was even dubbed 'The Cenotaph Choir', but the work, which had always been more of a popular than a critical success, proved less enduring than Lutyens' monument. Foulds was too unorthodox a figure to enter national life, and soon fell foul of the British Legion, in whose official history he does not even warrant a mention. For a start, he had not fought in the war. He had apparently volunteered, but was told he would be more useful remaining in England as a professional musician. Although already married, in 1915 he had begun living with a musician called Maud MacCarthy, with whom he had two children before she eventually became his second wife. He was both a Theosophist, believing less in the British Empire than in the eternal brotherhood of mankind, and was staunchly left-wing.

Although Foulds donated all the proceeds from performances of his *Requiem* to the Legion, in 1927 it was decided that something that veterans would themselves enjoy should replace this rather high-minded work at the centre of Armistice night. Sponsored by the *Daily Express*, the 'Empire Festival of Remembrance' was basically a sing-song for Legion members. Before the ever-popular Prince of Wales and numerous military dignitaries, 10,000 veterans belted out hymns and soldiers' songs, and the entire festival was broadcast on the radio to the farthest corners of the globe by the BBC. Such was the success of the event that it became an annual fixture which still continues. From 1929, a million paper poppies were released from the dome of the Albert Hall at the climax of the evening, each one representing an Empire life lost as it fluttered down. Meanwhile, Foulds and his *Requiem* sank into obscurity until the piece was revived eighty years later at the Festival of Remembrance in 2007.

From its somewhat haphazard beginnings, Armistice Day had become a fixture in the national calendar. Although it would remain principally a secular occasion for some years, it assumed a 'sacredness' of its own, conferred upon it by grieving widows and children. By 1925 the *Daily Mail* was declaring that: 'Of all the days in the calendar, excepting Good Friday, it has the most solemn associations.' The shift in people's attitudes to warfare caused by the losses suffered between 1914 and 1918 may be judged by the fact that Armistice Day more or less supplanted Trafalgar Day, the annual celebration of Nelson's great naval victory on 21 October 1805. Throughout the nineteenth century, right up until the outbreak of the First World War, Trafalgar Day had been marked by naval parades and banquets, but its popularity and significance subsequently declined. Just as after 1914 a literary tradition of martial verse extolling patriotism, chivalry and military prowess was usurped by what we now call 'War Poetry', which dwelt upon the terrible human cost of war, so Trafalgar Day, which unambiguously celebrated a crucial naval battle, paled into insignificance beside Armistice Day, which honoured the dead of many battles, some of which were a good deal less successful than Nelson's routing of the French navy. That this shift in attitude persists may be judged by an announcement made by the Conservative MP John Redwood, on the anniversary of Trafalgar Day in 2007: 'Today we mourn the deaths of 1,663 brave seamen and soldiers who died fighting to preserve the freedom of our country against Napoleon's imperialism 202 years ago.' Clearly, this statement has a Gallophobic slant one might expect from one of Britain's leading Euro-sceptics, but no one before 1914 would have imagined Trafalgar Day an occasion for counting the cost and mourning the dead.

The Cenotaph remained the focus of Armistice Day, though this appears to have been less at the behest of the authorities than in deference to popular sentiment. Indeed, there seems to have been a decision as early as 1922 that the ceremony at the Cenotaph should be abandoned. It is likely that this came from the Church authorities, who no doubt felt that since there was now a representative of the Empire's dead buried within a Christian church, this should be where the country's principal act of remembrance should be held. Capacious as the Abbey was, it could not accommodate anything like the number of people who thronged Whitehall, and services continued to be held both in Westminster Abbey and at the Cenotaph. The former was a full service with lessons and a sermon, whereas the liturgical content of the latter was restricted to a couple of prayers and a hymn – and this, from the Church's point of view, may have been the trouble. But it was also the point: as Lutyens intended, the Cenotaph was a place where anyone, regardless of creed, could pay homage to the dead. People of other religions, or of no religion at all, could stand politely during the brief Christian prayers and hymn and still feel that the greater part of the ceremony was inclusively secular. 'The ceremony at the Cenotaph has struck the imagination of the Empire,' *The Times* reported on the eve of Armistice Day in 1923, 'and there has been universal gratification that the first decision to abandon the service has been reversed.' This volte-face had the endorsement of Rudyard Kipling, who may not have been the Poet Laureate but was certainly regarded as a national poet, far more popular than the long-serving official incumbent, Robert Bridges. In the same edition of *The Times*, Kipling published a bleak poem called 'London Stone', placing the Cenotaph very firmly at the centre of Armistice Day observation. Far from making due obeisance to religious sentiment, the poem explicitly took and repudiated a biblical text. It further suggested that in the face of so much loss conventional religion had failed to provide answers or comfort, and that the only solace was a secular sense of community among the bereaved. The Cenotaph is designated 'the Place of Grieving', where people will come to lay flowers and take part in the two minutes' silence:

> For those minutes, tell no lie:–
>   (Grieving – grieving!)
> 'Grave, this is thy victory;
>   And the sting of Death is grieving.'
>
> Where's our help, from earth or Heaven?
>   (Grieving – grieving!)
> To comfort us for what we've given,
>   And only found the grieving.

Heaven's too far and Earth too near
    (Grieving – grieving!)
But our neighbours standing here,
    Grieve as we are grieving.

[...]

What's the tie betwixt us two
    (Grieving – grieving!)
That must last our whole lives through?
    'As I suffer so do you.'
That may ease your grieving.

It is not by any stretch Kipling's finest poem, but its almost intolerable tolling of 'Grieving – grieving!', from a man who had himself lost his only son in the war, and its laying of that grief, as it were, at the Cenotaph rather than in the Abbey, reflected the public mood.

This mood, and the placing of Lutyens' memorial at the centre of Armistice Day, was echoed by the appearance in 1923 of *Cenotaph*, 'A Book of Remembrance in Poetry and Prose for November the Eleventh', edited by the journalist and poet Thomas Moult. The frontispiece was a drawing by Joseph Pike depicting the Cenotaph on what looks like a rain-sodden English afternoon. Alongside such perennial favourites as Binyon's 'For the Fallen', McCrae's 'In Flanders Fields', Brooke's 'The Soldier' and Hardy's 'Men Who March Away', as well as many less enduring verses, Moult reproduces extracts from letters written at the front, newspaper accounts of the first Armistice Days, the last reported words of Nurse Cavell, General Pershing's speech when awarding the Congressional Medal of Honor to the Unknown Warrior, and Joseph Conrad's salute to 'the seamen of Great Britain'. Not all the selections are anodyne: Sassoon's 'Aftermath' includes references to 'the stench of corpses rotting' and the 'dying eyes and lolling heads' of stretcher cases, but is included perhaps because it ends with an exhortation never to forget the dead. There would be no further attempts to usurp the pre-eminence of the Cenotaph in the grieving hearts of the British people for some time to come.

Lutyens' austere memorial rapidly joined other buildings and monuments as a famous London sight, appearing in guidebooks and on postcards. Souvenir manufacturers such as Crest also provided ceramic models of the Cenotaph so that even those who could not visit the monument in person could display one on their mantelpieces. As its name suggested, the Crest company specialised in ceramics with garish and gilded coats of arms enamelled on their plain white surfaces, as did several other companies, including Carlton, Podmore and Arcadian. The standard model naturally bore the coat of arms of London, but you could often buy one bearing your own local crest, whether you lived in a large city such as Oxford or a small town such as Walton-on-the-Naze. Some manufacturers, evidently feeling that Lutyens' restrained reference to the Glorious Dead left something wanting, daubed their models with such inelegant if heartfelt slogans as 'The blood of heroes is the seed of freedom'. Quite what the architect himself would have made of such sentiments, or indeed these often fanciful models of his pure and unadorned design, is not known, but these commemorative gewgaws were evidently popular.

The Cenotaph got a chapter to itself in H.V. Morton's *The*

Heart of London (1925), Lutyens' comparatively new monument taking its place beside more ancient sights of London such as St Paul's, the Royal Mint and Cleopatra's Needle. Morton describes visiting the Cenotaph 'on a cold, grey February morning':

> A parcels delivery boy riding a tricycle takes off his worn cap. An omnibus goes by. The men lift their hats. Men passing with papers and documents under their arms and attaché and despatch cases in their hands – all the business of life – bare their heads as they hurry by.
>
> Six years [since the end of the war] have made no difference here. The Cenotaph – that mass of national emotion frozen in stone – is holy to this generation. Although I have seen it so many times on that day once a year when it comes alive to the accompaniment of pomp as simple and as beautiful as church ritual, I think I like it best just standing here in a grey morning, with its feet in flowers and ordinary folk going by, remembering.

The ordinary folk, members of the lower middle class, were Morton's intended readership, and many of his books started out as columns in the populist *Daily Express*, where he worked as a journalist throughout the 1920s. Morton became one of the most widely read travel writers of the twentieth century, and although his volumes now crowd the shelves of second-hand bookshops, during his lifetime his influence was considerable, particularly in the interwar period. His most famous book was *In Search of England* (1927), and all his books are very much concerned with a sense of national identity. The book's title suggested a spiritual as well as a geographical quest, and the England Morton goes in search of in his Morris Cowley is as much a repository of national values as it is a collection of fields and woods and towns and villages. Morton was himself a veteran of the war – though one whose military career remains something of an enigma – and, as his biographer Michael Bartholomew notes, *In Search of England* 'is in many ways the archetypal post-war record of a soldier, home from the trenches, going off to try to locate and define the country he'd been fighting for'.

It opens melodramatically 'I believed I was dying in Palestine', which at this period naturally makes the reader think of him as a serving soldier. Morton explains that he was worried that an acute pain he was suffering in his neck might be a symptom of spinal meningitis, but he is careful not to provide a date for these intimations of mortality, which were widely shared by the generation that had been to war. He describes climbing a hill overlooking Jerusalem and, 'turning as accurately as I could in the direction of England', giving in to a wave of homesickness.

Perhaps in instinctive contrast to the cold, unhappy mountains of Palestine there rose in my mind the picture of a village street at dusk with a smell of wood smoke lying in the still air and, here and there, little red blinds shining in the dusk under the thatch. I remembered how the church bells ring at home, and how, at that time of year, the sun leaves a dull red bar low down in the west, and against it the elms grow blacker minute by minute. Then the bats start to flicker like little bits of burnt paper and you hear the slow jingle of a team coming home from the fields … When you think like this sitting alone in a foreign country I think you know all there is to know about heartache.

Many servicemen must have entertained similar thoughts when they managed to find a quiet moment to themselves out of the noise and confusion of war. 'I took a vow that if my pain in the neck did not end for ever on the windy hills of Palestine I would go through the lanes of England and the little thatched villages of England, and I would lean over English bridges and lie on English grass watching an English sky.' The manner and language might be reminiscent of Rupert Brooke, but Morton was not on active service. He was in fact – as he is careful not to tell us – in Palestine as a tourist in 1923, returning from Egypt, where he had been on a journalistic assignment for the *Daily Express* to report the discovery of Tutankhamen's tomb.

The sleight of hand practised by Morton in the opening pages of *In Search of England* is not particularly reprehensible, and it gives the book an added force at a time when war memoirs were starting to appear. Unsurprisingly, Morton also wrote about the Unknown Warrior in *The Spell of London* (1926), in which jaunty character sketches mingle sometimes uneasily with overblown passages suggesting an almost religious sense of Englishness. The Unknown Warrior, he writes, 'lies not only at the heart of London, but also at the heart of England, here in magic earth, in this sacred soil, so warm in love, so safe in honour. No noise of traffic disturbs his sleep, no unkind wind whistles over him – no solitude of night. Instead, the silence of a mighty church, a silence as deep and lovely as though he were lying in some green country graveyard steeped in peace, above him a twilight in which the stored centuries seem to whisper happily of good things done for England.' Of course, the sacred soil in which the Warrior rests was not English at all, but specially imported from the battlefields, which may be why Morton liked to imagine this representative of all that is good about England as if he were in a country churchyard. Indeed, the England Morton came to value and think most representative of the nation was that of the smaller towns and villages. 'This village that symbolizes England sleeps in the sub-consciousness of many a townsman,' Morton observed.

> A little London factory hand I met during the war confessed to me when pressed, and after great mental difficulty, that he visualised the England he was fighting for – the England of the 'England wants you' poster – as not London, not his own street, but as Epping Forest, the green place where he had spent Bank Holidays. And I think most of us did. The village and the English country-side are the germs of all we are and all we have become: our manufacturing cities belong to the last century and a half; our villages stand with their roots in the Heptarchy.

Morton's England was essentially pre-war, even prelapsarian, but the villages he was visiting and writing about were acutely conscious of the changes wrought by the war. While Morton was extolling a sense of continuity, the radical break in history that the war represented was finding concrete form in the memorials being erected in such places to commemorate their dead. According to the Somerset volume of *The King's England* series of guidebooks founded by Arthur Mee in 1930, there were only thirty villages in the whole country in which all those who marched off to war returned. These were known as 'thankful villages' or 'luck parishes'. Morton's book ends in an English churchyard, where the vicar talks of the generations that have lived and died in the parish. He mentions Crusaders, but surprisingly no mention is made of the more recent dead, who by this time would almost certainly be commemorated in the church or churchyard. Like the Cenotaph, local war memorials were now added to tourist itineraries in other less rigidly nostalgic guidebooks with, for example, a whole chapter devoted to them in *Wonderful Britain: Its Highways, Byways and Historical Places*, published in parts between 1928 and 1929. Similarly, local war memorials joined grand civic buildings, picturesque street scenes and thatched cottages as suitable subjects for postcards.

Most war memorials were paid for by public subscription, local committees being formed to raise money and oversee planning and design. While some communities commemorated the dead with public buildings such as a new village hall or cottage hospital, or public recreation grounds, most erected a monument of some kind: a cross or obelisk, or a figurative statue. These were often in addition to the Roll of Honour displayed in churches, where the names of the parish's dead were listed on a brass wall plaque, a wooden board or occasionally in stained glass, as in the cloisters of Worcester Cathedral, where fallen bell-ringers and members of the choir are commemorated. Schools, universities, businesses and other organisations also erected their own memorials to commemorate former pupils, alumni, employees and other members of communities other than towns and villages. The unveiling of new memorials during services of dedication carried on for many years, right up until the eve of the Second World War. Thereafter they formed a focus for civic pride of a particular kind, not merely remembering the individual dead but demonstrating that each community had played its part and made its own sacrifices in the war.

These sacrifices were immediately and starkly apparent in Combe Down, the birthplace of Harry Patch, which might stand representative of local losses in the same way that Patch himself came to represent the British Tommy. Fifty-six names are carved on the limestone war memorial that was erected in 1921 on Firs Field, a public space purchased by public subscription for this purpose. Both Patch and his brother William had returned safely from the war, but many of the boys they had grown up with did not. These included their cousin Fred, a private in the Somerset Light Infantry (SLI) killed at the Battle of Arras in April 1917. His name is recorded on the Arras Memorial alongside those of some 35,000 servicemen who died in the sector between 1916 and 1918 and have no known grave. Patch had also lost several close friends, including Charlie Wherrett, who joined the Somerset Light Infantry at the outbreak of war, survived past the Armistice, but died while serving in India in June 1919 at the age of twenty-five and was buried far from Combe Down in Peshawar. Two other friends from Patch's schooldays, Stanley Pearce and Lionel Morris, also joined the local regiment when war was declared, and like Patch took part in the Third Battle of Ypres. Pearce was killed in July 1917, disappeared into the Passchendaele mud, and is listed among the 54,000 names of the missing on the Menin Gate. Morris was killed two months later at the age of twenty, and his name appears on the Tyne Cot Memorial to the Missing at Zonnebeke, which commemorates another 35,000 men whose bodies were never found. Another friend, Leslie Lush, joined the Royal Army Medical Corps along with his brother Lewis. Leslie returned, but Lewis was killed in France at the age of twenty-two, eleven days before the Armistice. He had been serving with a field ambulance unit and was buried at the St-Sever Cemetery Extension at Rouen, along with 8,345 other casualties, most of whom had been unsuccessfully treated for their wounds in the city's many military hospitals. Harold Chivers, who served with the Royal Engineers, died at the age of twenty-one in November 1917 and is buried along with 10,772 others at Etaples, the largest British war cemetery in France. Eric Barrow, too young to enlist when war broke out, lied about his age in order to join the Somerset Light Infantry in October 1915. He went to France in May 1916 and was killed on the Somme three months later, still only eighteen. Like Fred Patch, Stanley Pearce and Lionel Morris, he disappeared without trace: his name is recorded on the Memorial to the Missing at Thiepval.

Harry Patch also remembered other local men and boys who joined the local regiment at the outbreak of war. Frederick Gerrish died a year later in August 1915 and is buried at Hazebrouck in France, a cemetery beside one of the major casualty clearing stations. Kendrick Frankling, who sang with Patch in the church choir and whose father had been the station-master at nearby Midford, was killed on the Somme in August 1916 at the age of twenty-three; Albert Kellaway, who gained a lance corporal's stripe, died there at the age of twenty-eight in September 1916. Neither of their bodies was found and their names joined that of Lionel Morris on the crammed panels of Lutyens' vast memorial at Thiepval. Captain C.J.O. Daubeny, the only son of Captain C.W. Daubeny of The Brow, a large house built above Jackdaw Quarry, was killed in France at the age of twenty-one in June 1917 and is buried near Arras. A plaque was erected to him in Holy Trinity, the church in which his family sat in named pews and where his father frequently read the lesson. The vicar's son, Alfred, had served with the SLI at Gallipoli and in Egypt and was killed at the age of twenty-five in Palestine. He is buried at Beersheba, a place whose name would have been familiar to his father from the Bible.

Combe Down casualties continued to mount even after the war had officially ended. Eric Grant, who sang tenor in the choir and served with the Bedfordshire Regiment, was still in uniform when he died at the age of eighteen in March 1919. He is buried beneath an IWGC headstone in the churchyard of St Michael's, Monkton Combe, as is Patch's neighbour Victor Wilkinson, a policeman, who returned from serving as a gunner with the Royal Garrison Artillery but died in April 1919. These fourteen men are merely the ones whose names Patch recalled in extreme old age when he wrote his autobiography, but behind every single name on the Combe Down war memorial is a family and a story. As Patch himself observed, there was scarcely a family in the village who had not been affected by these losses. The same could be said of towns and villages across the land.

War memorials became the places where communities far from the Cenotaph gathered once a year on 11 November to observe the two minutes' silence, lay wreaths, and remember their dead. If Armistice Day had become a public holiday, as the British Legion had wanted, the two minutes' silence (by now usually referred to as 'the Silence') would have been a good deal less impressive. As it was, this tradition endured, sometimes to an absurd or even dangerous degree. It was reported in 1922, for instance, that the pilot of an aeroplane operated by the Daimler Hire Company travelling between Manchester and London on 11 November observed maroons marking the beginning of the Silence bursting in the air as he approached Rugby. 'He throttled down his engine, and glided silently through the air', while his four passengers stood to attention with bowed heads. Four years later *The Times* reported of the service at the Cenotaph that:

> It was probably the deepest Silence that has ever reigned even at this ceremony. Special care had been taken to keep it unbroken by the slightest noise. There was none of the avoidable interruptions that have sometimes marred a little the solemnity of the Two Minutes. An attentive ear could make out but two sounds – a stifled cough and a distant belated steam-whistle. Not a movement could be seen; if any had been seen it would have been felt, so immobile was the whole grey picture.

From 1928 almost the entire nation could join the Silence when the Cenotaph service was broadcast for the first time on BBC radio, something that became an annual event and around which programming had to be fitted. Radio existed to produce a more or less continual output of sound, so the Silence was particularly striking. It brought the whole nation together with what was happening at the Cenotaph at precisely the same moment. The notion of well-nigh universal participation in the observances of Armistice Day even provided the plot for a detective novel published that same year. Dorothy L. Sayers' *The Unpleasantness at the Bellona Club* could in fact be called an

Armistice Day novel; as a popular one, it provides a fascinating insight into prevailing attitudes.

The entire novel is suffused with the experience of the war, an experience that almost everyone at the Bellona Club, members and staff alike, has shared and which gives them a sense of comradeship regardless of class. The detective hero Lord Peter Wimsey (we are told in a prefatory biographical note) served throughout the war, winning the DSO 'for some reckless good intelligence work behind the German front'. In 1918 Wimsey had been 'blown up and buried in a shell-hole near Caudry' and suffered from severe shell shock from which it took him two years to recover. His convalescence was overseen by his former batman, Sergeant Mervyn Bunter, who becomes his invaluable valet and sidekick in the series of novels Sayers wrote about her aristocratic sleuth. *The Unpleasantness at the Bellona Club* was written against a background of Sayers' own experience of the after-effects of war: her husband, Atherton Fleming, had also served at the front and, shortly after their marriage in 1926, began suffering some form of delayed war trauma.

The notion that Armistice Day remained principally an occasion for the general public rather than veterans is clear from the novel's opening page. 'All this remembrance-day business gets on your nerves, don't it?' Wimsey says to Captain George Fentiman. 'It's my belief most of us would be only too pleased to chuck these community hysterics if the beastly newspapers didn't run it for all it's worth. However, it don't do to say so.' Fentiman, who is also a veteran of the trenches, agrees: 'What's the damn good of it, Wimsey? A man goes and fights for his country, gets his insides gassed out, and loses his job, and all they give him is the privilege of marching past the Cenotaph once a year and paying four shillings in the pound income-tax.' These characters are of course fictional, but it is striking that such sentiments could be voiced not only by the embittered, out-of-work and neurasthenic Captain Fentiman but also by someone as admirable and likeable as Sayers' detective hero.

The novel's complex plot hinges upon the exact time of the death of Captain Fentiman's grandfather, a general who fought in the Crimean War. This needs to be established in order to decide how his estate is to be divided. The general supposedly died in the club's smoking room on the morning of Armistice Day, but Wimsey discovers that he had in fact died the day before. A central clue to this discrepancy is that no poppy is found on the body. 'My dear sir,' Wimsey says to the family solicitor, Mr Murbles, 'consider what day it was. November the 11th. Is it conceivable that, if the old man had been walking the streets as a free agent on Armistice Day, he would have gone to the Club without his Flanders poppy?' Such a thing, he adds, would be 'unthinkable'.

Another element of the plot is whether or not a telephone booth in the club was out of order. A club member remembers that it was because he wanted 'to get through to a man down in Norfolk. Brother was a friend of mine – killed on the last day of the War, half an hour before the guns stopped firing – damnable shame – always ring up on Armistice Day, say a few words, don't you know.' Wimsey realises that the phone had not in fact been out of order, but that a notice had been put on the door of the booth to that effect while it was being used temporarily to store the general's corpse, which was then transferred to the chair in the smoking room where it was discovered. Murbles points out that there were people in the smoking room all morning; how on earth could anyone have moved the body without being observed? 'Were people there *all* morning, sir?' Wimsey replies. 'Are you sure? Wasn't there just one period when one could be certain that everybody would be either out in the street or upstairs on the big balcony that runs along in front of the first-floor windows, looking out – and listening? It was Armistice Day, remember.'

Mr Murbles was horror-struck.

'The two minutes' silence? – God bless my soul! How abominable! How – how blasphemous! Really, I cannot find words. This is the most disgraceful thing I ever heard of. At the moment when all our thoughts should be concentrated on the brave fellows who laid down their lives for us – to be engaged in perpetrating a fraud – an irreverent crime—'

The perpetrator, a veteran of the war, is unrepentant, which further outrages Murbles. 'I cannot, and I will not sit here and listen while you congratulate yourself, with a cynicism at which you should blush, on having employed those sacred moments, when every thought should have been consecrated,' he expostulates. 'Oh, punk!' replies the fraudster. 'My old pals are none the worse because I did a little bit of self-help.'

Much of the unravelling of the plot relies upon what people would normally be doing in the run-up to Armistice Day and on the day itself. Sayers also uses the character of George Fentiman to illustrate the difficulties faced by men of the officer class who returned after the war to find themselves unemployed. Their plight had been thoroughly aired in Warwick Deeping's hugely popular sentimental novel *Sorrell and Son* (1925), in which the eponymous hero undergoes the indignity of having to work as a hotel porter in order to pay for his son's education. Fentiman is a more extreme case. Heavily in debt, he lives in rented rooms in unfashionable Finsbury Park. Frequently ill as a result of gassing and shell shock, unable to find work, Fentiman is obliged to rely upon his wife's income as a cashier working long hours in a tea shop. This he finds deeply humiliating: it is the cause of frequent marital rows, of which he later feels very ashamed. He later applies for a job selling cars, one of the new but distinctly déclassé jobs available to former officers after the war.

The Unpleasantness at the Bellona Club makes ingenious use of the form and customs of Armistice Day while at the same time showing that attitudes towards it were not perhaps as universal as people liked to believe. Indeed, Armistice Day remained an event from which many real-life ex-servicemen continued to feel alienated. It was not merely those who were out of work and felt themselves forgotten, but others for whom the event seemed, as Harry Patch put it, 'nothing but a show of military force'. The presence of a steadily diminishing band of veterans proudly wearing their medals at the Cenotaph every year has become such a familiar feature of the ceremony that it is something of a surprise to discover that it was not until the early 1930s that the British Legion began to play a significant role in Whitehall each 11 November. There had always been debate as to how this ceremony should be conducted, and the increasing participation of politicians and other 'bigwigs' laying wreaths in order of precedence seemed to have little to do with the ordinary people it supposedly honoured. Some felt that the forces' march-past, which had survived since the very first Armistice Day, should be scaled down or removed altogether since it added a martial – or even militarist – emphasis to what should have been a commemoration of the human cost of war.

A further factor against excessive military participation in the Armistice Day ceremony in the interwar period was that those who were being remembered at the Cenotaph had been members of the armed forces only 'for the duration'. They may have died as soldiers, but they had lived as civilians, which is how many of their friends and families remembered them. It was the British Legion's patron, the Prince of Wales, who suggested in 1932 that the armed forces at the ceremony should be replaced by members of the Legion, who might sport medals, but would of course be in civilian dress. Both the government and the prince's father were opposed to the idea, and the Legion itself worried that the armed forces might resent their role being usurped by old soldiers. Furthermore, it was not clear whether enough veterans could be assembled to fill the gap left by the military.

The resurgence of militarism and fascism in Europe played a part in these shifts of attitude towards Armistice Day, but it may also have been significant that from 1928 onwards a large number of books more directly about the war than Sayers' novel began to appear. The generally pious and patriotic volumes commemorating the Fallen, which were often privately printed, gave way to frank accounts written for the general reader of the realities of trench warfare, enlivened by criticism of those whose principal strategy had been to pursue a war of attrition. Many of these war memoirs and autobiographical novels became bestsellers. Siegfried Sassoon's *Memoirs of a Fox-Hunting Man* and Edmund Blunden's *Undertones of War* both appeared in 1928, the year R.C. Sherriff's frequently revived trench play *Journey's End* was first performed. In 1929 came Robert Graves's *Goodbye to All That*, Richard Aldington's coruscating *Death of a Hero*, and the English translation of E.M. Remarque's *Im Westen nichts Neues* (*All Quiet on the Western Front*). Frederic Manning's bowdlerised but still stark account of life as a ranker, *Her Privates We*, appeared in 1930, as did Sassoon's *Memoirs of an Infantry Officer*, Henry Williamson's expressionist fable *A Patriot's Progress* and Sherriff's novelisation of *Journey's End*. While not all of these were strictly 'anti-war', most described all too vividly the realities of trench warfare and put individual faces to the already dreadful statistics.

Similarly, regimental histories and detailed accounts of individual battles and strategy, mostly aimed at a specialised audience, were supplemented by more popular historical and analytical accounts of the war. Particularly influential in shaping people's attitudes were official-sounding histories such as Winston Churchill's *The World Crisis* (1923–31) and B.H. Liddell Hart's *The Real War, 1914–1918* (1930), both of which were a good deal less objective than their titles suggested and undoubtedly fuelled a growing public perception of the war as ill conceived and badly conducted. Together with Lloyd George's six volumes of *War Memoirs* (1933–36), these books did much to make people question why and how the war had been fought and whether the cost was worth it.

That cost is frequently measured in these three books, with casualty figures given a prominent part in accounts of the principal battles. Churchill's chapter on the Somme in the third part of his book, which appeared in 1927, for example, outlines the losses suffered by a single division on the first day of the battle: 'In all, the Division lost in little more than two hours 218 out of 300 officers and 5,274 other ranks out of 8,500 who had gone into action. By the evening of July 1, the German 180th Infantry Regiment was again in possession of the whole of its trenches. Its losses during the day's fighting had been 8 officers killed and 273 soldiers killed, wounded or missing.' Although Churchill is at pains elsewhere to praise 'the phlegm, the temper and the fortitude of Sir Douglas Haig', he notes of J.H. Boraston's summary of the first day on the Somme in *Sir Douglas Haig's Command* (1922): 'It takes some hardihood for Col. Boraston to write: "The events of July 1 … bore out the conclusions of the British High Command and amply justified the tactical methods employed."' Churchill also criticises Haig's own account in his published *Despatches* (1919) of the gains made during the first five days of the battle, noting that these gains had 'been purchased by the loss of nearly a hundred thousand of our best troops'. In spite of such losses, he writes: 'The battle continued. The objectives now were pulverised villages and blasted woods, and the ground conquered at each stage was so limited both in width and depth as to exclude any strategic results.' He dismisses Haig's unwisely self-confident tally of casualties: 'Sir Douglas Haig, in his final despatch upon the Somme, committed himself to the following positive assertion: "There is nevertheless sufficient evidence to place it beyond doubt that the enemies' losses in men and material have been very considerably higher than those of the Allies."' Positive, but according to Churchill completely untrue: the figure, he says, was in fact roughly 2.27 British losses for every German loss. While he concedes that Haig could not take sole blame for what happened on the Somme, he added: 'Nevertheless the campaign of 1916 on the Western Front was from beginning to end a welter of slaughter, which after the issue was determined left the British and French armies weaker in relation to the Germans than when it opened, while the actual battle fronts were not appreciably altered, and except for the relief of Verdun, which relieved the Germans no less than the French, no strategic advantage of any kind had been gained.' The account ends with a fulsome paean to the bravery and determination of the troops whose lives, the reader could only conclude, had been profligately and more or less pointlessly sacrificed. Churchill's tribute to the front-line troops was not merely a piece of retrospective patriotic piety made from the comfort of a Whitehall armchair. In 1916, but before the Battle of the Somme, he had himself served briefly as a commanding officer in France, where he was noted not only for his leadership but also for the concern he showed for the well-being of the men in his battalion.

Similarly, it could be said that, as someone who had joined up at the age of nineteen in December 1914, served as a subaltern with the King's Own Yorkshire Light Infantry (KOYLI) on the Western Front, and been gassed at Mametz Wood in 1916, Captain B.H. Liddell Hart was amply qualified to write a book entitled *The Real War*. After his war service Liddell Hart embarked on a career in journalism and produced several volumes of military history, so his voice also had the authority of a seasoned professional historian. In his preface, he writes:

> Some may say the war depicted here is not 'the real war' – that is to be discovered in the torn bodies and minds of individuals. It is far from my purpose to ignore or deny this aspect of the truth. But for anyone who seeks, as I seek here, to view the war as an episode in human history, it is a secondary aspect. Because the war affected individual lives so greatly, because these individuals were numbered by millions, because the roots of their fate lay so deep in the past, it is all the more necessary to see the war in perspective, and to disentangle its main threads from the accidents of human misery.

The perspective, however, was clearly coloured by Liddell Hart's own experiences: he may have been a professional historian, but he was also a veteran of the conflict he was writing about.

He admits that his book (which in 1934 he revised, expanded and retitled less combatively *History of the First World War*) is not perfect, but suggests it

> may at least claim one merit, and one contrast to most war 'histories'. I have as little desire to hide its imperfections as to hide the imperfections of any who are portrayed in its pages. Hence in writing it my pursuit of the truth has not been interrupted by recourse to the pot of hypocritical varnish that is miscalled 'good taste'. In my judgement of values it is more important to provide material for a true verdict than to gloss over disturbing facts so

that individual reputations may be preserved at the price of another holocaust of young lives. Taking a long view of history, I cannot regard the repute of a few embodied handfuls of dust as worth more than the fate of a nation and a generation.

Reading this, it is impossible to forget that Liddell Hart had fought on the first day of the Somme, by the end of which he was one of only three second lieutenants in the 9th KOYLI surviving of the eight who had been present when the attack started. Though he scrupulously avoids bringing his own experiences explicitly into his history, this is clearly an account of the Western Front by someone who had served there and witnessed at first hand the results on the ground of decisions made at GHQ.

In an early chapter, he outlines the individual qualities of the generals, noting that 'the process of selection had not succeeded in bringing to the fore the officers best fitted for leadership'. He quotes Sir John French's observation in 1912 that Haig and General Sir John Grierson ('a man of full figure and sedentary habits' who perhaps fortunately dropped dead on his way to the front) would 'always shine more and show to greater advantage as superior staff officers than as commanders'. Liddell Hart adds that although, when serving in the South African War, Haig's 'thoroughness and methodicity had made him an ideal staff officer to French', his appointment to command a mobile column caused Colonel Woolls-Sampson, 'an incomparable Intelligence officer and fighter scout', to remark: 'He's quite all right, but he's too —— cautious: he will be so fixed on not giving the Boers a chance, he'll never give himself one.' Liddell Hart notes that according to the *Official History* of the 1914–18 war, 'Haig's excessive caution on reaching the Aisne [in September 1914] allowed the day of opportunity to slip away, and the enemy to establish their four-years' tenure of the position beyond', a judgement he repeats and enlarges upon when he comes to writing about that episode in the main narrative.

Liddell Hart does at least acknowledge that 'the ill-fated Loos-offensive [in September 1915] was undertaken directly against the opinion of Haig, the man who, as commander of the First Army, had to carry it out', but this allows him to criticise the British and French commanders-in-chief, Sir John French and General Joffre. He quotes Lord Kitchener, who as Britain's Secretary of State for War had political responsibility for the overall conduct of the war, complaining that these two men 'told me in November [1914] they were going to push the Germans back over the frontier; they gave me the same assurances in December, March, and May. What have they done? The attacks are very costly and end in nothing.' It was this impatience which was partly responsible for the attack at Loos being launched with less than a quarter of the troops French and Haig deemed necessary to make it a success. Gradually, a picture emerges from Liddell Hart's account, a picture that would become the prevailing view of the war: political and military misjudgements led to the needless slaughter of thousands upon thousands of soldiers. Indeed, by the end of the battle in mid-October British casualties amounted to 60,392 compared with German losses of fewer than 20,000. Even so, Liddell Hart writes, Haig (whose concern about inadequate troops had evidently waned) 'was working up a new general attack for November 7th, an operation whose inevitable cost does not seem to have any adequate excuse.

Happily, Generals Winter and Weather intervened.' This little flourish is characteristic of Liddell Hart's style, which manages to remain lively and readable without ever losing an authority he reinforces by frequently quoting from the compendious *Official History* of the war. Even this work, more properly *The History of the Great War Based on Historical Documents*, concluded that the Battle of Loos 'had not improved the general situation in any way and had brought nothing but useless slaughter of infantry', but Liddell Hart was more inclined to apportion blame, believing that 'the historian's task is to distil experience as a medicinal warning to future generations'. And it was his history of the war, rather than the official one running to a daunting twenty-eight volumes, that the general public would read. The book retained its popularity for decades and was still being republished in the 1990s.

Liddell Hart's account of the Battle of the Somme is, as one would expect, equally critical of the High Command, while that of Passchendaele ('so fruitless in its result, so depressing in its direction [that it has become] a synonym for military failure – a name black-bordered in the records of the British Army') continues the criticism of Haig's 'lofty optimism' and records the many deaths that were the result. Ninety years later, a veteran of that battle, Harry Patch, was still alive to remember those deaths. It was at the Battle of Passchendaele that he first saw action, saw a young man torn open by shrapnel begging to be put out of his misery, and subsequently lost three of his closest friends. These were experiences from which he said he never really recovered. 'Some nights I dream of that first battle,' he said. 'I can't forget it.'

Liddell Hart's reservations about the competence of Haig (who had died in 1928) were as nothing to those of Lloyd George in his *War Memoirs*. Lloyd George had replaced Asquith as Prime Minister in December 1916, having already taken an active part in the conduct of the war as successively Chancellor, a spectacularly effective Minister of Munitions, and Secretary of State for War. He was appointed to this last post in July 1916 as the Battle of the Somme was taking place in France. Although he believed in 'total war', he had already spoken out in January 1915 against the strategy of attrition. His relations with the generals, never cordial, grew worse once he was Prime Minister – to the point that, since members of the High Command were virtually unsackable, he used the press to undermine their position. He failed, however, to prevent Haig from mounting a new offensive at Passchendaele in the conspicuously wet summer of 1917, and the massive loss of life that resulted preyed on his conscience thereafter, further alienating him from the High Command. He was nevertheless widely seen as 'the man who won the war', and his re-election in December 1918 had in part been a reflection of this belief. After a bruising few years, he left office in October 1922, remaining an influential political figure thereafter.

Like most political autobiographies, Lloyd George's *War Memoirs* were in part an exercise in vindication and self-exculpation. The author had no qualms whatsoever in criticising the military leaders with whom he had so often disagreed while in office. In part the memoirs read like an account by the man who won the war of the stubbornness and ineptitude of those who very nearly lost it. Anyone who might innocently imagine the book would provide a first-hand but objective account of the war need only look up the very long entry under 'Haig, Field-Marshal Earl' in the index that forms part of Volume VI, as someone evidently did in a copy at the London Library, pencil in hand. Running to over four pages in double columns, entries begin reasonably neutrally though perhaps pointedly with 'his reputation founded on cavalry exploits' and conclude on the qualified commendation of 'no conspicuous officer better qualified for highest command than'. In between these two entries, however, is a comprehensive catalogue of Haig's professional and personal failings, which the reader at the London Library has helpfully underlined: 'his refusal to face unpleasant facts', 'his limited vision', 'Germans accustomed to his heavy-footed movements', 'his stubborn mind transfixed on Somme', 'his misconceptions concerning morale of German army', 'obsessed with Passchendaele and optimistic as to military outlook', 'none of his essential conditions for success prevail at Passchendaele', 'misrepresents French attitude', 'his plans strongly condemned by Foch', 'misleads Cabinet about Italian Front', 'prefers to gamble his hopes on men's lives than to admit an error', 'completely ignorant of state of ground at Passchendaele', 'fails to appreciate the value of tanks', 'not anxious for success on Italian Front', 'a mere name to men in the trenches', 'narrowness of his outlook', 'incapable of changing his plans', 'his judgement on general situation warped by his immediate interests', 'his fanciful estimates of man-power', 'jealous of Foch', 'does not expect big German attack in 1918', 'distributes his reserves very unwisely', 'his conduct towards Fifth Army not strictly honourable', 'his unwise staff appointments', 'his defeatist memorandum of 25/3/18', 'unfairly removes Gough from command of Fifth Army', 'his complaints as to lack of men unjustified', 'does not envisage Americans being of use in 1918', 'stubbornness', 'unreliability of his judgements', 'launches successful attack of

8/8/18 […] but fails to follow it up', 'his censorious criticism of his associates', 'his attempt to shirk blame for March, 1918, defeat', 'only took part in one battle during War'… and so on. It is something of a surprise to find the entry 'Lloyd George has no personal quarrel with', but this is wittily placed since the entries immediately following it read: 'unequal to his task', 'industrious but uninspired', 'did not inspire his men', 'entirely dependent on others for essential information', 'the two documents that prove his incapacity', 'unselfish but self-centred', 'his inability to judge men', 'liked his associates to be silent and gentlemanly', 'his contempt for Foch', 'his intrigues against Lord French and Kitchener', 'his failure at Loos', 'his ingenuity in shifting blame to other shoulders than his own', 'his shabby treatment of Gough', 'his conspiracy to destroy General Reserve'.

Some commentators thought it in poor taste to attack Haig, who was no longer in a position to answer back, but by a stroke of good fortune Lloyd George was still at work on the final two volumes of his *War Memoirs* when extracts from Haig's diaries were published, edited by Duff Cooper. This allowed him to add a late chapter, 'Lord Haig's Diaries and After'. Of Haig's diaries he writes: 'The publication of these intimate reflections – or rather aspersions – by Lord Haig on the men, some now living, some dead, with whom he was associated in the service of his country during the War, must silence the reproof directed against my Memoirs on the absurd ground that they occasionally express adverse opinions on the strategy of Generals who have now passed away.' Delighted to have the opportunity of returning to the attack, Lloyd George savages Haig's prose as well as his conduct: 'Considering that the Diaries contained a daily record of momentous events in which Lord Haig took a leading part and of his impressions and reflections upon them in the quiet of his study at dusk, the extracts are not only meagre but remarkably sterile and undistinguished. If this represents the best which Mr Duff Cooper could find, what must be the quality of the rest?' Haig's diaries, he says, are the result of 'a sustained egoism which is almost a disease', before slyly adding: 'I certainly had no time or inclination amidst the labour and anxiety of the War for sitting down every evening to write for the enlightenment of posterity the tale of my accomplishments during the day. It could not have been of any assistance to me or anyone else in the discharge of our onerous duties.' He is at pains to point out (not altogether truthfully) that:

During the critical days of the War, when it was important not to undermine public confidence in the Commander-in-Chief of our own Army, I made no public attack on his personal fitness for so immense a responsibility [...] but I never concealed from myself or my colleagues that I thought Sir Douglas Haig was intellectually and temperamentally unequal to the command of an Army of millions fighting battles on fields which were invisible to any Commander [...] He had long training on lines which were irrelevant to the experiences and exigencies of this War. That was not his fault. There never had been such a war, and the narrow and rigid system which he had learnt and taught made it difficult for so unsupple a mind to adapt himself readily to any other ideas.

Far more than Churchill, Lloyd George had the trick of appearing to make every excuse for Haig as a man in an impossible position before undercutting any faint praise with a deadly rider. This makes his *War Memoirs* very entertaining, and certainly a far livelier read than poor old Haig's pompous and ponderous diaries. This quickness and imagination that Haig so signally lacked are apparent on virtually every page of Lloyd George's book, and it is this which makes it persuasive even though highly partisan and self-serving. Within a year of the publication of the final volume, the *War Memoirs* had sold over 54,000 copies. Along with Churchill's and Liddell Hart's books, they did enormous damage to Haig's reputation in particular, and fixed in people's minds the inadequacies of the High Command and the huge losses that resulted. The fact that two of these authors had served in the government during the war, one of them as Prime Minister, while the other was a respected historian who had seen active service on the Western Front, lent these books considerable authority.

These three accounts of the war, and the novels and memoirs already mentioned, were merely the most famous of the period, and represent a very small portion of the torrent pouring from the presses. Some of these novels and memoirs, mostly forgotten or little read now, were quite as graphic and savage as anything produced by Graves, Sassoon or Aldington. Indeed, so many 'War Books' had appeared by 1930 that the military historian Cyril Falls was able to compile a descriptive bibliography, in which nearly two hundred of the 690 titles he included were either memoirs or novels. As Falls acknowledged in the book's preface, almost as much ink had been spilled since the war as blood had been spilled during it. Of the 188 volumes of 'reminiscence' he listed alphabetically from J. Johnston

Abraham's *My Balkan Log* (1921) to Francis Brett Young's *Marching on Tanga* (1917), he observed:

> These books are of the most diverse kinds. Some are bald records, a few works of genius. Some are inspired by the historical spirit, some by the desire to tell a good story. Some by the spirit of propaganda, to prove that their side was the right and the other wrong, or – but these, as might be expected, are English only – that their side was wrong and the other side right, more often still to make an end of war. On the whole it may be said that as time goes on they become more and more critical of their own country's political and military leadership, more and more bitter in tone, more and more filled with loathing of war.

Falls found war novels rather more consistent: 'One may say that to an overwhelming extent "War fiction" is concerned with the junior officer or man in the ranks, and especially the infantryman, the worst sufferer. And in the case of five books out of six it is not only bitterly opposed to war but marked by certain characteristics which are worth examination.' These characteristics are remarkably similar to those that continue to colour the general public's view of the war, and Falls was one of the very earliest military historians to formulate what later scholars would call the 'myth of the First World War' and challenge it. What is particularly interesting about this is that, unlike many of his successors, Falls had actually fought in the war. Having joined the Royal Inniskilling Fusiliers in 1914 and spent much of the war on the Western Front (he was twice mentioned in dispatches and twice nominated for the Croix de Guerre),

Falls was well aware of what service in the front line had been like:

> The general conditions of the War, especially on the Western Front, were horrible, and the infantryman had a worse time of it than anyone who did not serve in the ranks or as a junior officer can realise [...] while the private was setting forth on a working-party, [the general behind the lines] might sympathise with him but he was so far off that he might have been in England. It may also be said that there is ample room for criticism regarding the manner in which many British offensives were conducted. The War was a ghastly experience, and everyone should do all that in him lies to ensure that it is not repeated.

Falls nevertheless felt that the authors of war fiction were determined by whatever means available to them 'to prove that the Great War was engineered by knaves or fools on both sides, that the men who died in it were driven like beasts to the slaughter, and died like beasts, without their deaths helping any cause or doing any good'. He questions much of the 'incidental details' such novels provide by way of evidence for this thesis, and complains that: 'Every sector becomes a bad one, every working-party is shot to pieces; if a man is killed or wounded his brains or his entrails always protrude from his body; no one ever seems to have a rest.' It should be said, however, that this genuinely reflects the experiences of many of those who wrote about their time in the trenches.

Falls did not include poetry in his bibliography, but this too was appearing during the period and having its impact on people's perception of the war. As with the novels and memoirs, these were poems written by people who had been in – and in some cases not survived – the trenches. Isaac Rosenberg was a diminutive working-class recruit from the East End of London, who had joined up simply in order to supplement his mother's meagre income. He loathed the army, was bullied because he was both Jewish and an inept soldier, and was killed while on night patrol near Arras on April Fool's Day 1918. His poems, some of the finest to emerge from the war, were edited by Gordon Bottomley in 1922 and his *Collected Works* were published in 1937. The *Selected Poems* of Siegfried Sassoon, whose entire life and work would be shaped by his service on the Western Front, were published in 1925. Edmund Blunden's previously mentioned *Undertones of War* contained 'A Supplement of Poetical Interpretations and Variations', and his *Poems 1914–1930* were published in 1930. Herbert Read, who served as a second lieutenant in the Yorkshire Regiment, and described himself as 'in a literal sense, a living witness of the slaughter', published several books during this period: *The End of War* (1931) was sandwiched between the two collections, *Poems 1913–1925* (1926) and *Poems 1914–1934* (1935). Robert Graves, Sassoon's sometime friend and fellow officer in the Royal Welch Fusiliers, published his *Poems 1914–1927* in 1927, and a revised edition of *The Collected Poems* of Rupert Brooke, that icon of self-sacrificial youth, was published the following year. Not all these volumes were restricted to war poetry, although in each the war provided part – often a significant part – of the individual poet's journey. Equally, they did not present a blanket response to the war – Brooke and Rosenberg, for example, being at opposite ends of the spectrum.

The poet most influential on public opinion was undoubtedly Wilfred Owen, whose subject, he wrote memorably in a preface, was 'the pity of War'. The first collection of Owen's *Poems*, edited by Sassoon, had been published in 1920, but a new and expanded edition, edited by Blunden, appeared in 1931, with a curious table of contents in which the twenty-seven poems that would still be taken to be the core of his output are categorised by 'motive', almost every one of which is negative: 'Heroic Lies', 'Inhumanity of war', 'Willingness of old to sacrifice the young', 'Grief', 'The insupportability of war', 'The unnaturalness of weapons', 'Mentality of Troops and vastness of Losses, with reflection on Civilians'.

The very first 'motive' listed in Owen's *Poems* is 'How the Future will forget the dead in war', and even war memorials, those most tangible reminders to the Future of the war's dead, did not escape criticism in what had begun to be termed 'War Poetry'. Siegfried Sassoon's largely meditative and tranquil *The Heart's Journey* (1928) included a poem 'To One in Prison', which showed scant respect for the ceremonies at the Cenotaph, and in another, 'On Passing the New Menin Gate', Sir Reginald Blomfield's memorial to the missing at Ypres is dismissed as 'a pile of peace-complacent stone'. The 54,388 dead whose 'name liveth for ever' are imagined rising from 'the slime' in which they were lost to 'deride this sepulchre of crime'. This, clearly, was not a majority view, but many people felt that the notion of war memorials having a warning function in addition to a commemorative one was not helped by massed parades of those currently in the armed forces, which continued to play their by now traditional role on Armistice Day. In 1933 a new symbol of remembrance appeared for the first time: the white poppy. A suggestion by a member of the No More War Movement (which grew out of, and in 1921 replaced, the No Conscription Fellowship) that the central bosses of the British Legion's poppies should bear the legend 'No More War' rather than 'Haig Fund' received a dusty answer, and so in 1933 the long-established Women's Co-operative Guild began manufacturing and distributing white poppies. Founded in 1883 as a means of alleviating the lot of working-class families, the Guild had taken on an increasingly political role and participated in the International Women's Congress at The Hague in April 1914, where a resolution opposing war was passed. Unable to stop history in its tracks, the Guild nevertheless continued to campaign for peace, demanding for example that militarism should be banned in schools. In 1934, the Peace Pledge Union joined forces with the Guild in the promotion and distribution of the white poppy with the single word 'Peace' imprinted on its silver central boss. By 1938 the sale of white poppies had reached 85,000 a year, but these sales were still minute compared with the 40 million red poppies sold that year by some 360,000 volunteers. The white poppy would never catch on in quite the same way, but it has survived to the present day and is an emblem that remains controversial.

In spite of a difficulty caused by the new threepenny bit, which proved too thick to go through the slot of the British Legion's collecting boxes (whose design was thereafter adapted), 'the wearing of Haig's poppies by the public in London' was reported in 1937 to be 'so general that to be without one in the streets was to be conspicuous' – not merely for military men in Dorothy L.

Sayers novels. The continuing need for the funds raised by the sales of poppies is shown by the fact that even two decades after the Armistice, around 639,000 officers and men were still receiving disability allowances. Even so, the universal observation of Armistice Day declined during the 1930s. If the service at the Cenotaph was intended to warn the future as well as commemorate the past, this message began to look increasingly forlorn as the decade wore on. Furthermore, the Great War had begun to seem distant and irrelevant to the new generation, which had been too young to take part in it. It was already becoming history. Even the tomb of the Unknown Warrior was not quite the sacred site it had initially been, and it was reported in 1938 that the stone was 'to be "elevated" because people walked heedlessly over it': 'There have even been instances of wreaths and flowers on the tomb being trampled on' by 'thoughtless or unobservant visitors'. A proposal that an eternal flame should be kept burning on the newly elevated tombstone, as it is in Paris beneath the Arc de Triomphe, came to nothing because it would have caused a fire hazard in a building often crowded with visitors. In the end low railings were reinstalled around the tomb.

A survey carried out by Mass Observation, the anthropological group set up in 1937 to study British life and attitudes, discovered that by 1938 20 per cent of the population no longer observed the two minutes' silence but simply carried on with work. There was still a certain amount of peer pressure at work: of those who were alone at 11 a.m., 30 per cent ignored the Silence compared with a mere 10 per cent of those who found themselves in company at that hour. The day itself nevertheless continued to exert an influence and act as a reminder. In the late October run-up to Armistice Day in 1938 69 per cent of those men interviewed admitted they no longer doffed their hats when passing the Cenotaph; but of another sample taken two days after 11 November this had dramatically reduced to a mere 5 per cent. Similarly, 43 per cent of people interviewed on 29 October 1938 proclaimed themselves against the continuation of the two minutes' silence, whereas on 11 November itself this percentage had 'fallen to 20%, with 11% doubtful, 69% pro'. The survey nevertheless concluded that there was a 'widespread feeling that the ceremony was already out-of-date and should be stopped'.

There was some support for this in the press, started by Hannen Swaffer writing in the socialist *Daily Herald* in November 1937. Swaffer was known as the Pope of Fleet Street because of his many pronouncements on all matters, and he now declared: 'Armistice Day's formal Empire service at the Cenotaph, with its Two Minutes' Silence, should never be held again! Yesterday's happenings made this even more obvious.' What had happened on 11 November 1937 was that the Silence had been interrupted by a man who burst through the supposedly restraining phalanx of sailors in Whitehall shouting 'All this hypocrisy!' and something else rather less audible that was reported as 'You are deliberately conniving at another war!' He then ran in the direction of the Prime Minister and the new king, George VI, but was leapt upon by several policemen before he reached an impassive Neville Chamberlain. From beneath the collapsed scrum he could still be heard repeating his mantra, while everyone else remained silent and tried to concentrate. When the Silence finally ended, the man was led struggling back through the reassembled line of bluejackets to an ambulance station. From the crowd cries of anger (including a shout of 'Kill him!' – hardly in tune with the mood of the day, one would have thought) were heard above the solemn roll of drums preceding the sounding of the Last Post. The episode was described as causing 'no more than a little pool of violence at the centre of a motionless and soundless sea'. One senses that it was with some relief that newspapers subsequently reported that the man was 'an escaped patient from a mental asylum'. What was not immediately reported was that the man, whose name was Stanley Storey, was also a war veteran, who may well have been incarcerated, as so many had been, as a result of shell shock or some other kind of battle trauma. He was a reminder of a cost of the war that had often been hidden from the public. In the year of his protest, there were still some 35,000 veterans receiving disability pensions on the grounds of mental health. Many of these men were confined to lunatic asylums around the country, out of sight and out of both the public's mind and their own. Some were still there, or at any rate in special hospitals and under psychiatric care, in the 1990s. 'My experiences of the First World War have haunted me all my life,' Edmund Blunden confessed some fifty-five years after the Armistice, 'and for many days I have, it seems, lived in that world rather than this.' For veterans locked away in county asylums, there really was no escape from the war and what it had done to them. One soldier, for example, wounded at Cambrai in 1918, was admitted to Colney Hatch Lunatic Asylum in 1920. By 1987 this institution had long since been more tactfully renamed Friern Psychiatric Hospital, but the old soldier was still there, eventually dying at the age of ninety-two in December of that year.

* * *

The supposed warning provided by the million dead was ignored and on 3 September 1939 England once again declared war on Germany. On 11 October the Home Office announced that the King had decided that no service would be held at the Cenotaph on Armistice Day, and that 'in the present circumstances it would be preferable that other large services which it has been the custom to hold throughout the country on Armistice Day should not be held'. It was felt, among other things, that the sirens used to mark the end of the Silence might be confused with those signalling the air raids everyone expected to be an early feature of the war. Poppies, however, would be sold and worn as usual, and wreaths could be laid at the Cenotaph and other war memorials – which was just as well since 50,000 had already been made at the Poppy Factory at Richmond when war broke out. Special showrooms had been opened in Bond Street and on the Cromwell Road, where people could inspect and order from fifty different designs, and in the event orders for 35,000 additional wreaths were placed after war was declared. Sales of poppies generally were in fact up on the previous year, with gross receipts of £595,188 compared with £578,188 in 1938.

The service at Westminster Abbey would take place as usual. A two minutes' silence would be observed there at 11 a.m., and those listening to the broadcast at home on the radio – including the King and Queen at Buckingham Palace – could join in. The Archbishop of Canterbury advised that services of remembrance might be held as usual, but that the Sunday immediately following Armistice Day (which happened to fall on a Saturday that year) 'should be observed as a Day of Remembrance and Dedication'. The Archbishop went on to quote Abraham Lincoln:

It is for us to be dedicated to the great task remaining before us; that from these honoured dead we take increased devotion to the cause for which they gave the last full measure of devotion.

Anyone who thought that the war might be used as an excuse to remove Armistice Day from the national calendar altogether would be disappointed, *The Times* declared in an editorial head-lined 'The Faith of Armistice Day'. While there would be 'no stately gathering at the Cenotaph, no prescribed minutes of silence to hush the whole land', such ceremonies were 'merely symbols and it is not upon their unbroken continuance that the real observance of the Day depends'. Those who wanted Armistice Day 'expunged from the national calendar' complained that 'the price paid [...] to secure a victory which failed and a truce which never became a real peace can scarcely be thought to justify an annual thanksgiving'. *The Times* felt that 'there is little reason for supposing this view to be widely held, and none at all for doubting that it is profoundly foolish. It wholly misconceives the purpose of Armistice Day':

What Armistice Day chiefly commemorates is a victory not of arms but of the spirit, a victory won not through war but in war. [...] No doubt the men who served spoke seldom of this their inward faith; to do so was not their habit. Yet the record of it was found in intimate letters and diaries of many who fell, and it was shared by multitudes quite incapable of expressing it in words. To remember this spirit gratefully, to honour the men loyal to it in life and death, is the real purpose of Armistice Day.

The low-key observation of the day continued throughout the war years. 'There was no pageantry; there were no crowds,' it was reported in 1940. 'Instead, as Big Ben chimed the hours, two elderly women, each with medals pinned across her coat, laid at the foot of the Cenotaph a simple wreath in memory of a Guardsman who fell in the last War. Omnibuses and motor-cars rumbled on, but a group of people standing around the Cenotaph stood still in silence for the usual two minutes.' The silence was not absolute because shortly before 11 a.m. the air-raid sirens had gone off, 'and the drone of British aircraft filled the air during the two minutes when in normal time London is locked in silence honouring the Empire's dead'. Almost as the two minutes came to an end, 'the sirens sounded "raiders passed" and, coming just then, the signal seemed like a prophecy of the final "all clear" for which the nation works'.

Old Soldiers
1939–1945

'Here we are! here we are!! here we are again!!!
We're fit and well, and feeling as right as rain.
Never mind the weather. Now then, altogether:
Hullo! Hullo! Here we are again!'

from *Cinderella* (1914) by
CHARLES KNIGHT and KENNETH LYLE

The all-clear would not sound for several years yet, and before the war ended in 1945 many veterans would find themselves once again in uniform. The upper age limit for war service was fixed at forty-one, which meant that the youngest of those who fought in the earlier conflict were eligible for conscription. The majority of the veterans were a good deal older than that, and of those who survived into the twenty-first century only Kenneth Cummings saw active service in both wars. The son of a merchant seaman, Cummings was just fourteen when the First World War broke out, but the following year he won a P&O scholarship to become a naval cadet and received training aboard HMS *Worcester*. He subsequently served as a midshipman of the Royal Naval Reserve on HMS *Morea*, an armed escort for troopships and Atlantic convoys. On his very first voyage the *Morea* passed the point in the Bristol Channel where a hospital ship had been sunk by the Germans, and Cummings remembered the unreassuring sight of the bodies of nurses and patients floating on the water. After the war he left the Royal Navy and joined P&O as a cadet, qualifying as an officer in 1921. He was serving on the *Macedonia* in 1923 when it brought back from Egypt the body of Lord Carnarvon, who had financed the dig that uncovered the tomb of Tutankhamen. During the Second World War P&O's liners were commandeered as troop carriers, and Cummings was serving on board the *Viceroy of India* when it was sunk off the North African coast in November 1942, having just delivered 2,000 troops to Algeria. He got away safely on a lifeboat and then became chief officer on another troop carrier, the *Ile de France*. Having survived both wars, Cummings lived to 106, becoming one of the very last handful of First World War veterans still alive eighty-eight years after the Armistice.

For some, whether or not they went to war again was down to chance. In 1939 Tom Kirk, who during the First World War had served in the Royal Navy as a surgeon probationer on ships escorting Norwegian convoys, was in practice as a GP in Lincolnshire. Both he and his partner wanted to volunteer, but the British Medical Association decided only one of them could be spared. They tossed a coin for it and Kirk remained in the practice, a 'decision' approved by the BMA because Kirk's partner had not been in the earlier war. Kirk's luck continued to hold, and he lived to be 105. Other veterans who survived into the twenty-first century, such as George Hardy, who had been a cavalry instructor with the Inniskilling Dragoons, and Charles Watson, who had served with the Royal Flying Corps, found themselves in reserved occupations during the Second World War – respectively as a chartered accountant in Hull and as draughtsman and designer for a well-known engineering company in Bedford. Hardy was, however, also the director of a shipping yard in Hull and had to spend every night sleeping there in order to raise the alarm during bombing raids. In the event of the Germans managing to land and attempting to capture the yard, it was Hardy's job to blow it up to prevent it falling into enemy hands. Watson, meanwhile, volunteered as an air-raid warden. The threat of air raids and the possibility of invasion were of course very real from the outset of the war, and an opportunity for older veterans to serve their country again was provided by the formation of the Local Defence Volunteers (LDV), later renamed the Home Guard.

As early as 1936 plans were mooted by the government to organise volunteer battalions consisting of 'ex-servicemen capable of guarding vulnerable parts of Britain in the event of war'. Nothing further was done about this until October 1939, when Winston Churchill, as First Lord of the Admiralty, asked the Home Secretary: 'Why do we not form a Home Guard of half a million men over forty?' This would naturally include 'many [who] served in the last war', which would in turn ensure that younger men were reserved for service abroad. The period from the outbreak of war in September 1939 until the German invasion of Belgium and Holland in May 1940 was dubbed the Phoney War because nothing much seemed to be happening. It looked rather different, of course, in Poland, where the Germans were very busy indeed, but the initial fears for Britain's national security were temporarily allayed. Although the Luftwaffe had attacked British warships in Scotland, the predicted air raids on major cities had not materialised and children who had been evacuated to the comparative safety of the countryside began to trickle back to their urban homes. Once the Germans had occupied the Low Countries, however, it became clear that their next objective was to march into France. The air of phoniness rapidly evaporated and the threat of invasion in Britain became far more pressing. The Secretary of State for War, Anthony Eden, made a broadcast on BBC radio on 14 May in which he announced the formation of the Local Defence Volunteers, asking for those between the ages of seventeen and sixty-five not already in military service to go to their local police station and sign up for home defence duties. Some people did so even before the broadcast had finished, and the appeal brought around 250,000 volunteers within the week. By the end of July 1,500,000 people had reported for duty. One of the suggested requirements for joining this force was 'a knowledge of firearms', which could of course have suggested that poachers and gamekeepers would be of use (two sixteen-year-old volunteers said they had 'knowledge of the use of an air-gun'); but it was evident that Eden as much as Churchill was hoping that those who had seen service in the trenches would come forward.

And come forward they did. 'The rally to Mr Eden's call was proving worthy of the days of Queen Elizabeth or the Napoleonic Wars, and just as natural,' wrote Charles Graves, father of the war poet Robert Graves, in his account of *The Home Guard of Britain*, published in 1943. 'Hundreds and thousands of men had been waiting patiently for a chance to do something though they were too old for active service.' Quite what these men were to do once they had volunteered remained something of a mystery. A major problem was lack of equipment, and the image of members of the Local Defence Volunteers still in civilian clothing reporting for duty armed with pitchforks is not entirely a caricature. Even the War Office was obliged to admit in an official pamphlet published in June 1940 that the LDV was 'neither trained nor equipped to offer strong prolonged resistance to highly trained German troops'. It was felt that Volunteers would 'therefore best fulfil their role by observation, by the rapid transmission of information, and by confining the enemy's activities. They will also act as guards at places of tactical or industrial importance.' Reports of units which had a mere 190 rifles for 15,000 men were not unusual, and there was an element of pragmatism in a government memorandum that declared that the LDV was '*not* designed for serious offensive fighting'. To those who had experienced front-line action on the Western Front and had volunteered to serve their country again, this seemed a waste of resources, and some former officers made a nuisance of themselves by lobbying the War Office or writing to the press demanding proper equipment and training. Rifles were hastily imported from Canada and America, but in the summer of the rout at Dunkirk, Britain's Local Defence Volunteers were still hopelessly short of arms.

Churchill, by now Prime Minister, had taken a personal interest in the LDV, and in a radio broadcast on 14 July 1940 he emphasised the vital role they would play in the event of an invasion. His preferred name, the Home Guard, was now adopted, and he insisted that its members had 'the strongest desire to attack and come to close quarters with the enemy, wherever he may appear'. Keenness was not always matched by competence, and the popular and enduring image of the Home Guard is the one provided by the BBC television comedy series *Dad's Army* (broadcast 1968–77), in which the very English coastal town of Walmington-on-Sea relies upon a motley assortment of non-combatants to keep it safe. Several members of Walmington-on-Sea's troop are veterans not only of the First World War but of even earlier conflicts. Corporal Jones had fought in Sudan in the 1890s, and seen action on the Northwest Frontier and in the Boer War as well as in the trenches. He is supposedly in his early seventies and was based on a genuine veteran of the Battle of Omdurman (1898) with whom one of the series' writers, Jim Perry, served in the Watford Home Guard. The doddering Jones's famous catch phrase, 'They don't like it up 'em', was used by this old professional when teaching Perry and his fellow volunteers bayonet drill. Almost as ancient were Private Frazer, the gloomy local undertaker, and Private Godfrey, a weak-bladdered former employee of the Army & Navy Stores who acts as the platoon's medical orderly. Whereas Jones was played by a heavily made-up Clive Dunn, who was only in his late forties at the beginning of the series' run, both Godfrey and Frazer were played by actors in their seventies who, like their characters, had seen active service in the First World War. Godfrey had been a conscientious objector who had nevertheless served as a medical orderly and won the Military Medal on the Somme. He was played by Arnold Ridley, who was eighty-one by the time the series ended. Himself a veteran of the Somme, where he had been severely wounded, Ridley had also seen active service in the Second World War, taking part in the evacuation of Dunkirk before being discharged on health grounds. John Laurie, who played Frazer, was a year younger and, like his character, had seen active service in the First World War and served with the Home Guard in the Second World War.

Although these three characters were comic caricatures, many people who served in the Home Guard recalled similar fellow volunteers, some of whom were well beyond the official upper age limit. Charles Graves noted that the medical standard for service was merely that volunteers had to be 'capable of free movement'. Furthermore,

> The generous age-limit for LDVs attracted a considerable number of elderly gentlemen whose spirit and enthusiasm were not easily to be overcome. Those gallants showed an astonishing vagueness when the awkward question, 'Date of birth?', came to be answered. It was not infrequently suggested by the sympathetic but sceptical people attending to the task of enrolment that some of them had first been in action at Bannockburn or Agincourt.

As in the First World War, many volunteers, both old and young, lied about their age in order to serve. A presumably youthful-looking member of the 10th London Battalion gave his age as thirty-nine because he believed the upper age limit to be forty. He was in fact seventy-one, but when this was discovered he was allowed to remain a member of the LDV. Attempts by several other ancient veterans to do their bit became causes célèbres. According to Graves, the oldest volunteer accepted by the Home Guard was Alexander Taylor, an eighty-year-old veteran of the Egyptian campaign of 1884–85. Not only had he been sent to relieve General Gordon at Khartoum, but he had also served in the Boer War and seen action in the First World War as an RSM. It was reported that he still possessed 'the clear, agile, adaptable and soldierly mind which enables him to appreciate the new and deadly weapons' of the present war, and so he was allowed to join the Crieff LDV in Perthshire. Taylor was generally agreed to be Britain's oldest serving soldier, but when a fellow Scot called Harold Breen, who had been decorated in the First World War, was rejected by the Greenock Home Guard on the grounds that he was seventy, questions were raised about him in the House of Commons. Eden commended Breen for his 'patriotic spirit' but suggested it was inappropriate for men over sixty-five to serve with the Home Guard.

Age was not the only barrier to veterans who wanted to join this volunteer force. A man called Jack White, who had been awarded the VC in the First World War, had been initially accepted but was then asked to leave when it was revealed that in spite of his very English name he was technically a 'foreign national' and therefore debarred from service. His father had come to Britain from Russia at the age of seven, but had never taken out naturalisation papers. For this reason, even though he had been born in Britain, White was deemed 'foreign'. White himself believed that the fact that he was Jewish counted against him. The case was taken up by the *News Chronicle*, and once again questions were raised in Parliament, where in July 1940 Sir Edward Grigg, the Under-Secretary for War, decreed that former war service would in future overrule 'foreign' nationality as a qualification for serving with the Home Guard.

In contrast to the bumbling hopelessness of the Walmington-on-Sea veterans in *Dad's Army*, many ex-servicemen were considered valuable assets in the Home Guard. Clearly those who had seen active service and become used to drilling, parades and route marches could form a useful backbone to any new part-time force. Furthermore, many veterans of the First World War were still only in their forties. A high proportion of those who volunteered were former officers: in Northamptonshire, for example, twenty-seven of the county's fifty-five platoon commanders had held commissions in the First World War. In spite of (or perhaps because of) previous service, not all veterans wanted to command platoons, or even take a sergeant's or lance corporal's stripes. Many 'old sweats' who had kept their heads down during the First World War were content to do the same in the Home Guard and remain in the ranks. Though estimates varied, veterans undoubtedly formed a significant proportion of Home Guard volunteers. In July 1940 Lloyd George (by now in his late seventies, but still taking an active interest in politics) announced that veterans formed 40 per cent of the force, while in November Churchill put the figure at 50 per cent. The following year one newspaper upped the figure to 75 per cent, but a War Office estimate that same year remained at 40 per cent.

It was in the Home Guard that several men who lived on to become Britain's last surviving veterans served: Alfred Anderson (1896–2005), William Elder (1897–2005), Fred Lloyd (1898–2005) and Arthur 'Smiler' Marshall (1897–2005) all joined the force, even though the last named had lost an eye between the wars. Others – Bert Clark (1899–2005), John Oborne (1900–2004), Harry Patch (1898–2009), Ted Rayns (1899–2004) and Charles Watson (1899–2005) – joined other civil defence organisations such as the ARP (Air Raid Precautions) and the AFS (Auxiliary Fire Service), did a spot of fire-watching for their employers, or became temporary members of the police force as special constables. Harold Lawton (1899–2005), who had been taken prisoner by the Germans in 1918, and subsequently became a lecturer in modern languages at Southampton University, spent part of the war patrolling the city's docks as a special constable. He then gave lectures to troops, including some who would take part in SOE (Special Operations Executive) operations, about French customs and language. This resulted in his name being placed on one of the Nazis' lists of 'wanted' men. These lists were widely thought to exist to identify people the Nazis would target should they successfully invade Britain. The alarmingly well-informed *Gestapo Handbook for the Invasion of Britain*, produced in 1940 by the SS general Walter Schellenberg, was just such a book, though its existence was kept a secret for some fifty years after the war. The principal reason the book remained classified was that it had been compiled from information provided under duress by two captured British agents, with additional material supplied for a fee by a rogue British intelligence officer. It included a Special Wanted List containing the names of 2,820 politicians, writers, academics, scientists, entertainers and trade union officials who were to be seized the moment the Nazis invaded Britain. One name on it was undoubtedly that of Arthur Halestrap, who had been working since the end of the First World War for Marconi and joined the Royal Corps of Signals in 1939. From 1942, he was seconded to the SOE, sending agents behind enemy lines in Europe. He became chief signals officer at Grendon Hall in Buckinghamshire, the communications centre for the SOE and its agents in the field. His son, serving as a navigator with the RAF, was killed at the age of twenty in 1945. At the end of the war in Europe, Halestrap went to Germany as a member of the Allied Control Commission, but after a motor accident he returned to England to join the Diplomatic Wireless Service. In 1963 he was appointed MBE for his work with this organisation, from which he retired in 1970 at the age of seventy-two.

Other veterans were in jobs of national importance and found themselves supporting the war effort as part of their everyday jobs. Henry Allingham (1896–2009), who had become an engineer after service in the First World War with the Royal Naval Air Service, worked on ways of dealing with the magnetic mines the Germans were using to destroy British ships. These had to be safely disabled, but Allingham also worked on a device to be placed in ships to neutralise the mines. Having served in the front line with the Durham Light Infantry, George Rice (1897–2005) found a job with Austin at their plant in Longbridge. During the Second World War he worked in a factory in Coventry producing anti-barrage-balloon devices to be installed in Halifax bombers. Scenes of devastation produced by air raids on Coventry, with injured people crying out for help from beneath the rubble, revived with horrible vividness his grim memories of the trenches in France.

Harry Patch was similarly affected, and spoke for many veterans when he recalled that 'for those of us who had been through the 1914–1918 war, the idea that we were going to go through it all again was difficult to accept'. He was just too old for military service, but wishing to do something for his country in the event of war, he had joined the Auxiliary Fire Service around the time of the Munich Crisis in 1938. As someone who 'knew about water' from his long experience as a plumber, this seemed the obvious service for him. He was still living in Combe Down, the Somerset village in which he was born, and as a member of the AFS was in the third line of defence as outlined by the government, the first line being the navy, the second being troops in training in combination with the Home Guard. Apart from iron railings being removed and melted down for the war effort and people being made to observe the blackout, the war did not greatly affect Combe Down at the beginning of the war. The AFS nevertheless had regular training on Sunday mornings, often demonstrating their skills to local crowds by way of entertainment and reassurance, and sometimes going on exercise with the professional firefighters of nearby Bath. Dealing with major blazes caused by air raids on Bristol, which began in 1940, would remain the duty of the regular force, while the AFS were left to deal with any other emergencies that might arise while the Bath professionals were assisting their Bristol colleagues. There were three AFS fire crews at Combe Down, and they operated not unlike troops in the front line in Patch's own war: No. 1 crew would attend any fires that broke out, No. 2 crew would stand by in reserve, and No. 3 crew would be resting. A temporary fire station was created in one of the vicarage's stables: the fire engine was kept on the ground level, while the hayloft above was converted to sleeping quarters for the crews.

Bath remained poorly defended and so was unprepared for the so-called Baedeker Raids in April 1942, when the Germans targeted British cities of cultural importance in revenge for RAF raids on the medieval city of Lübeck. The British targets – Exeter, Bath, Norwich, York and Canterbury – were supposedly selected according to the high ratings given to them in the famous Baedeker guidebooks, first published in the 1820s. The target on 25 and 26 April may have been the stately crescents of Bath, but bombs dropped rather closer to home on Wells Way, part of the old pilgrims' road which led from Combe Down to Bath. It was not merely the fires and the damaged buildings which were dangerous: a bomber dropping flares for illumination flew low over Patch's crew as they were trying to douse some flames and opened fire on them with a machine gun. In all, Patch dealt with four major raids. 'Did the bombs remind me of Ypres?' he asked sixty-four years later. 'Of course they did; I was going through it again, and it was tough.'

When not working for the AFS, Patch was attempting to pursue his ordinary job as a plumber. He had built up his own small company during the 1930s, but all three plumbers who were working for him in 1939 were called up and he had been forced to sell the business. In 1942 he saw a newspaper advertisement placed by the Ministry of Works for someone too old for war service to oversee the plumbing and sanitation of several military camps in Somerset, which were being prepared for the arrival of American troops. Patch described the job of Garrison Camp Engineer as 'money for old rope, really', but because it made him privy to troop movements during the build-up to D-Day, he had to sign the Official Secrets Act. The actual date for the Allied invasion of France was of course kept from everyone: Patch arrived for work on 6 June 1944 to find the camps, which had been packed to bursting with troops the previous evening, entirely deserted. Assisted by POWs from a nearby camp, he was subsequently employed to dismantle the sites and return the sheets of corrugated iron that had been used to construct the huts to an army depot at Shepton Mallet. Told at the depot that this material could not be accepted because it was of American origin, Patch tried another one at Taunton, only to be given the same answer. He ended up selling the sheets and anything else he found lying about in the deserted camps to local farmers, donating some of the proceeds to police funds and pocketing the rest. A further unexpected bonus came at a camp where there were four petrol pumps which the Americans had disabled before they left. Putting his plumbing skills to good use, Patch managed to extract gallons of petrol, storing it for future use in old hot-water cylinders which he kept in some Nissen huts in nearby Street. Since petrol was strictly rationed, this hoard was very valuable: as well as using it for his own car, Patch joined the black market economy by selling it, his main customer being the chief superintendent of police at Glastonbury.

Some veterans, too old for service themselves, learned what their parents had been through in the First World War when their own sons enlisted. Patch was naturally anxious about his two boys, both teenagers as he had been in 1914. They both served in the war, but returned safely. Others were less lucky. Cecil Withers, born in Rotherhithe in London in 1898, recalled his mother's anxiety when he and his brother were both serving in the 1914–18 war. She was naturally – and as it turned out justifiably

– anxious because another son had died of bronchitis at the age of seven. Withers and his brother both returned safely from the front, but another, older brother who had been unfit for army service had died of tuberculosis during their absence. During the Second World War, the elder of Withers' two sons joined the RAF as a flight sergeant and was killed at the age of twenty-four in 1944. That same year one of his sisters and her husband had been killed by a flying bomb while on duty as ARP wardens. Those of his family not killed or struck down with disease were blessed with longevity: two of his sisters lived to be ninety and 100, while Withers himself outlived them all, dying in 2005 at the age of 106.

Alfred Finnigan (1896–2005) had joined up at the beginning of the First World War, in September 1914, and served with the Royal Field Artillery at Passchendaele. What he experienced in 1917 was so appalling, the losses of both fellow soldiers and the horses with which he was working so devastating, that when he married after the war he decided not to have children: 'I was not prepared to produce cannon fodder for the army,' he recalled towards the end of his long life, without apparently having had cause to regret this decision. During the Second World War he acted as a fire-watcher for a firm of London printers and shortly found himself in a similar situation to those too old for service in the earlier war: he became an assistant cashier because the man who had this position in the company had been called up. He held this job until his retirement in 1961.

A rather grimmer picture of the role of the Home Guard than the nostalgic *Dad's Army* was provided in 1942 by Alberto

Cavalcanti's film *Went the Day Well?* Based on a short story by Graham Greene, the film opens with a resident of the fictional village of Bramley End speaking directly to the camera and showing the viewer a memorial in the churchyard. The memorial commemorates 'the Battle of Bramley End' in which a group of Germans disguised as British soldiers were defeated and (at some cost) slaughtered by the residents of this emblematic village over the Whitsun weekend of 1942. In Greene's story, 'The Lieutenant Died Last', the principal character is a veteran of the Boer War, who more or less single-handedly repels a German invasion; but in the film the villagers have to overcome the enemy. This is all the more necessary when the Home Guard, in a scene that was both shocking and propagandist, are machine-gunned to death by the Germans as they return on their bicycles from a day's manoeuvres. The final assault, however, is led by the Home Guard of a neighbouring village, joining forces with the regular army. These troops, it is announced at the beginning of the film, were played by real soldiers: 'Men of the Gloucestershire Regiment, by kind permission of the War Office'.

By the time Cavalcanti's film was released in November 1942, the threat of invasion had receded considerably, although, as Churchill had already warned, 'until Hitler and Hitlerism are beaten into unconditional surrender the danger of invasion will never pass away'. As more and more troops were sent overseas to pursue this end, the Home Guard was in theory becoming increasingly important in its role of safeguarding Britain, and many of its members were by now manning anti-aircraft facilities and coastal batteries as enlisted troops prepared for the Allied invasion of France. By the end of 1944 the Home Guard had officially been stood down, but it was not until December 1945, several months after the war ended, that it was formally disbanded.

Both in the Home Guard and in other forms of civil defence, many veterans of the First World War had done further valuable service between 1939 and 1945. The popular notion that their own war had been 'a war to end wars' had proved unduly optimistic, and additional cemeteries were being constructed in Europe to hold the new harvest of the dead. It remained to be seen how this later conflict would be commemorated and whether the veterans of 1914–18 would find themselves usurped by those who came home after demobilisation.

THREE

Fifty Years On
1945–2000

And when they ask us, how dangerous it was,
Oh, we'll never tell them, no, we'll never tell them …

First World War song

On 11 November 1945, after its six-year suspension during the
Second World War, Armistice Day was reinstated. It happened
that year to fall on a Sunday – which meant that it coincided with
Remembrance Sunday, the day suggested by the recently
enthroned Archbishop of Canterbury, Geoffrey Fisher, for
wartime observance – and it was initially announced as
'Remembrance Day'. 'The change of title enriches the Day with
a wider scope and a heightened significance,' *The Times* decided.
'Tomorrow and through years to come all who fell whether
between 1914 and 1918 or 1939 and 1945 will be united by a
single commemoration, as in life they were united by a single aim.
Remembrance Day is to have a fixed place in the national
calendar, with the hope that it may be observed throughout the
Commonwealth and Empire, and possibly in the United States

also.' That place in the calendar had not, however, been settled. In fact no final decision had yet been taken about the name either, or indeed whether the dead of the two wars should be remembered on the same or different days.

Everyone agreed that the massive losses recently suffered – many of them civilian losses – should be commemorated in the way the losses of the previous war had been. Some argued that an entirely separate day should be designated, but choosing one proved complicated. Because the Second World War had been fought on many more fronts and in many more countries than the First World War, there was no exact equivalent of 1918's Armistice Day, a day on which it could be said that the war conclusively ended and hostilities ceased around the world. Instead there was VE Day marking the Victory in Europe on 8 May 1945 and VJ Day marking Victory over Japan on 15 August 1945. Neither of these seemed satisfactory for what it was hoped would be international observance in the Commonwealth and Empire. *The Times* further noted that VJ Day was 'inconvenient and unsuitable, occurring as it does in the middle of August holidays'; VE Day was a better choice, 'though its possible if very infrequent coincidence with Ascension Day has to be remembered'. Equally pragmatic objections were raised by the paper over continuing with 11 November, which carried with it the 'risk of weather unfavourable to outdoor ceremonies', a factor that also 'may be thought to rule out All Souls' Day, November 2, which otherwise seems an excellent choice' – excellent because the Church's designation for the day is *Commemoratio omnium Fidelium Defunctorum*, the Commemoration of all the Faithful Departed.

Even given these difficulties, the paper still felt that the 'union of commemorations is well advised. Personal memories of the late war are vivid and poignant for all, while those of the earlier belong now to older folk alone.' To categorise those who had lost husbands and fiancés in that war, and might still be in their forties, let alone those younger people who as children had lost fathers, as 'older folk' seems wide of the mark. In spite of what Britain had been through during the past six years, there would almost certainly have been considerable resistance to changing the date of national commemoration among those who had fought in or been directly affected by the First World War. The lessons for the future may not have been learned, as had been piously hoped, but this did not mean the sacrifices of the generation of 1914–18 should be forgotten or even superseded by those of the generation of 1939–45. *The Times* did at least agree this point: 'What is owed to those who fought and died in 1914–18 must never be forgotten. In a real sense, indeed, the two wars were but separate parts of one, being waged against the same enemy in defence of the same principles and ennobled by the same spirit of self-sacrifice.' This may have been historically and politically questionable, but was also the view in France, where, as *The Times* itself had earlier reported, the two conflicts were generally regarded 'as one war interrupted by an armed and uneasy truce'.

France was at that very moment arranging a particularly sombre commemoration of Armistice Day in which the bodies of three members of the Resistance (two men and a woman), two presumably Jewish 'deportees', a prisoner of war who had died in a German camp, and 'nine soldiers from France and her territories overseas killed in the military campaigns' would be brought to

Paris on the evening of 10 November. Entering through the three city gates, they would be taken in a torchlit procession to Les Invalides, where they would spend the night. The following morning the coffins would be conducted to the Arc de Triomphe, where, beneath an eternally burning flame, France's Unknown Warrior was buried. This would allow crowds to file past to pay their respects to the representative dead of both wars. In the evening, the coffins would be escorted on gun carriages to the fortress of Mont Valérian, where 4,500 French men and women had been executed by Germans during the war. There they would wait until they could be laid in a special shrine being built for them.

Unlike Britain, France had been a battleground in both wars, and it had suffered even greater casualties. Its losses in the First World War outstripped even those of Germany, while its occupation by the Nazis during the Second World War and subsequent questions about the extent to which its citizens had collaborated with the enemy were a national trauma Britain was fortunate enough not to have had to confront. There appears to have been no move in France to commemorate these national catastrophes separately, and the Armistice Day ceremony there in 1945 seemed designed to emphasise a sense of continuity. It was certainly a very different occasion to the somewhat muted and business-as-usual one planned at the Cenotaph. Whatever the politicians and *The Times* may have thought, the continuity of sacrifice would be emphasised in Britain when communities planned how they were to commemorate the new casualties of war. In general, sculptors lost out to letterers since, rather than commissioning new war memorials, most towns and villages merely added the later dates and a further, though almost always shorter, list of names to existing memorials. A similar decision would be taken about the Cenotaph. Lutyens had died on 1 January 1944, but he would no doubt have been pleased that the only alteration made to his elegant pylon would be the addition of dates: 'MCMXXXIX' and 'MCMXLV'.

On the first Remembrance Sunday after the war, 11 November 1945, huge crowds gathered in Whitehall just as they had between the wars, though conspicuous by his absence from the proceedings was the new Labour Prime Minister, Clement Attlee. Perhaps appropriately, given the role America had played in the recently concluded war, Attlee was visiting President Truman for talks in Washington. It was announced that he would attend a ceremony held in Arlington National Cemetery, where America's Unknown Soldier had been buried on 11 November 1921. Meanwhile, James Chuter-Ede, who had been appointed Home Secretary and was spending Remembrance Sunday in Epsom, chose the day to announce that this would probably be the last year in which the commemoration would take place in November.

The debate continued throughout the remainder of the year and well into 1946. Elements of both the British Legion and the Federation of Townswomen's Guilds (the latter representing the bereaved women who had traditionally been a focus of Armistice Day) wanted to retain 11 November, but on 19 June the Prime Minister told Parliament that from now on Armistice Day would be replaced permanently in the calendar by Remembrance Sunday, held on the second Sunday of November. This was something of a triumph for the Church, which had always been concerned that insufficient religious emphasis had been placed on Armistice Day. Given that the Second World War had broken out less than twenty-one years after 'the war to end wars' had concluded, and was characterised by the indiscriminate bombings of civilians by both sides, the brutalities of Japanese prisoner-of-war camps, the genocidal policies conducted by the Nazis, and the destruction of Hiroshima and Nagasaki by nuclear weapons, it might be thought that the Church had little reason to want to appropriate the day. God's infinite mercy had, after all, seemed in short supply recently. The Archbishop of Canterbury, Geoffrey Fisher, nevertheless proclaimed: 'Remembrance of all those who died in the two wars and of all that was done and suffered; thanksgiving for deliverance and for the good hand of God upon us; dedication in the strength of God to all true purposes – these will be uppermost in hearts and prayers on that day.' He and the Archbishop of York, Cyril Forster Garbett, had approved orders of service for the new day, copies of which, it was announced, were available from the SPCK (Society for Promoting Christian Knowledge).

Apparently forgetting that it had originally advised against a November date, *The Times* now decided nothing could be more appropriate:

Some of the world's greatest poets – HOMER, VIRGIL, DANTE, MILTON – have seen in the falling of autumnal leaves the image of fleeting generations of men; and from before the dawn of history our ancestors seem to have dedicated the month of November to thoughts of the beloved dead. In their proud festival of All Saints, as well as the more sombre commemoration of All

Souls, the Christian church has made this immemorial cult its own, giving it richer, nobler, and in a deep sense happier significance. So in the quiet of the falling year we shall remember the valour and the sacrifice, and continue to give thanks.

The two minutes' silence was retained as part of the Remembrance Sunday ceremonies, but its impact was massively reduced. This was chiefly because the whole idea of the Silence was to bring the country to a stop, whatever it was doing, and on a Sunday morning the country was usually doing very little. Shops, offices and factories were closed and a considerable percentage of the population was either in church, or at home preparing Sunday lunch or relaxing over the Sunday papers. Those who had televisions could, if they wished, watch a live broadcast of the ceremony at the Cenotaph, which took place in lovely autumnal weather that year. 'The setting, architectural and human, of the service was as it has always been, but with Whitehall looking its most beautiful,' *The Times* reported.

No accident of weather marred the ceremony; there cannot have been a finer late autumn morning in London. Certainly it was cold, but it was also exhilarating while the sun shone, and that was till half an hour or more after the Silence. All through the service the Cenotaph, like the gnomon of a giant sundial, threw a long, deep shadow that moved slowly eastward across the roadway north of the monument, where the King and Princess Elizabeth had their posts.

The future Queen, who had served in the Auxiliary Territorial Service (ATS) during the war, was there in her khaki uniform to represent future generations, and her father wore the uniform of the Admiral of the Fleet. The remainder of the Royal Family, dressed in black and sporting scarlet poppies, looked down upon the ceremony from a first-floor window of the Home Office building.

Part of that ceremony was the unveiling of the two new dates carved on the east and west faces of the Cenotaph to match MCMXIV and MCMXIX on the north and south ones. Just before 11 a.m., the King stepped forward and 'pulled a gold-tasselled cord, so drawing apart two pairs of small shutters, apparently made of close-packed laurel leaves, which had hidden the two halves of the new inscription'. He then stepped back as Big Ben began sounding the hour and a gun went off to mark the beginning of the Silence. The crowd heard the 'dull explosions of belated maroons in the distance. After that a quiet all but complete, chiefly disturbed by the noise of heavy aircraft somewhere to the west. As the throb of engines swelled and died away some who heard may have felt the sounds to be not wholly irrelevant.' *The Times* drew a comparison with this day and the unveiling of the original, temporary Cenotaph by the King's father, George V. 'Looking back to 1919, it was surely still possible then to feel with something like certainty, however mistakenly, that the world must and could determine that the catastrophe should never recur. But to-day? There seemed plenty of time in the Silence for some not very satisfactory thoughts, mixed with private memories that rustled with the last leaves on the Whitehall plane trees.'

Wreaths were laid by the King and Princess Elizabeth, and on behalf of Queen Mary, the Queen Mother. Then came the

Prime Minister, characteristically upstaged by the Leader of the Opposition, Winston Churchill, 'with many medals pinned on his overcoat'. The massed bands of the Brigade of Guards and the choir of the Chapel Royal sang the hymn 'O God, Our Help in Ages Past', and the Archbishop of Canterbury said a short prayer before leading the crowd in the Lord's Prayer. It may have been Remembrance Sunday, but the Church's role at the Cenotaph remained small. 'As the white-helmeted buglers of the Royal Marines sounded a gay and lovely Reveille the Cenotaph flags were stilled again as if listening.' There followed a march-past led by 2,000 men and women of the British Legion and representatives of what were now the four services, civil defence joining the army, navy and air force. The police then moved into position and members of the public were 'marshalled into endless moving streams along Whitehall': 'The civilian pilgrimage past the Cenotaph went on for many hours. Many tributes, from wreaths to single poppies, were left at its base by men and women, themselves wearing poppies and often medals, who had also brought with them many memories.' After a service at Westminster Abbey, the congregation, mainly made up of 'ordinary men and women in sombre dress', filed past the tomb of the Unknown Warrior, where they laid 'wreaths and bunches of poppies in memory of those who had fallen in old campaigns as well as the two world wars'. The commemoration of the dead of earlier military campaigns suggests that Remembrance Sunday would take on a broader historical significance than Armistice Day: as the blood-soaked twentieth century moved into its second half, the dead of all wars would be remembered.

*   *   *

Although newspaper reports in the later 1940s and 1950s suggest that Remembrance Sunday had indeed replaced Armistice Day in the national calendar and was marked much as 11 November had been, there remained those who felt that the whole observance had been downgraded now that it no longer had a fixed date. At the British Legion's conference in Great Yarmouth in June 1949, a call was made for the reinstatement of Armistice Day on 11 November, with Remembrance Sunday maintained as a subsidiary occasion held on the first Sunday after the main event. Four years later, by which time Britain also had casualties from the Korean War to remember, there were still arguments going on about changing the date. A correspondent wrote to *The Times* to propose that Remembrance Sunday be moved to the second Sunday in May, 'an approximate date for the end of the 1939–45 war': 'The weather in November is often cold and wet, and a great physical strain is imposed on the older men as they stand bareheaded for a period of nearly five minutes during the service of remembrance.' (Indeed, it was widely rumoured that the death of George V in January 1936 had been the result of his standing bare-headed at the Cenotaph in what *Time* magazine called Britain's 'murderous November damp'.) Those about whom this correspondent was so concerned were in fact the last people to want a change of date. The vice-chair of the Kent branch of the British Legion replied that the notion of changing Remembrance Sunday to what he referred to scathingly as 'a more convenient date in early summer' had been 'fully debated' at his local conference and 'heavily defeated'. 'The older members were adamant that whatever the weather they would continue to pay their homage in November. The younger generation of war veterans felt that they had been steeped in the November tradition since childhood and that in view of the discrepancy between VE and VJ days, they would prefer the present arrangement to stand.' And stand it did.

Nevertheless, by the 1960s people began to question whether Remembrance Sunday should be observed at all. Once again, the Church weighed in, this time in the shape of a clergyman who was keen to appear attuned to the modern world. In November 1963, Archdeacon Edward Carpenter, Canon in Residence at Westminster Abbey, called for a new approach to Remembrance Sunday, 'hinged somehow to the hopes of people throughout the world'. He proposed that it might 'become a day of dedication to idealism' and expressed the hope for 'some bold, imaginative move, which would give it a new name'. Meanwhile, at St Paul's the controversial precentor, Canon John Collins (an active opponent of apartheid and a sponsor of the Campaign for Nuclear Disarmament), complained: 'We tend always to look backwards to think too much of our finest hour and too little of the purpose for which the sacrifices were made.' This 'interference from clerical busybodies', as one correspondent in *The Times* put it, gained support in a Hampshire vicarage, from where G.A. Potter wrote that Remembrance Sunday was indeed becoming meaningless: 'All through the "Silence" yesterday cars were roaring past our church. Parades were attended mostly by local officials, The British Legion (mostly 1914–18 vintage), and uniformed youth organizations who are under orders to attend.' He suggested that the day should be moved to become part of All Souls' Day, which he said was kept by Christians the whole world over and on which prayers for the souls of the dead were offered. By contrast, 'the parades, poppies and platitudes of the present observance can only help the living'.

This was to misunderstand the whole meaning of Remembrance Sunday, which from the very start (as Armistice Day) may have commemorated the dead but was organised for the living. Armistice Day had also commemorated the dead whatever their religion may have been. It was bad enough to move the day to the Christian Sabbath; to align it with All Souls' Day, recognised only in the Christian calendar, would have been a further step towards appropriating this supposedly inclusive and secular national occasion and marginalising those grieving for the dead of other faiths. The bereaved had always been a focus of the ceremonies, augmented by those veterans who cared to take part. To suggest that the members of the British Legion designated as '1914–18 vintage' were somehow irrelevant was insultingly dismissive, while poppies served a practical purpose, having always been made by severely disabled veterans and sold in order to help those left physically or financially in need because of war service.

The debate continued the following year, when the Reverend N.D. Stacey, rector of Woolwich, declared that Remembrance Sunday 'should be discontinued before it becomes an empty and meaningless event'. This comment introduced the report of the day's ceremony at the Cenotaph in *The Times* under the headline: 'Memorial Service Losing Grip?' The paper also reported that a British Legion spokesman had announced that 'early Poppy Day returns [for 1964] showed a considerable decrease over last year's figures'. Where once the annual coverage of this event would have been extensive, taking up several columns, it was now reduced to a few inches tucked away inconspicuously among other home news. The following year the report appeared in only one of the paper's eight editions.

By 1965 even the anonymous correspondent (or correspondents) who every November, year in, year out, contributed a meditation to *The Times* on the meaning of Remembrance Sunday and what was being remembered began to express doubts about its continuation in the present form. A particularly unenticing headline to this column, which one imagines even in a good year attracted few readers, ran 'Remembrancetide: Adjusting Observance to Changed Needs' – an adjustment in which, the correspondent felt, the Church should be leading the way. The intention was to find a way of altering Remembrance Sunday in a way that would 'be true to the insights of the Gospel, adjusted to the contemporary world-consciousness of mankind's fundamental unity while still preserving the solemn meaning of a colossal sacrifice of human life on both sides of the conflict in two world wars'. Once again, the 'traditionalism of the British Legion and the various old comrades' associations' was accused of standing in the way of progress, 'hold[ing] back the proper movement of this solemn remembrance towards a new annual expression of the nation's resolve to give itself to the task of reconciliation'.

In a 1965 edition of *Theology*, Britain's leading journal of religious debate, the Reverend Ronald Coppin suggested that Remembrance Sunday should be quietly dropped from the calendar. 'Since the passing of the 1914–18 war generation the public desire to remember has slowly withered, and the very different character of the 1939–45 war means that for very many, perhaps the majority, there is no desire to remember,' he observed.

Perhaps most important of all is the fact that for anyone under the age of thirty Remembrance Day has no meaning and, as it has been conceived, can have no meaning. The observance is in decline and should be allowed gradually to fall away until it becomes as significant or insignificant as Trafalgar Day or November 5th. Any attempt to rescue it or to change it into an occasion for edification on the evils of war or the cause of peace would be doomed to failure, as is shown by the general indifference to United Nations Day, Shakespeare's birthday, etc.

In the meantime, he felt, 'it would be quite wrong for us as a Church to pull out of the existing observance'. Indeed, the Church should take an active part in altering the character of Remembrance Sunday, ensuring that while it continued it became 'much more international in ethos, and much more realistic about the [presumably fallen] nature of man'. Many Church members, he felt, disliked such 'pseudo-Christian details' of the observance as 'the equating of the valiant dead with saints [and] the paralleling of the soldiers' deaths with Christ's' – two notions that had popular currency during the First World War itself, as numerous religiose postcards depicting military calvaries testified. He listed some 'practical suggestions in changing the form of observance':

1. In every major city at the Cathedral, parish church or Cenotaph there should be an ex-enemy national taking an official part in the ceremonies. If this were too great a pill to swallow in one go, then at least a national from a non-Commonwealth allied country.

2. The hymns and prayers, especially at church services, should be carefully chosen, and certainly they should not draw uneasy parallels between servicemen's deaths and the cross, as in, e.g., 'O valiant hearts', nor assume that death in battle is a martyr's death.

3. The lessons chosen should have more bite: the Beatitudes would be a good New Testament lesson; for they set forth the ideals for which we were supposedly fighting and they remind us how both the servicemen and ourselves fail to measure up to Jesus's demands.

Dulce et decorum est pro patria mori is no longer an acceptable motto; perhaps *decorum est pro orbe terrarum mori* more accurately expresses the feelings and needs of our age. We can only then both expect and welcome the gradual disappearance of Remembrance Sunday; but while it is still with us let us redeem it as far as we may.

This attempted act of redemption would in part take place three years later, when the traditional church service for Remembrance Sunday was picked over by a small committee of churchmen and a single representative of the British Legion. The idea was to bring the service 'into line with modern thinking now that 50 years have passed since the first Armistice'. The Reverend Coppin's ambitious notion of inviting ex-enemy nationals to participate in Remembrance Sunday in every church in the land was not adopted, but his advice about hymns was taken up. No specific directions were given to bin John Arkwright's touchingly chivalric 'O Valiant Hearts', written in 1917 to a beautiful mid-Victorian tune by Edward J. Hopkins, but Cecil Spring-Rice's hugely popular 'I Vow to Thee, My Country', set to music by

Gustav Holst in 1921, was banished. The original meaning of Armistice Day was once more diluted, and while the act of remembrance was retained, it was augmented by 'an act of commitment to serve God and all mankind in the cause of peace and for the relief of want and suffering'. This widening of the brief to include more general social ills that had nothing whatever to do with warfare was approved in 1968 not only by the Church of England but also by the Free Churches and the Roman Catholic Church. 'It comes in response to criticism that the older form of service was too patriotic and warlike in tone, and too narrow and retrospective in its import to engage the interest of any but the elderly,' *The Times* reported. 'In general the emphasis is much less on remembrance and much more forward looking with its specific acts of penitence and commitment'. In other words, the interests of the people for whom Armistice Day was inaugurated, the generation of 1914, were once again being ignored in the Church's attempts to seem youthful and up to date. Some veterans protested in particular at that part of the new service concerning penitence: 'Having spent four years in the mud and blood of Flanders, they said, not unreasonably, they did not entirely see what they had to be penitent about.'

Rather than a period of reflection and remembrance, the days surrounding Remembrance Sunday during the 1960s had become a time for debates about the nature and future of a date in the calendar that had once been compared with Good Friday. The abolition of National Service at the beginning of the 1960s certainly played a part in shifting attitudes. Conscription, reintroduced at the beginning of the Second World War, had persisted beyond the end of the hostilities in 1945 and was still referred to as 'war service'. The National Service Act of 1948 obliged all young men between the ages of seventeen and twenty-one, unless they were working in farming, coal mining or the merchant navy, to serve in one of the armed forces for a period of eighteen months. The length of service had been extended to two years at the outbreak of the Korean War in 1950, and this remained the term until National Service officially ended on 31 December 1960. For many diehards, the abolition of National Service was when the rot set in and long-haired youths no longer obliged to sport a military short-back-and-sides set out to undermine British society with their amoral views and behaviour – a notion that conveniently overlooks the often violent Teddy boy culture of the 1950s. At the same time as abandoning compulsory military service, Britain also abandoned its policy of unilateral nuclear disarmament. The decision by the government to manufacture a hydrogen bomb as a nuclear deterrent was widely criticised and led to the founding of the Campaign for Nuclear Disarmament in 1958. The inaugural meeting of the CND was attended by 5,000 people and it soon attracted a rapidly growing band of supporters. It became the most prominent and vocal protest group of the period, numbering many leading figures in politics, the Church, education and the arts among its members.

The nuclear threat was given additional force after the Cuban Missile Crisis of 1962, when the United States and the Soviet Union had momentarily teetered on the brink of all-out war. Some idea of what a nuclear strike on Britain might look like was given by Peter Watkins in *The War Game* (1965). This film was commissioned by the BBC, for whom Watkins had earlier made

Culloden (1964), about the notorious Scottish battle of 1746 in which a well-armed English force led by the Duke of Cumberland defeated and subsequently massacred the makeshift Jacobite army of Bonnie Prince Charlie, largely made up of sword-wielding Highlanders. An assistant producer for BBC2, Watkins had been given the opportunity to direct a film by the Corporation's Head of Documentary Film, Huw Wheldon. This highly original drama, made in Scotland using local non-professional actors, was shot as if it were a news documentary, complete with commentary. Few who saw the film would forget the scenes in which the narrator described various sorts of weapons and showed in graphic detail what they did to human beings. If this determination to look war in the face and to show its lethal effects upon individuals seemed reminiscent of prevailing attitudes to the First World War, this is hardly surprising. While a drama student in the 1950s Watkins had acted in a production of R.C. Sherriff's often-revived Western Front play *Journey's End*. He had subsequently and reluctantly done National Service, and after his release had made a seventeen-minute amateur film, *Diary of an Unknown Soldier* (1959). Set in the trenches of the Western Front, it opened with the diarist stating in voice-over 'Last day of my life', and showed this day from the doomed soldier's point of view.

Although *Culloden* was highly praised, *The War Game* proved too harrowing and contentious even for the innovative and often controversial Wednesday Play slot, and the BBC refused to broadcast it. Watkins' film was unashamedly propagandist, once again showing graphically the effects of warfare upon suffering individuals, but also highly critical of the government's nuclear policy and the utterly inadequate contingency plans the Home

Office had in place in the event of what seemed at the time a not altogether unlikely catastrophe. The BBC always denied that any political pressure had been put upon it to ban the film but had in fact arranged a private screening for senior government and military figures before coming to its decision. Instead the Corporation announced that the film had been shelved because it was an 'artistic failure' – a statement that was both untrue and looked pretty silly when, after a cinema release in 1966, *The War Game* went on to win an Oscar for best documentary, a BAFTA for best short film, a Special Prize at the Venice Film Festival, and a UN Award.

It is no coincidence that these films appeared in the same decade as the fiftieth anniversary of the outbreak of the First World War. A revival of interest in the war had already been apparent at the beginning of the 1960s, but that interest was now more critical. One of the best-known works to emerge from this period was Benjamin Britten's *War Requiem*, commissioned for the dedication in May 1962 of the new cathedral at Coventry, replacing the one that had been destroyed by the Luftwaffe during the devastating air raids of November 1940. In spite of the occasion for which the *Requiem* was commissioned, and the fact that it was dedicated to the memory of four men who had served in the Second World War, the piece looked back to the earlier conflict. Britten decided to set war poetry alongside the Latin mass for the dead, and although there were many fine poems of the Second World War from which he could have chosen, he went back to Wilfred Owen. A lifelong pacifist, Britten evidently felt that Owen was the principal voice raised against the horror of warfare, as well as the principal elegist for the youth who died as

171

cattle, and so a natural choice for a *War Requiem*. The origins of the work are often forgotten and any illustrations for recordings or performance programmes tend to take their iconography from the trenches of 1914–18 rather than the ruined British cities of 1940.

Britten's work is not so much an attack upon the war as a lament for its consequences. Some idea of how images of the First World War could be used to subversive effect is given by Ken Russell's film about another British composer, Edward Elgar, made that same year for the BBC's flagship arts series, *Monitor*. *Elgar* was a celebration of a man not only regarded as Britain's greatest composer, but one who (whatever his own views may have been) was seen as representing both Englishness and Empire. Such works as the *Enigma Variations* and the *Introduction and Allegro for Strings* (played here at the very opening of the film as a small boy galloped across the Malvern Hills on horseback) seemed to sum up a distinctively English strain of rural lyricism, while the *Pomp and Circumstance* marches had become associated with Britain's imperial might. It was appropriate, therefore, that Russell's film should be the 100th edition of *Monitor*. Even more significant was the date of its broadcast: 11 November.

Although a patriot who believed in composing stirring tunes for stirring times, Elgar was also a man who had many friends in Germany, a country in which his reputation as a composer stood very high. It was, for example, a German, Hans Richter, who had conducted the first performance of the quintessentially English *Enigma Variations* in 1899. Elgar's feelings about the First World War were, therefore, equivocal, and he grew very much to dislike the fact that 'Land of Hope and Glory' (the major tune in his

Pomp and Circumstance March No. 1 with words added, to the composer's dissatisfaction, by A.C. Benson) became Britain's 'second national anthem'. Russell developed this notion by using the march to represent the First World War in his film. Although a commentary outlined Elgar's unhappiness about the way the piece had been appropriated, for the most part the march is played without comment over archive footage from the First World War, starting with jubilant crowds greeting the outbreak of war in London and ending, inevitably, in the war cemeteries. As the first notes of the piece are heard, we see film of a recruitment rally in Trafalgar Square, followed by footage of men marching through the streets. In a scene in which new recruits in civilian clothes march over one of the city's bridges, a boy watches them and keeps turning to look at the camera. It is perhaps a mark of the way people by now thought about the war that it is impossible to look at this boy without wondering what became of him, a plausible supposition being that he was killed in the trenches. As the music progresses, the action moves to the Western Front, with footage of men going over the top and the injured being carried along the trenches. As the 'Land of Hope and Glory' tune swells on the soundtrack, Russell uses footage of a long procession of soldiers, blinded victims of gas attacks. There is also footage of the temporary cemeteries, row upon row of crosses stretching to the horizon, with a close-up of a single marker for the grave of an unidentified body. The sequence ends with a panning shot of the permanent gravestones in a war cemetery, the pan quickening in pace until stone after stone rushes past in almost unimaginable profusion. The overall effect of this sequence, as Elgar's biographer Michael Kennedy put it to

Russell many years later, was that it was almost as if 'Land of Hope and Glory' was being *blamed* for the First World War. It is a highly skilful, and highly manipulative, piece of film-making.

The real blame for the First World War, however, had been laid firmly at the door of the politicians who started it and the generals who conducted it, known collectively and unaffectionately as the Frock-coats and Brass-hats. Just as in the late 1920s and early 1930s, when public opinion was influenced by Churchill's *The World Crisis*, Liddell Hart's *The Real War* and Lloyd George's *War Memoirs*, three seminal accounts of the war published in the 1960s attacked the reputations of those who had conducted the First World War. The first and most controversial book to put this case in the run-up to the fiftieth anniversary of the war was Alan Clark's *The Donkeys: A History of the B.E.F. in 1915*, published in 1961. The title was taken from an observation attributed to the German commander and strategist General Hoffman, who described the British troops in the First World War as 'lions led by donkeys'. Unlike the War Poets, the lions in Clark's book were not civilian volunteers and conscripts but professional soldiers. They were members of the regular army, whose service and traditions stretched back over the centuries but who, according to Clark, were betrayed by their commanders in 1915, most seriously at the costly Battle of Loos. Aptly described by *The Economist* as 'a shell-burst of a book', it opened: 'This is the story of the destruction of an army – the old professional army of the United Kingdom that always won the last battle, whose regiments had fought at Quebec, Corunna, in the Indies, were trained in musketry at Hythe, drilled on the parched earth of Chuddapore, and were machine-gunned, gassed and finally buried in 1915.' As a prelude to this dismal story, Clark argued that in September 1914, in the wake of the German defeat at the First Battle of the Marne, a chance had arisen for the British cavalry to break through the enemy lines, but this had been frittered away by overcautious and indecisive commanders, thus condemning the army to the four years of attritional trench warfare that followed. 'A resolute thrust, pressed with even a semblance of the disregard for casualties that characterized later operations under the same commanders,' Clark insisted, would have isolated the tired and hungry German First Army of General von Kluck, which had been separated from the Second Army led by General von Bülow, and would have resulted in 'wholesale surrenders.'

Clark's main narrative begins with an unflattering account of relationships within the British High Command as background to the events of 1915, in which 'considerations of personal vanity and prestige led to much bloodshed that might have been avoided by a dispassionate consideration of the military principles involved'. His book is anything but dispassionate, repeatedly accusing the generals of being ill prepared, 'ignoring [...] the repeated warnings of the Intelligence Section and, indeed, the evidence that presented itself to the naked eye of any observer in the front line'. The text is enlivened by such asides as: 'The battle – if the afternoon's massacre may be dignified by such a term – lasted three hours.' Just as in the book's plates section Clark juxtaposes a photograph of Joffre, Poincaré, Foch, Haig and George V standing smartly uniformed on the steps of a chateau (and captioned: 'Polished boots') with one of the devastated landscape around the village of Loos, so the bickering and infighting that took place among the High Command (sarcastically referred to as a 'Band of Brothers') is contrasted with the stoicism of front-line soldiers holed up in winter trenches. Clark vividly evokes the cold and sodden conditions in which troops 'starved of the equipment necessary in trench warfare, with little pretence even of artillery support and seriously short of trained junior officers and N.C.O.s' endured these conditions, before noting that: 'In the warmth and comfort of the Allied Headquarters, however, the mood was one of optimism.'

That such optimism was unjustified, and was supported neither by clear strategy or a proper consideration of what was happening in the front line, is a principal theme of the book. Even before the main narrative of the battles of 1915 begins, Clark undermines Haig's reputation, gleefully outlining the general's inglorious early career. His conclusion is that Haig's ascension to high command 'owed more to influential connections than to natural ability', an unfortunate result of which was that 'the Army seemed to contain many people who had tried to thwart [him] or who had, on account of superior quality, excelled him'. The whole of the High Command is portrayed as petty, scheming and rivalrous, but Clark retains his strongest criticism for Haig, frequently and damningly quoting from official papers in order to bolster his attack.

An example of Clark's method is the chapter dealing with the Battle of Aubers Ridge in May 1915. It is prefaced by an epigraph reproducing an exchange taken from the *Rifle Brigade Official History*:

GENERAL RAWLINSON: This is most unsatisfactory. Where are the Sherwood Foresters? Where are the East Lancashires on the right?

BRIGADIER-GENERAL OXLEY: They are lying out in No-Man's-
Land, sir, and most of them will never stand again.

In the wake of the partially successful first attack, Clark reports,
men from the Irish Rifles attempting to return to their own
trenches with a large party of Germans they had taken prisoner
were being fired upon not only by the enemy but also by the
British, who imagined that a counter-attack was taking place.
Losses had been considerable and the communication trenches,
which were known to have been insufficiently deep, were now
clogged with stretcher-bearers and the walking wounded. Back at
HQ, Haig nevertheless gave orders to renew the attack. By the
time these orders were received, 'it was plain to all the commanders on the spot that it was physically impossible to mount
an attack with the shattered remnants of the assaulting battalions
that remained in the front trenches, while the acute congestion in
the immediate rear made the task of relieving them with fresh
troops, and that of evacuating the large number of wounded that
impeded free circulation, laborious and costly'. The orders for an
immediate attack were, therefore, ignored: 'It was plainly
impossible to achieve a state of readiness before the afternoon.'
This did not, however, deter the 'impatient' Haig, who shortly
before noon 'issued further orders insisting that the attack should
be pressed "immediately"'. Desperate attempts were made to
follow these orders, but the Germans were firing on the assembly
trenches: 'The majority of men never even climbed out into No-
Man's-Land, although many companies were reduced by more
than half as they huddled in the shallow, crowded forming-up
places waiting for the whistle. By two o'clock the position had

changed not at all, except that the 8th Division had suffered a further 2,000 casualties.'

In a characteristic shift of perspective, Clark moves immediately from this account to the operational centre for the attack at Lestrem to find Haig attending a luncheon where 'the talk was mainly of horses and hunting'. Clark quotes from an unidentified diary of someone there who reported that when news was brought of the failure of this attack, 'launched as a result of Haig's insistent orders' and 'attended by serious losses': 'the Chief took it very hard. We had been getting reports all morning of how well the French had been doing and he must have felt that they would be laughing at our efforts.' The clear implication is that Haig was more concerned about being laughed at by the French than about the massive casualties among his own men that were a direct result of his stubbornness.

Returning his narrative to the front, Clark once again juxtaposes the circumstances of the generals and their troops: 'While Haig was motoring from Lestrem to Aire, the position of the 2nd London, the Munsters and the Northants, still holding on inside the enemy lines, was becoming hourly more desperate.' Haig was in fact merely returning to his own headquarters, but Clark's deliberate use of the verb 'motoring' makes the journey sound like a jaunt. In spite of receiving a report from General Gough, commander of the 7th Division, who had made a 'personal reconnaissance' of the front line and was convinced that no renewed assault during daylight had any hope of succeeding, Haig ordered another attack for 4 p.m. The bombardment that preceded this killed all but three of the hapless Munsters, who had managed to break through the German line. The attack itself was a costly failure and the day's British losses were 458 officers and 11,161 men: 'It had been a disastrous fifteen hours of squandered heroism, unredeemed by the faintest glimmer of success.'

Clark's account of the Battle of Loos is equally dispiriting, leaving readers with the indelible impression that in the First World War gallant troops were repeatedly and pointlessly sacrificed by pig-headed generals. It was a version of history that reinforced the one handed down by the War Poets – and the historical accounts of Churchill, Liddell Hart and Lloyd George. Liddell Hart was still a hugely influential figure in First World War studies, and it comes as no surprise to find in Clark's book a fulsome acknowledgement to 'that acknowledged master of military history, Captain B.H. Liddell Hart, who has allowed me access to his private files on the period and has been of the greatest help at every stage in the development of the book'. *The Donkeys* was Clark's first work of non-fiction and it won him few friends among professional military historians, who challenged its reliability and disliked its anti-authoritarian tone. It was perhaps made worse by the fact that Clark was not a tiresome young pacifist lefty from a redbrick university, from whom little better could be expected. He had been educated at Eton and Christ Church, Oxford (where he studied under leading historians Robert Blake, who would edit Haig's diaries, and Hugh Trevor-Roper, who would become Haig's son-in-law); had briefly been in training with the cavalry during the Second World War and been a member of the Royal Auxiliary Air Force in the 1950s; and had trained for the bar. The leading military historian Michael Howard, however, was unimpressed by these credentials, writing in *The Listener* that:

> Military history, more than any other branch of historical studies, lends itself to the journalist and the populariser. This is not to belittle the work of either, for journalism and literary entertainment are respectable professions calling for great skills and hard work. But what these practitioners write is not history [...] Mr Clark is not a historian. Neither the tuition of Professor Trevor-Roper nor the access to the files of Captain Liddell Hart of which his publishers boast have made him one.

While acknowledging that Clark was 'a vivid writer with considerable gifts both of description and narrative', Howard also accused him of bias and poor scholarship: 'Like other con-temporary works on the first world war, [the book] accepts unquestioningly a popular stereotype of brave British lives being squandered by stupid generals and fills out the picture by selective quotation from a very limited number of sources used without any sort of critical acumen.' He conceded that the book was 'good value' as 'entertainment', but added: 'As history it is worthless.'

The Donkeys nevertheless remains an important historical document – if not of 1915, then certainly of the 1960s. It was very popular with the general reader, and its ferocious attack on the leadership of the generals and its portrayal of the front-line soldiers as courageous men sent heedlessly to their inevitable doom set the tone of debate for the entire decade. It fixed even more firmly in the public mind the mud-blood-and-futility view of the war.

Clark was a fledgling historian, easy for those who regarded themselves as his elders and betters to dismiss; but equally popular, even more influential and almost as controversial as *The*

Donkeys was A.J.P. Taylor's *The First World War: An Illustrated History* (1963). Frowned upon by many of his peers for his outspoken and occasionally eccentric views and manner, and challenged by his successors over his reliability, Taylor was a genuinely populist historian and an excellent communicator, who had a long career both on television and as a newspaper columnist. With his heavy-framed spectacles and jauntily askew bow tie, he was perhaps the one historian most people would have recognised, and his book on the First World War was written for the general rather than the specialist reader. It was produced by the 'packager' George Rainbird, who took advantage of the advances in printing technology that had resulted in the colour supplements to Sunday newspapers to produce at affordable prices beautifully designed and lavishly illustrated books for mainstream publishers – in this instance Hamish Hamilton. The democratic aim of these books was to popularise such subjects as history by leavening serious and well-researched texts, usually by well-known authors, with contemporary illustrations, often in full colour. In Taylor's case, the illustrations were all black and white, in keeping with the subject matter, and were used by the author with subversive wit. Even without reading the full text, one would have a pretty clear idea of Taylor's general thesis just by looking at the illustrations and the captions he provided to highlight his arguments – or, some would argue, score cheap points.

Although most captions to photographs of the war zones were reasonably neutral, Taylor sometimes uses them as an offensive weapon to blast wartime clichés: 'The wicked Hun' beneath a picture of one of the Kaiser's less terrifying conscripts, a bespectacled and exhausted soldier who looks like a mild-mannered clerk; 'Civilization triumphs again' beneath a now famous photograph of a long line of shuffling men blinded in a gas attack. Taylor reserves his biggest guns, however, for the Frock-coats and Brass-hats. A photograph of French in morning dress, complete with glossy top hat and cane, presumably late for some appointment since he is running past a crowd of onlookers, is captioned: 'Sir John French, commander of the B.E.F., in training for the retreat from Mons'; a portrait photograph of Haig posing in his uniform, his cap under one arm, is tagged: 'He relied upon divine help, became an earl and received £100,000 from parliament'. 'He could have lost the war in an afternoon' accompanies a photo of Admiral Jellicoe aboard his flagship; a picture of the French High Command, their embonpoint barely contained by their uniforms, is labelled: 'French generals suffering from undernourishment'. Politicians fare no better than the military: Lloyd George being conducted along a line of munitions workers – as well he might be since he was after all Minister of Munitions – is captioned: 'Lloyd George casts an expert eye over munitions girls'; 'Lloyd George and Churchill on the march to the top' runs another caption – that march being along a London street in formal wear rather than the one through a shattered landscape to the front endured by the soldiers carrying out their bidding.

These figures are treated with equal disrespect in the text, a text which – it by now seems almost inevitably – had been submitted in draft to the doyen of First World War studies, B.H. Liddell Hart. The disasters on the Western Front are duly itemised and blame apportioned. The Battle of Loos was fought largely because Kitchener thought that 'unless the British gave full support [to the French], Joffre would be overthrown and the French politicians would then make peace. Hence, British soldiers died so that France could be kept in the war.' At the end of the battle, the Allies had 'made no gain strategically or even on the most limited scale; there had simply been useless slaughter'. The Battle of Verdun was 'the most senseless episode in a war not distinguished for sense anywhere', but the Battle of the Somme was not much better: 'Nothing had been learnt from previous failures except how to repeat them on a large scale.' Taylor itemises the casualties (420,000 British, 200,000 French) and throws doubt upon the *Official History*:

> The Germans probably lost about 450,000; and would have lost less if it had not been for the order of [the German commander] Falkenhayn, rivalling Haig in obstinacy, that every yard of lost trench must be taken in counter-attacks. Many years later, the editor of the British official history performed a conjuring trick on the German figures, and blew them up to 650,000, thus making out against all experience that the attackers suffered less than the defence. There is no need to take those figures seriously.

Taylor was right: the generally agreed figure for German losses is 465,000.

Passchendaele comes at a period when 'British strategy, if such it can be called, reached its lowest level. Haig had come through three years of war still in high command and having learnt little from experience.' Taylor dismisses most of the strategical thinking that led to Passchendaele, listing the 'excuses' that Haig subsequently 'manufactured' as to 'why the Ypres offensive had to be made'. These are described as simply 'untrue'. 'The truth was simple: Haig had resolved blindly that this was the place where he could win the war. He never inspected the front line. He disregarded the warnings of his own Intelligence Staff against the mud. No one else shared his confidence.' In sum, Haig 'preferred an unsuccessful offensive under his own command to a successful one under someone else'. This account of Haig preparing to send his troops, among whom was Private Harry Patch, into the mud and misery of Passchendaele is accompanied by a photograph of the general standing on the steps of a country house being offered an overcoat by a chauffeur, captioned: 'Sir Douglas Haig feels the cold'.

Many writers critical of the conduct of the First World War have been accused by revisionist historians of not dealing with the war beyond the Western Front. Taylor covers all theatres of war, including Italy, the Balkans, the Middle East and Turkey, but his account of these campaigns is often quite as critical as it is of those conducted by Haig. General Sir Ian Hamilton, entrusted by Kitchener with the Gallipoli campaign, sets off for the Dardanelles in 1915 'without a staff, with no proper maps, and with no information later than 1906 about Turkish defences'. Apart from one division from the regular army, the troops allotted to Hamilton were 'colonials and territorials, with no previous experience'. Furthermore, 'The British army had never rehearsed landing on a hostile coast and had no equipment for this purpose […] The attack on the Dardanelles was a brilliant idea in theory. But even the best idea brings disaster when it is carried out hastily and inadequately.'

Later military historians would argue that (in the words of

Gary Sheffield) the Allied counter-offensive of 1918 rates as 'one of the greatest series of victories in British history', partly secured through enormous improvements in strategy; but in Taylor's view 'Foch and Haig stumbled unwillingly on a newer and wiser method – to attack at weak points, not strong ones; they quickly took credit for it'. No one reading Taylor's book could be left in any doubt as to who was to 'blame' for the First World War. The fact that, like Clark's *The Donkeys*, it was strongly criticised by later historians has done little to diminish its popularity among the reading public. Over forty years and many editions later, it almost certainly remains the most widely read book ever written about the war.

In his preface, Taylor declared: 'The unknown soldier was the hero of the First World War. He has vanished, except as a cipher, from the written records. He lives again in these photographs.' He was also about to live again on the stage. Taylor's book was dedicated to Joan Littlewood, whose Theatre Workshop production of *Oh What a Lovely War!* received its premiere that same year at the Theatre Royal, Stratford, in London's East End. Like Taylor, Littlewood was left-wing and populist, and she had founded her company to bring theatre to the masses. It was hardly surprising, therefore, that *Oh What a Lovely War!* turned out to be a savage satire in which idiotic upper-class generals sent stoical and cheerily singing working-class rankers to certain death.* It transferred from Stratford to the West End, later played

* Both Taylor and Littlewood were prominent supporters of the CND: when Canon John Collins decided to hold a rally in support of the CND at the Albert Hall, he had invited Littlewood to stage it, and the proceedings included Taylor receiving a march-past of Scottish pipers.

on Broadway and in Paris, and remains perhaps the best-known play ever written about the war. Essentially an ensemble piece staged as 'a pierrot show of fifty years ago', it was created as the result of extensive research by the writer-producer Charles Chilton (whose father had been killed in the First World War at the age of nineteen) and members of the cast. The title is taken from one of the characteristically ironic and fatalistic soldiers' songs of the period, and further examples of these songs are used throughout the play, often to devastating effect. The production also made use of archive photographs and newspaper headlines giving casualty figures. In one scene, representative of the whole play, a burial party is seen at work in front of a news panel stating: 'BY NOV 1916 ... TWO AND A HALF MILLION MEN KILLED ON WESTERN FRONT'. They are watched from a balcony by Haig, who makes a speech beginning, 'I thank you, God; the attack is a great success.' As the soldiers work, they sing 'The bells of hell go ting-a-ling-a-ling', which Haig, donning a pierrot's cap, begins to conduct as another news panel appears: 'APRIL 17 ... AISNE ... ALLIED LOSS 180,000 MEN ... GAIN NIL'.

This may not have been particularly subtle, but it was agitprop theatre of the most effective kind, lent authority not only by the use of genuine songs and documents of the period, but also by the fact that it boasted in its programme and in the published text a 'military adviser' and a long list of source material, which included official publications and the diaries of General Haig alongside *The Donkeys* and the works of Sassoon, Graves and Blunden. It was tuneful, it was funny and at times extremely moving. It made no attempt to be even handed, but it caught the public imagination and further reinforced the way people thought about the war. '*Oh What a Lovely War!* awakened race memory in our audiences,' Littlewood recalled of the Stratford run. 'At the end of each performance people would come on stage, bringing memories and mementoes, even lines of dialogue which sometimes turned up in the show.' One local woman brought along one of Princess Mary's tins, embossed brass boxes variously containing cigarettes, sweets, pencils and chocolates which had been given to every serving soldier as 'a gift from the nation' at Christmas 1914. 'I've had this on my mantelpiece forty-five years,' she said. 'It was Dad's, for 'is Woodbines, he carried it with 'im wherever 'e went till 'e got killed. You can keep it.' One of the actors carried it in his pocket throughout the run.

Not everyone was impressed. The military historian John Terraine wrote to *The Spectator* to complain that the claim in the programme that every word uttered by Haig in the play was taken from his diaries was misleading since the quotations were highly selective: no doubt *Mein Kampf* 'could provide impeccable "evidence" that the late A. Hitler was a misjudged saint', he concluded. Terraine was on dangerous ground here, since a year earlier in the same magazine he had himself been accused by the historian and journalist Robert Kee of quoting selectively from Haig's diaries in his admiring and controversial biography of the general. Terraine also protested about one of the 'scoreboards' used in the play. He admitted he had not in fact seen the production, but had read reports of one scoreboard that stated that on the first day of the Battle of Passchendaele, British losses were 135,000 for a gain of 100 yards. This, he objected, was grossly inaccurate: the British losses for that day were not known, but those for the first *three* days of the battle did not exceed

31,850. It seems, however, that Terraine may have been misled: certainly, no statistics for Passchendaele are given in the published text of the play. His dim view of *Oh What a Lovely War!* would nevertheless be echoed by many military historians over the years. Correlli Barnett described it as 'a highly partisan, and often grossly unfair, presentation of the war from an extreme anti-Brasshat point of view', while in *The Unquiet Western Front* (2002) Brian Bond concurred, complaining of the play's 'blatant anti-military bias and historical distortions'. This view, he suggested, was supported by 'a distinguished general and military historian' (named in the notes as General Sir Anthony Farrar-Hockley, author of many books, including a 1966 account of *The Somme*), who in a private letter to Bond opined that 'taken as history, the play is not even serious enough to be called a travesty'. Bond acknowledged that Liddell Hart, something of a bête noire in his book, believed that 'there was more of the real war in the play than in recent "whitewash history"; it *did* faithfully reflect what his generation thought of the war', but Bond's own generation of military historians begged to differ. When it was later revealed that the Theatre Workshop's 'military adviser', Raymond Fletcher, had been recruited to the KGB the previous year, this merely confirmed many historians' suspicion that the play, though admittedly entertaining, was little more than Marxist propaganda. Not that any of this had much effect on its enduring popularity with theatregoers.

By the time the fiftieth anniversary of the outbreak of the war arrived, the ground had been laid for a distinctly 1960s anti-Establishment approach to the proceedings. The anniversary was widely marked, but the most notable event was BBC television's epic documentary series, *The Great War*, which was both scholarly and sober but nevertheless attracted audiences averaging eight million for each of its twenty-six episodes. This figure is even more remarkable, since the series was being shown on the recently launched 'highbrow' channel BBC2; such was its success that it started being repeated on BBC1 even before it had finished broadcasting on the new sister channel. The series was hugely ambitious, covering every aspect and theatre of the war. For some historians, it appeared to provide an opportunity to redress the balance and present a more even-handed account of the war than the lions-and-donkeys approach of Clark, Taylor and Littlewood. Indeed, among those who wrote the scripts were John Terraine and Correlli Barnett, neither of whom was inclined to this supposedly simplistic view of the war. Terraine's attempt to rehabilitate the reputation of General Haig has already been mentioned, while Barnett (author of *The Swordbearers: Supreme Command in the First World War*, published the previous year) would become a scourge of what he saw as the 'whingeing' school of First World War studies. Between them they were credited with writing or co-writing twenty of the twenty-six episodes, and both served as 'historical and research consultants', while Terraine was also appointed as associate producer. Liddell Hart had agreed to act as 'military adviser', but resigned over Terraine's episode on the Somme and eventually had his name removed from the credits for the entire series. He explained his reasons for doing so publicly, writing a letter to *The Times* in which he explained that when he read the script for the Somme episode, he 'immediately pointed out that it was wrongly slanted – for it repeatedly emphasised the supposed inexperience and unskilfulness of the British troops while not making any mention of the indisputable faults of the High Command's planning and conduct of the offensive'. The programme was, however, broadcast 'without any adequate correction of the commentary'. He was told that he would be sent Terraine's script for the episode on Third Ypres, but since he would receive it only a few days ahead of the broadcast, it would be impossible for him to offer any advice that could be implemented. He wrote that he regretted having to explain publicly his reasons for asking to have his name removed from the series 'because many of the earlier programmes were good, as well as graphic, examples of how history could be treated on television'.

In spite of the best efforts of the principal scriptwriters, however, the overwhelming impression left by the series with viewers was one of waste and futility. Never before had people seen so much archive footage, most of which vividly depicted the conditions in which men had fought and died. What is surprising is that even those episodes scripted by Terraine seem to reinforce the impression of the war he was supposedly attempting to dispel. The episode dealing with Ypres in 1917, for example, was given the title 'Surely we have perished', a line from Wilfred Owen. Extensive footage of troops slogging along waterlogged trenches and mules floundering helplessly in the Ypres quagmire was accompanied by such observations as 'the miseries of the war multiplied and heaped upon the soldiers' and 'this was the slough of despond'. Some scenes were accompanied on the soundtrack by extracts from such poems as Owen's 'Dulce et decorum est …' and Sassoon's 'Attack' with its final plea, 'O Jesus, make it stop!' Although the programme went on to describe how the Canadians eventually took Passchendaele, it concluded by recording that at the end of Third Ypres, the British had suffered almost a quarter of a million casualties without their reaching even their first objective. A journalist was quoted as saying that for the first time the British army had lost its spirit of optimism and saw no future except 'continuous slaughter'. This was followed by more images of corpses, and the episode's final words were given to Sassoon, an extract from his poem 'To Any Dead Officer', which ends with the regretful line 'I wish they'd killed you in a decent show'.

The use of poems, beautifully read, now looks like something of an own goal by Terraine, and it is hardly surprising he failed to confound people's notion that the war was almost uniquely squalid and tragic, given that the abiding memory of this particular episode was a montage of photos all too vividly illustrating lines from Sassoon's poem 'Counter-Attack' in which he describes in repulsive detail an area of the front 'rotten with dead'. The images are shocking even today, when we are more inured than people in the 1960s to death and destruction as a staple of television news reporting and documentary.

The most striking thing about *The Great War*, however, was that this footage was intercut with the stark testimonies of veterans of these campaigns, by now mostly in their late sixties and beyond and wearing the standard 1960s mufti of jackets and ties. Filmed in a studio in front of blown-up photos of the trenches, they spoke calmly but frankly of the dreadful conditions at the front, of shell craters brimming with corpses that were gradually decomposing into the surrounding slime, of the wounded slipping off duckboards to drown in the mud, and of the bitterness such deaths caused. Here were perfectly ordinary-looking men, who (to use a metaphor endorsed by the programme) had seen and survived hell. They looked just like the people at home watching their testimonies, providing a tangible link between the present and the horrendous cavalcade of images from what by 1964 must have seemed to most viewers a distant, almost unimaginable world. They were evidence that what we were seeing was not something that could simply be consigned to history; they had been there and could recall it as if it were indeed yesterday rather than half a century ago. It was perhaps the first time for many years that some of these veterans had spoken publicly (or even privately) of their experiences, and it marked the beginning of a more general public interest in them as living witnesses to an event that had shaped the century and seared the collective consciousness. Harry Patch did not take part, nor did any of those who would some forty years later be fêted as the 'last veterans'. In spite of this widespread revival of interest in the war, many of those who had fought in it maintained the long silence they had already kept for half a century.

The marking of the fiftieth anniversary of the First World War coincided with the birth of a new, post-Austerity youth culture in Britain, and there are surprising parallels between these two events. In the 1960s Britain could once again consider itself a world leader, as it had in 1914, though this time it was not as an imperial power but as a cultural force. The pop culture of the period drew heavily upon Britain's imperial past, and enjoyed a similar sense of national self-confidence. The Union Jack was adopted as the symbol of what became known as the Swinging Sixties, but rather than fluttering dutifully from flagpoles, it lent its distinctive red, white and blue to T-shirts and other fashion items, posters and postcards, lapel pins, and decals to stick on cars and motorbikes. Alexander Issigonis's Mini, launched in 1959, became the classic 1960s vehicle, and during this period these cars often boasted Union Jack decorations on their roofs or even on their headlights. The eccentric and pseudonymous pop singer Screaming Lord Sutch, later to become a colourful figure in British general elections as leader of the Monster Raving Loony Party, drove around in a Rolls-Royce painted in Union Jack stripes. Some older people were affronted that a national symbol should become a fashion accessory among the disrespectful young, and perhaps its most symbolic appropriation was that of Pete Townshend, who sported a Union Jack jacket on the sleeve of the Who's assertively titled 1965 album *My Generation*.

One of the most familiar images of Swinging London was a First World War recruiting poster. On 6 August 1914, two days after the outbreak of war, the recently ennobled military hero Earl Kitchener of Khartoum had joined the cabinet. Appointed Secretary of State for War, he became the face of recruitment when a poster was produced depicting his sternly mustachioed likeness in military uniform pointing a huge accusing finger at the viewer with the reminder 'Your Country Needs You'. It became perhaps the best-known image of the war, and sixty years later was subversively appropriated by Britain's thriving pop culture. One of London's most celebrated and fashionable shops in the mid-1960s was called I Was Lord Kitchener's Valet and sold second-hand and antique military clothing at 293 Portobello

Road. Describing itself as 'London's First Second Hand Boutique', specialising in 'Kinky, Period & Military Gear', the shop adopted and adapted the 1914 recruiting poster as its trademark. The earl was seen pointing at passers-by from a sign hanging outside the shop, and some of the world's leading pop groups bought their clothes here. Perhaps its most iconic moment was the day Brian Jones of the Rolling Stones took Jimi Hendrix to the shop to kit him out in the braided, frogged and colourful military jackets that became his trademark. Such was the success of the shop that it subsequently opened branches in the other two streets that epitomised Swinging London, Carnaby Street and the King's Road in Chelsea. On their 1966 album, *Winchester Cathedral*, the New Vaudeville Band, who wrote and played songs that were mostly pastiches of the music of the 1920s and 1930s, included a number called 'I was Lord Kitchener's Valet', imagining what his lordship would make of this cheeky appropriation of his image and wardrobe.

The taste for fanciful military gear, most famously adopted by the Beatles for their seminal 1967 album *Sgt Pepper's Lonely Hearts Club Band*, arose directly from the renewed, if largely satirical or critical, interest in the First World War. This reached its apogee at the end of the decade when, as *Oh! What a Lovely War*, Littlewood and Chilton's celebrated play reached an even wider audience when it was adapted for the cinema.* Directed by Richard Attenborough, the film boasted a cast that included some

---

* It is unclear why the exclamation mark shifted, but Littlewood herself sometimes included it at the end of the title and sometimes didn't, and seems also to have been indecisive about the comma she sometimes but not always placed after the 'Oh'. The published text of the play dispenses with both.

of Britain's most distinguished and popular actors (Laurence Olivier, John Gielgud, Ralph Richardson, Michael Redgrave, John Mills, Kenneth More, Jack Hawkins, Dirk Bogarde, Phyllis Calvert, Maggie Smith), two of whom had already lent their resonant voices to the BBC's *The Great War*. The script by Len Deighton differs markedly from that of the play, although the central idea of a pierrot show is maintained by setting much of the film on Brighton Pier. It opens with crowds milling on the promenade on that famously sunny August Bank Holiday in 1914. Among them is the Smith family, emblems of the ordinary people of Britain whose lives would be shattered by the actions of the politicians and generals. The gulf that separated these two groups is suggested in the title sequence, with the names of those actors playing the Smiths appearing above the title, while the theatrical luminaries who play the political and military grandees are listed as 'guest stars' at the end of a cast list, culminating in 'and John Mills as Sir Douglas Haig'. The film's essential theatricality is emphasised by the image of Haig selling tickets for the war from a kiosk. All the male members of the Smith family enlist and are duly killed – though this must be the only war film in which not a single death is actually shown: people die off-screen or, like old soldiers, they simply fade away.

In spite of the deliberate artificiality of its conception, the film is prefaced with a carefully worded announcement suggesting historical authenticity: 'The principal statements made by the historical characters in this film are based on documentary evidence and the words of the songs are those sung by the troops during the First World War.' An early sequence depicts the uniformed representatives of the main combatant countries more or less blundering into war, propelled by the scheming Austro-Hungarian foreign minister, Count von Berchtold (played by a gleeful John Gielgud), who dupes the silent and it seems senile Emperor Franz-Josef into declaring war on Serbia. This is a version of events that few professional historians would endorse, and indeed neither the crucial role allotted here to von Berchtold, nor even his name, features in such modern histories as Michael Howard's *The First World War* (2002) or Norman Stone's *World War One: A Short History* (2007). As in Clark's *The Donkeys*, the generals are depicted as rivalrous, snobbish and backstabbing, and the casualties of both the Somme and Passchendaele are recorded on cricket scoreboards at Haig's headquarters. The conversation between Rawlinson and Oxley used by Clark as the epigraph to his chapter on Aubers Ridge is reproduced accurately but ascribed to Haig and one of his ADCs. The film also made use of a notorious passage from Clark's book in which, as one dissenting historian puts it, the author 'maliciously suggests [...] that Haig was more upset by King George V being thrown from his (Haig's) horse than by the tragedy of the battle of Loos'. What many people remember as the movie's most memorable shot did not in fact appear in the film but gained widespread distribution as a publicity photograph. It depicted Mills as Haig standing in front of the row upon row of white crosses, which (lined up on the Sussex Downs and without Haig) supplied the film's final and enduring image.

Another successful anti-war play that transferred to the screen was John Wilson's *Hamp*, about a private serving in the trenches who is court-martialled and shot for desertion. It opened in Edinburgh in 1964 and was filmed that same year by Joseph

Losey under the fiercely ironic title *King and Country*. A concern with the lives of 'ordinary' people that characterised the 'new wave' of British cinema in the late 1950s and 1960s was very similar to the growing interest in the 'ordinary' soldiers of the First World War, which is to say those serving in the ranks rather than the officer class. Directors such as Tony Richardson, John Schlesinger, Lindsay Anderson and Karel Reisz were keen to portray the working classes as complicated individuals rather than the cheerful Cockneys and chippy Northerners who had traditionally populated British films. In *King and Country* Private Hamp is just such an individual, at first suspected by the captain called upon to defend him of being a typical product of his lowly background, feckless and unreliable. It turns out, however, that Hamp is suffering from shell shock. He is nevertheless condemned to death as an example to others, and both he and the captain are seen as victims of not only the British class system but also the impersonal and implacable military machine. It is not without significance that Losey was an American who had come to work in Britain after being blacklisted in Hollywood in the wake of the McCarthy hearings. Equally significant was the casting of Tom Courtenay, a contemporary icon of rebellious youth after his roles in *The Loneliness of the Long Distance Runner* (1962) and *Billy Liar* (1963), as the hapless victim of military justice.

Renewed interest in the war continued to influence cinema throughout the decade. Although set in the Second World War, Richard Lester's *How I Won the War* (1967) is about a group of soldiers suffering at the hands of an inept commander and owes much to common perceptions about the earlier conflict. Its release in the so-called Summer of Love, in which hippies and flower children demanded people make love not war, was timely, and the casting in a leading role of John Lennon when the Beatles were at the height of their popularity ensured enthusiastic and youthful audiences. Equally, Tony Richardson's *The Charge of the Light Brigade* (1968) – which had the same scriptwriter, Charles Wood – may have been set in the Crimean War, but its account of heroic British cavalrymen sent by incompetent commanders to their certain deaths against a lethally armed enemy had distinct echoes of the Battle of the Somme. As in *Oh! What a Lovely War*, the older generation of distinguished actors (Richardson, Gielgud, Trevor Howard, Harry Andrews) took the roles of the generals and commanders, while David Hemmings – another youth icon of the period, who had made his reputation playing a photographer in Swinging London in Michelangelo Antonioni's *Blowup* (1966) – was cast as the doomed young Captain Nolan.

Widespread concern about the Vietnam War was also a contributing factor to people's views of wars. America's involvement in this costly debacle caused protests not only in the United States but also in Britain. Such prominent public figures as Vanessa Redgrave, when not appearing alongside her father as the pacifist feminist Sylvia Pankhurst in *Oh! What a Lovely War*, could be found leading protests against America's involvement in Vietnam outside the country's embassy in Grosvenor Square. Peter Watkins' *Culloden* had drawn upon Vietnam as well as the First World War, since the director saw parallels between what the English did in the Highlands in the eighteenth century and what the Americans were now doing in Vietnam. As in the First World

War, young men were being conscripted and there was a sense that another generation was being sacrificed by politicians for no very good reason. One of the great anti-war anthems of the period, Country Joe and the Fish's 'I-Feel-Like-I'm-Fixin'-to-Die Rag', which everyone sang along to at Woodstock, asked the same questions about Vietnam that people were asking about the First World War and had some of the ironic fatality of soldiers' songs from that earlier conflict:

> And it's one, two, three, what are we fighting for?
> Don't ask me, I don't give a damn,
> Next stop is Vietnam.
> And it's five, six, seven, open up the pearly gates.
> Well there ain't no time to wonder why,
> Whoopee! we're all gonna die.

To some extent, then, revisionist military historians such as Brian Bond and Gary Sheffield are correct in complaining that attitudes to the First World War in the 1960s were anachronistic, more a reflection of the period than of 1914–18. Robert Kee, reviewing the American historian Barbara Tuchman's *August 1914* in 1962, wrote about the various generations and their attitude towards the First World War: 'First there are the elderly who suffered in it and who in spite of many fine attempts to "work it out of themselves" in the years afterwards are still indelibly marked by it'; next came the middle aged, brought up after 1918, like Kee himself: 'Later one read Sassoon, Blunden, Owen, Graves, Aldington, turned pacifist for a week, fought in a new war, voted Labour, anti-Labour, but always "The Great

War" remained at the back of one's mind, obscurely unfathomed.'
Finally came the new generation, for whom

> it is probably simpler. They are the first generation since the old
> order foundered in the Flanders mud for whom it has been
> relatively easy to grow up not taking anything that comes from
> 'higher authority' for granted. The history of the First World War
> (very much more than the Second) is a marvellous example of the
> inadvisability of doing so and it is close enough to be breathing
> down their necks. To the extent that the very young today
> automatically use their own minds more than their fathers and
> grandfathers did at their age, they are particularly sane and the
> madness of the First World War must seem to them particularly
> incredible.

In Tuchman's book, which concentrated on the political
background to the outbreak of war and the first few weeks of the
conflict, 'the First World War mentality is out in the open: the
complacency, the high morale and astonishing courage, the
stupidity, the lack of imagination amounting in the context of so
much lack of imagination all round to a dogged military virtue,
the fantastic refusal to recognize reality when it clashed with
preconceived notions of what really ought to be'.

At the end of the decade, the historian Michael Howard wrote
a leading article for the *Times Literary Supplement* on 'The
Demand for Military History', particularly the history of the First
World War, which appeared to have grown throughout the
1960s. Readers of military history, he felt, used to fall into two
categories: 'nostalgic senior citizens and bellicose children of all

ages'. A new audience for military history, comprising people between the ages of eighteen and forty (that is, born between 1929 and 1951), was of course welcome to those who wrote military history for their living, but he questioned the interest of such readers in this subject. It was, he felt,

> compounded of fascination and disgust with values and habits of the past from which succeeding generations feel it necessary, at fairly regular intervals, to make prolonged and emphatic declarations of independence. As the generation of the 1920s felt it necessary to make clear by their literature and their habits their emancipation from the Victorian Age, so that of the 1960s feels, apparently, compelled to dance on the grave of the era of military imperialism which effectively ended with the Second World War: a dance inspired not by a joyful sentiment of liberation but by a determination to stamp the earth down as hard as possible on the coffin underneath.

Like *Oh! What a Lovely War* and *The Charge of the Light Brigade*, 'numerous instant histories of the First World War seem designed neither to provide the colourful excitement of popular military history nor a careful and sympathetic reconstruction of a bygone historical period. Their object is primarily iconoclastic.' This was undoubtedly true, as was Howard's assertion that the motive was not specifically pacifist: 'Lord Raglan, Lord Kitchener and Lord Haig are held up as figures of fun not because they were soldiers but because they are seen as representatives of a particular social system.'

As well as 'instant histories' of the sort Howard disparaged, the

1960s were also marked by numerous memoirs, biographies, anthologies and volumes of poetry concerned with the war. A new edition of Wilfred Owen's poems, edited by C. Day Lewis, appeared in 1963, along with the first volume of his brother Harold's trilogy of memoirs, *Journey from Obscurity*. That same year saw the publication of *The Contrary Experience*, an auto-biographical volume by the poet and art critic Herbert Read, which included extracts from the diary he kept in the trenches and the letters he sent home. The second and third volumes of Harold Owen's trilogy were published in 1964 and 1965, while Wilfred Owen's *Collected Letters* appeared in 1967. There was also a major biography of Rupert Brooke by Christopher Hassall, published in 1964, followed by a huge volume of his letters in 1968. Michael Thorpe's critical study of Siegfried Sassoon appeared in 1966, a year before the poet's death. Two of the best-known anthologies of war poetry, Brian Gardner's *Up the Line to Death* and I.M. Parsons' *Men Who March Away*, appeared in 1964 and 1965 respectively, alongside John H. Johnston's *English Poetry of the First World War: A study in the evolution of narrative form* (1964) and Bernard Bergonzi's *Heroes' Twilight: A Study of the Literature of the Great War* (1965). Those who wanted poetry of a rather less elevated kind could turn to John Brophy and Eric Partridge's *The Long Trail* (1965), which collected soldiers' songs, many of which had become familiar from *Oh What a Lovely War!*, alongside an extensive dictionary of soldiers' slang.

The surge of interest in the War Poets would continue through-out the following decade, which saw books on David Jones and Julian Grenfell; the collected poems and biographies of both Ivor

Gurney and Edward Thomas; the *Collected Works* and three biographies of Isaac Rosenberg; Jon Silkin's critical study *Out of Battle* and his *Penguin Book of First World War Poetry*; and various other books on the literature of the First World War, most notably Paul Fussell's seminal *The Great War and Modern Memory* (1975). It was also during this period that the testimony of veterans began to be regarded as invaluable sources for understanding or studying the 1914–18 conflict. As we have seen, the 1960s were marked by an increasing interest in the lives and history of ordinary people. History no longer belonged to the well educated and the articulate, those who could write and publish their own versions of events. In the preface to his *History of the Germanic People* (1824) the German historian Leopold von Ranke (a forebear of the soldier-poet Robert Graves) wrote: 'You have reckoned that history ought to judge the past and to instruct the contemporary world as to the future. The present attempt does not yield to that high office. It will merely tell you how it really was.' Since the world had apparently ignored the warnings of history provided by the First World War, those who had taken part in it were increasingly called upon to tell later generations how it really was. Oral history became popular as a way of preserving people's experiences, and the spoken rather than the written word was seen as adding a new layer of authenticity to the way we reconstructed the past. Unprepared and unmediated, words spoken into a tape recorder were felt to have an urgency no written text could match. Furthermore, the testimonies of those without either the education or inclination to put down their memories on paper could now be preserved, so that the data-base was becoming socially much broader, rankers beginning to contribute as much as the officers had previously done. Recordings also preserved the different ways in which people of different classes and from different parts of the country expressed themselves, which again made the rapidly accumulating data seem wider in its scope.

Given that the generation of 1914 was now ageing fast, institutions and individuals began amassing material for dedicated archives. The Imperial War Museum had been collecting written testimonies and other artefacts ever since it was founded, but it was in the early 1970s that it began building a sound archive in which veterans of the First World War recorded their experiences for posterity. Although the recordings now in the museum's collections span a considerable period, there was a large surge in acquisitions between 1973 and 1975, when these veterans would on average be in their seventies and eighties. The largest private archive of material about the war was established in 1967 by the historian and academic Peter H. Liddle, specifically 'to preserve permanently evidence of personal experience in the 1914–1918 war in order that this important aspect of British, Commonwealth and European heritage shall never be lost'. Since it became a national archive (now housed at the University of Leeds), this collection has amassed the written and spoken recollections of well over 3,500 veterans. Liddle himself has published numerous books drawing upon his archive, which is now used by scholars from all over the world.

One of the first books to make extensive use of the testimony of veterans was Martin Middlebrook's *The First Day on the Somme* (1971). In order to trace men who had been present on 1 July 1916, Middlebrook placed advertisements in ninety national and local newspapers and journals. As a result he managed to track down 526 British survivors, but many of them died while he was carrying out his research: 'I failed to get replies to an increasing proportion of the letters written during the three years it took to prepare the book for publication.' Even forty years ago, then, these living witnesses were beginning to thin out. Although Middlebrook outlined the military strategy of the battle and provided detailed maps, the sense that this was history from the bottom up, as it were, was indicated by the book's emphatic and empathetic dedication to the 'front-line soldiers of all nations, 1914–1918'. Of the ten soldiers Middlebrook chose as the principal representatives of the British army on 1 July 1916, there was one lieutenant colonel, two lieutenants, one lance corporal, one RSM, four privates and a bugler.

Middlebrook's approach was shared by several other historians, notably Lyn Macdonald, who has written a series of books about the First World War, starting in 1978 with *They Called It Passchendaele*. Subsequent titles include *The Roses of No Man's Land* (1980), dealing with nursing at the front, *Somme* (1983), *1914: The Days of Hope* (1988), *1915: The Death of Innocence* (1993), *To the Last Man: Spring 1918* (1998). These are all compiled from the reminiscences of veterans, linked by Macdonald's own commentary, while her *1914–1918: Voices and Images of the Great War* (1988) combined personal testimony with haunting photographs, contemporary cartoons, advertisements and newspaper clippings, and even the death certificate of a soldier 'Shot by sentence of FGCM [court martial] for "Desertion"'. Denis Winter's resonantly titled *Death's Men* (1978) is an account of 'the infantryman's war […] made up of small details and large emotions'. Winter emphasised that in this book the war would be 'described by men who had little idea of time, place or importance' – just as Harry Patch had little idea of the 'bigger picture' during the Battle of Passchendaele. It is significant than none of these three authors started out as professional or academic historians. Middlebrook was a Lincolnshire farmer who was inspired to write his book (and several others subsequently) after visiting the war cemeteries in France and Belgium. Lyn Macdonald was a BBC producer who first became interested in the oral testimony of veterans while making a radio documentary, and Denis Winter was a schoolmaster who, as his author note in *Death's Men* puts it, 'still attempts to teach history'. Naturally, professional military historians remain suspicious of such 'amateurs' and indeed of any kind of oral history, but such books have enormous public appeal. It was Winter who provided the most eloquent defence of the kind of history he wrote in the epigraph to *Death's Men*, which was taken from Aron du Picq, a 'pioneer writer on the behaviour of men in war and Crimean war veteran who died in battle in the Franco-Prussian war', who compared his own method with that of two well-known historians of the Napoleonic era:

> The smallest detail taken from an actual incident in war is more instructive to me, as a soldier, than all the Thiers and Jominis in the world. They speak for the heads of states and armies, but they never show me what I wish to know – a battalion, company or platoon in action. The man is the first weapon of battle. Let us study the soldier for it is he who brings reality to it.

It was this sense of the 'reality' of war which caught the public imagination. It gave veterans of the First World War, most of whom had kept their experiences to themselves, their voice – and, increasingly, their status.

FOUR
Head Count
2000–2009

Old soldiers never never die;
They simply fade away …

First World War song

There remain large parts of France and Belgium where it is impossible to forget the First World War. It is a haunted landscape, where the dead are ever present. This is precisely what the Imperial War Graves Commission intended. When in 1937 Fabian Ware reported on 'the work and policy' of the IWGC during its first twenty years in a slender volume called *The Immortal Heritage*, he calculated that in France and Belgium alone there were nearly a thousand specially built cemeteries. Within them were some 600,000 uniform headstones, supported by 250 miles of buried concrete beams and set in 540 acres of lawn, the grass of which had all been grown from seed. The cemeteries were enclosed by 50 miles of walls, and a further 63 miles of hedging had been planted. In addition, eighteen monuments to the missing had been erected, with some 54,000 names

(40,000 of them British) recorded on the Menin Gate, another 35,150 (34,000 of them British) on the Tyne Cot Memorial, 22,500 (all British) on the Ploegsteert Memorial, 35,080 (all but eighty British) on the Arras Memorial, and an overwhelming 70,830 (70,000 of them British) on Lutyens' Memorial to the Missing of the Somme, which dominates the skyline at Thiepval. In 1937 the missing themselves were still turning up at a rate of twenty to thirty a week, and some 38,000 of them had been discovered 'by accident' since official searches had been abandoned in September 1921. Even in the late 1980s the land would give up some twenty to thirty bodies a year.

Great Britain has nothing to compare with these acres of the dead. The few casualties buried here mostly died in hospitals after being invalided home. Small clusters of IWGC headstones are occasionally found in churchyards or cemeteries, but there are very few cemeteries containing multiple casualties of the First World War: the largest is the Brookwood Military Cemetery in Surrey, which contains 1,601 burials; the St James's Cemetery, Dover, contains 392 bodies, including those of nine unidentified men killed in the Zeebrugge naval raid in 1918; while the Cliveden War Cemetery in Buckinghamshire contains the graves of forty of those who died while supposedly recuperating from wounds on Lady Astor's estate, most of them Canadian.

Even so, reminders of the dead of the First World War are everywhere. Almost every city, town or village has its war memorial, either in the churchyard, on the village green, or at some other focal point of the community. Carved in stone or cast in bronze, Tommies stand with heads bowed and rifles reversed, remain on guard challenging all comers, wave encouragement to their comrades, or – as in Cambridge – stride off to battle bare headed with an almost unbearably jaunty optimism. Elsewhere angels and eagles stretch their wings protectively or fiercely, St Georges slay dragons, and victors flourish palms. Crosses, obelisks and urn-topped columns display their overfilled ledgers of the dead. In addition, most churches have a Roll of Honour listing 'the men of this parish' who died in the Great War. With their columns of names, war memorials may seem little more than inventories; but they can also tell a story. The memorial cloister at Eton College and the memorials to the 'Pals' Battalions' in the industrial North commemorate the disproportionate casualties suffered by very different individual communities. On memorials in rural villages are carved names still locally familiar, suggesting that descendants have not moved far; or the same names repeated, suggesting families who lost more than one member, perhaps brothers, perhaps fathers and sons. The dead of the First World War may not be present in Britain the way they are in France and Belgium, but their memorials are so ubiquitous that we scarcely notice them as we drive or walk past. Most of the thousands of commuters who pour every day through the elaborate main entrance of Waterloo Station no more realise that they are passing beneath the London and South Western Railway's War Memorial than they think about the Belgian battlefield of an earlier war that gave the station its name.

Even so, the First World War has become a point of reference, so much a part of our lives that we scarcely need allusions to it explained to us. An installation at the Royal Horticultural Society's garden at Hyde Hall in Essex in 2008, for example, consisted of nine headstones standing in isolation on a sloping

211

hillside. On each of the headstones is incised the botanical name of a native plant species that has become extinct. The shape of the headstones is instantly recognisable as that adopted by the Imperial War Graves Commission, and the installation was given the title 'The Fallen'. From a distance the stones do indeed resemble one of the many tiny war cemeteries found in northern France and Flanders. Few people now refer to those who are killed in action as 'The Fallen', but this was the title chosen by Morgan Matthews for an extraordinary television film in which he attempted to commemorate every single British soldier killed during the continuing conflicts in Iraq and Afghanistan. Broadcast in November 2008, in the wake of widespread coverage of the ninetieth anniversary of the Armistice, it ran over three hours, listing every lost soldier by name and interviewing grieving families and friends. The names loomed out of a dark screen which appeared to have moving golden flecks in it, a motif explained towards the end of the film when a lone sculptor was depicted adding names to the national Armed Forces Memorial in Staffordshire, stone debris flying from beneath his chisel. This memorial is a huge Portland stone circle which at the time of its unveiling by the Queen in October 2007 bore the names of some 16,000 service personnel who have been killed while on duty since the end of the Second World War. Room had been left on the curved walls for 15,000 additional names, including those being added by the letterer in Matthews' emotionally wrenching film. Widespread disquiet about Britain's involvement in Iraq and Afghanistan has meant that the general public has been less ready to give the dead of these wars their due than was the case in 1918. By calling his documentary *The Fallen*, Matthews provided an instantly recognisable historical reference point which aligned those who had died in these controversial conflicts with those of an earlier generation whose war had been far more popular. Similarly, if more light-heartedly, everyone understood the grim humour of an advert for the London Transport Museum that appeared in newspapers in August 2008, in the run-up to the ninetieth anniversary of the end of the war. Above the words 'Hundreds of London buses took troops to the trenches in the First World War. Discover this and other moving stories at the new museum' was a crumpled, period bus ticket: 'Ypres. One Way from Dover via Calais'.

The First World War has also become a staple of the national curriculum for British schools, though as part of the English literature rather than the history course. Wilfred Owen, Siegfried Sassoon and even R.C. Sherriff are listed as major writers to be studied for Key Stage 3, presumably falling into the Qualification and Curriculum Authority's desired category of writers who have 'influenced culture and thinking'. As a sample of how teachers might approach the literature of the First World War, the QCA's website provides a 'case study' from a sixth-form college in Hampshire:

> In preparing students for unit 6 on war literature, the department organises a visit to Ypres. There is a substantial role-play of a military court, deciding on the question of the court-martialling and execution of deserters, based on a range of documents, from letters, poems and interviews to statistics and visual images. The role-play helps students enter the mindset of people at the time, rather than relying solely on the view of the war of the

First World War poets and it comes as a surprise to the students themselves that many of their role-plays end with decisions to execute.

This somewhat macabre exercise is balanced by the more mainstream literary task of compiling 'anthologies of war poetry, drawing on their knowledge of themes and content to present the poetry to a wider audience'.

Trips to the battlefields of France and Belgium are no longer the preserve of veterans and historians or relatives of the dead. Not only are groups of schoolchildren conducted round these sites as an adjunct to their studies of the war, or the War Poets, but many other people are simply interested in seeing where an earlier generation had fought and died. Numerous books suggest walking tours of the battlefields, and specialist travel companies provide guided tours for coachloads of those who may not have any direct family link with the war but nevertheless want to learn something about it. It is possible, for example, to learn the extent of the war, which is neatly though coincidentally illustrated in the St-Symphorien Military Cemetery near Mons, where two headstones a few feet apart mark the final resting places of the first and last British soldiers to be killed in the war: Private John Parr, who died on 21 August 1914, and Private George Ellison, killed on 11 November 1918. The notorious ability of recruiting officers to be hoodwinked about the age of volunteers is apparent at Dartmoor Cemetery near Albert, where the oldest British casualty of the war, Lieutenant Henry Webber, killed by a stray shell on the Somme in July 1916 at the age of sixty-seven, is buried; or at Poelkappelle British Cemetery, which contains the remains of the youngest British casualty, Private John Condon, killed in August 1914 at the age of thirteen. A memorial stone in the Devonshire Cemetery at Mametz bears eloquent witness to the losses on the first day on the Somme: it was here on 4 July 1916 that the remnants of the 8th and 9th Battalions of the Devonshire Regiment buried 161 of their comrades in a trench beneath a sign that read 'The Devonshires held this trench, the Devonshires hold it still'. The Commonwealth War Graves Commission has an online 'Debt of Honour Register', which allows anyone to look up the names of all those who died and to find their grave or memorial. Individual entries list the name, rank, service number, date of death, age, regiment and nationality, give a grave or memorial reference, and describe the cemetery where the subject is buried or the memorial on which his or her name is inscribed.

Anniversaries of the beginning and end of the war, or of major battles, are regularly marked not only in the press and on television and radio, but even by the morning post. The Royal Mail produced three sets of commemorative stamps under the collective title 'Lest We Forget', all featuring Flanders poppies. The first marked the ninetieth anniversary of the Battle of the Somme in July 2006, the second the ninetieth anniversary of the Battle of Passchendaele in November 2007, the third the ninetieth anniversary of the Armistice in November 2008. Collectors could purchase commemorative sheets, bordered with lines from Binyon's 'For the Fallen' on which the stamps were accompanied by extracts from letters written home from the trenches of Passchendaele and photographs of artefacts such as a whistle blown to mark the start of an attack at Ypres by an officer who was subsequently awarded a VC, and the football dribbled towards the German lines by men of the 8th East Surrey Regiment on the first day of the Somme. A surge of interest in family history, fostered by such television programmes as *Who Do You Think You Are?*, in which famous people go in search of their forebears, has also led people to take a particular interest in what their parents, grandparents and great-grandparents did in the war. As part of its 'Ninety Years of Remembrance' season in November 2008, the BBC launched a website in which users were invited to 'trace your WW1 family history', the results of which could be posted on a Remembrance Wall, which at the time of writing had 5,837 combatants recorded on it.

The Internet has indeed made such searches easier and has become a conduit for a great deal of often esoteric information about the war. There are innumerable websites dedicated to the subject, providing a host of facts, statistics and images for the interested browser. Long-established organisations such as the Western Front Association (WFA) have used websites to reach a new and younger audience. Founded in 1980 'with the aim of furthering interest in the period 1914–1918, to perpetuate the memory, courage and comradeship of all those who served their countries in France and Flanders and their own countries during The Great War', the Association is at pains to stress that it 'does not seek to justify or glorify war' and 'is entirely non-political': its object is simply 'to educate the public in the history of The Great War with particular reference to the Western Front'. It has some sixty-five branches, not only in Britain, but in most of the Allied countries, has the leading military historian Correlli Barnett as its president, and has boasted descendants of both Haig and

Kitchener on its board. Its current membership stands at around 6,500 members worldwide and it produces its own magazine, *Stand To!*, published three times a year, as well as an in-house *Bulletin*.

Along with the British Legion, the WFA played a significant role in the restoration of the two minutes' silence on 11 November. While acknowledging the importance of Remembrance Sunday, the Legion had been campaigning for some time for the actual anniversary of the Armistice to be marked once more, precisely because it more often than not fell on a working day when any cessation of activity would be more impressive than it would be in the middle of divine service on a Sunday. There seemed to be considerable public support for this idea: in 2002 the Legion announced that independent research they had commissioned reported back that 92 per cent of the population (including, significantly, 91 per cent of young people between the ages of sixteen and twenty-four) thought the Silence should be observed on 11 November and that Remembrance should be part of the national calendar. In a letter to the Legion, the Prime Minister, Tony Blair, lent his support, and this was echoed by the Lord Chancellor, who that year invited all courts to observe the Silence. A large number of local authorities followed suit, suggesting meetings should be halted for two minutes, and leading employers, including shops and supermarkets, banks and building societies, power and transport companies, encouraged their staff to stop work for two minutes' silent reflection. All aircraft movement was halted at Manchester Airport, while trains and buses would also stop where possible. It was estimated that some forty-five million people observed the Silence that year, and in subsequent years the Silence at 11 a.m. on 11 November has indeed become a national ritual.

The resurgence of interest in the First World War at the beginning of the twenty-first century came about partly because there was a sense that what linked us directly to this vital part of our history was about to slip from our grasp. For much of the twentieth century, those who fought in the war and survived it had been very much part of the fabric of our lives in Britain. It was not merely that they appeared wearing ribbons and medals with their poppies every Remembrance Sunday, but they were our fathers and grandfathers, a living link with this increasingly distant event that nevertheless continued to cast its long shadow over the century. Reviewing a clutch of books about the First World War in May 2008, the historian Francis Beckett suggested that 'The war's extraordinary vividness is because it left a whole generation deeply and irreparably damaged, and that generation is close enough for many of us to have known members of it.' Beckett did not in fact know his maternal grandfather, who died in March 1918 after being hit by a shell the previous month. He did, however, witness the effect of that death on his mother, who had been nine at the time 'and never got over it'. 'In her last years, in the 1980s, her once fine brain so crippled by dementia that she could not remember the names of her children, she could still remember his dreadful, lingering, useless death. She could still talk of his last leave, when he was so shell-shocked he could hardly speak and my grandmother ironed his uniform every day in the vain hope of killing the lice.'

While over the years some veterans learned to speak of their experiences, others never did. The urge not to inflict harrowing stories on children and grandchildren as well as a more self-protective sense that some memories were better left undisturbed and unexamined meant that the link between history and its living witnesses was in many cases never forged. To take an example close to hand, both my grandfathers fought in the war but died when I was too young to formulate let alone ask the sort of questions I would like to put to them now. They might not have answered anyway. One of them served as an officer in Palestine with the Royal Army Medical Corps and was awarded the Military Cross, but when asked about this distinction would reply that they gave medals out to whoever came down to breakfast first. He was a stalwart of the village's British Legion, the annual fete of which was held in the garden of his house. He may have survived the war, but it got him in the end. He had been wounded by a shell and over half a century later the shrapnel left in his body led to his having a leg amputated. He survived the operation but succumbed to a heart attack while recuperating in hospital. My other grandfather served as a private in the Honourable Artillery Company in France, was also wounded, and was taken prisoner in 1917. Every Armistice Day he would lock himself in his study, speaking to no one. I don't remember this, but something of the dismal atmosphere he created must have communicated itself to me: as a child with no sense of history, I believed that he had suffered the terrible fate of a later generation and had been a prisoner of war of the Japanese. The fact that neither man ever spoke of his experiences if anything gave the war an even more terrible because hidden presence.

Any awareness of the First World War came by a less direct

route. We did not learn about the war in history classes at my preparatory school, but boys spent long hours in the hobby room constructing a huge papier-mâché trench system, from which miniature Airfix model soldiers clambered out to stagger across no man's land. Model aircraft were suspended by cotton from the ceiling over the battlefield, and their names – Sopwith Camel, de Havilland, Handley Page – became familiar even to a boy as uninterested in warfare as I was, and remain with me even though I could not actually identify one in a museum. Model aeroplanes and troops of the Second World War were also available, but were for some reason much less popular. Even so, I made no connection between the miniature battles recreated in the hobby room and the experiences my grandfathers had undergone in real life.

Nor did I readily connect war memorials with my grand-fathers. I was brought up in the Marches, so when we went on picnics or to the seaside we usually headed into Wales. Along the route were markers by which we measured our progress: the garage where we always stopped to buy ice lollies, the field in Pen-y-bont where there were always donkeys, and so on. For me there was another marker, one I never commented on but which haunted me. It was the New Radnor war memorial, a stone soldier standing sentinel above the road leading west out of the town. This lone figure filled me with a sort of dread. Even though I was too young to understand what he represented, I knew instinctively that it was something sad or frightening. Many years later, while writing this book, I remembered this memorial and went to look at it again. The town has long since had a bypass, which is why I hadn't seen the statue for such a long time. There are a mere six names, but someone thought they deserved this striking monument. The soldier is an ordinary Tommy, his head lowered, his rifle reversed, with some sort of stylised plant – perhaps an olive branch – growing from it. I cannot have seen much detail as a child being driven past in a car, but I now recognise that the expression on the soldier's face beneath his tin helmet is indeed haunting. The look is less reverent than desolate, with heavy lids lowered over sorrowful eyes as if drawn down under a weight of grief.

As the twentieth century drew to its close the group of First World War veterans who, their medals clinking, marched past and saluted the Cenotaph every Remembrance Sunday became smaller and smaller. Often referred to inaccurately as the 'Old Contemptibles' (a name in fact adopted by the BEF regulars in 1914 after Kaiser Wilhelm II had unwisely referred to them as 'Sir John French's contemptible little army'), these men had become a notable but increasingly aged and infirm element of the yearly commemoration, many on sticks and some in wheelchairs. Not all veterans took part in these proceedings, though Harry Patch was more vehement than most in his rejection of the annual commemoration. 'For me, 11 November is just show business,' he wrote late in his long life. This was clearly a minority view, but anything veterans could tell us not only about their experiences of the war but also their attitudes to its aftermath and commemoration began to seem increasingly vital as their numbers dwindled. People began compiling national statistics of survivors and the yearly headcount began.

The notion of a Last Veteran was not entirely new, but had in the past been a minor curiosity rather than a major news story. This was partly because in the past the media had been less sophisticated and widespread, but it is also a fact that no war had left such a mark upon so many people as the First World War. Astonishingly the last veteran of the Boer War long outlived many veterans of both world wars, not dying until 12 April 1993, aged 111. George Frederick Ives was born on 17 November 1881 and was working in his father's grocery business in Bristol when British forces suffered three consecutive defeats at the Battles of Stomberg, Magersfontein and Colenso during the so-called 'Black Week' of December 1899. One reaction to this disaster was a rush to enlist back in Britain, and Ives was among the new intake of volunteers, serving with the 1st Imperial Yeomanry as a mounted infantryman. Only seventeen of the 122 men who enlisted with him at Cheltenham survived and, as many veterans would do after the First World War, Ives returned to England to find widespread unemployment. He emigrated to Canada, where he remained for the rest of his life – although he returned briefly to Britain in 1992 in order to attend the Albert Hall Festival of Remembrance. There he experienced something of the attention the last veterans of the First World War would receive.

Farther back, the last survivor of the Charge of the Light Brigade in the Crimean War, Edwin Hughes from Wrexham in Wales, also became something of a celebrity. Popularly known as 'Balaclava Ned', he had been injured in the famous and foolhardy assault on the Russian guns on 25 October 1854 when his horse had been killed under him. He managed to extricate himself from under his dead charger and make his way back to his own lines. He left the regular army in 1873, after over twenty-one years' service, but immediately re-enlisted as a sergeant-instructor in a volunteer regiment, remaining there until forcibly retired at the age of sixty-five. He died in 1927 at the age of ninety-six, out-living by four months the last survivor of the Thin Red Line, which famously held off a Russian cavalry charge at Balaclava on that same day, Charles Ellingworth of the 93rd Sutherland Highlanders. Neither man was in fact the last British survivor of the Crimean War, since both were long outlived by the splendidly named Rookes Evelyn Bell Crompton, who enlisted as a naval cadet at the age of eleven and took part in the Siege of Sebastopol. The proud possessor of two campaign medals by the age of twelve, he returned to England to continue his education at Harrow, became a well-known engineer and did not die until 1940.

The farther back you go, the less easy it is to establish who the last veteran of any conflict or battle really is. The last British veteran of the Battle of Trafalgar was once thought to be a rating called John Rome or Roome, who died in December 1860. He had served on board HMS *Victory* and in old age claimed to have been the person who hoisted Nelson's signal 'England expects that every man will do his duty'. Since he had subsequently deserted, then rejoined the navy under a pseudonym, it is not at all clear whether his claim could be trusted. In any case, even if he had been the last survivor to have served on the *Victory*, he certainly wasn't the last veteran of Trafalgar. Stephen Hilton, who had been a master's mate on HMS *Minotaur* and was one of three brothers who all served at Trafalgar, died in 1872. Meanwhile, a tomb-stone in the churchyard of St Laurence at Cholesbury in Hertfordshire marks the grave of David Newton, who survived being wounded while serving on HMS *Revenge* and died at the age of ninety-six in July 1878. It seems, however, that all these claimants were outlived by one Joseph Sutherland, who was probably born in 1790, which would have made him around fifteen at Trafalgar, and died in 1890 at the age of 100. This would seem to clinch the matter, but powder monkeys could be as young as twelve, and there may well have been one who lived on longer than Sutherland but never identified himself.

Seeking out and verifying veterans of the first war of the Modern Age also has its problems, but matters were made easier in 1987 when Dennis Goodwin and his son Stephen founded the World War One Veterans' Association. The impetus for this was less idle curiosity than a concern for the welfare of those who had fought in the war. Both Goodwins were professionally involved with residential care homes, Stephen as a registrar and Dennis as a lay inspector, and in the course of their work met large numbers of elderly men who seemed to be rapidly and unresistingly fading away. They gradually realised that these old men had one thing in common: they had all fought in the First World War. Although the war had taken place in their increasingly distant youth, it often remained the most significant experience of their lives; but it was something neither the much younger staff nor the women residents, who greatly outnumbered the men, could share or understand. As Dennis Goodwin put it, these men 'simply retreated into their own shell hole of memories as the effects of benign institutionalism eroded their willingness to fight the ravages of the ageing process'. He recognised that getting old soldiers to talk about their war service was genuinely therapeutic for them, giving meaning to their experiences. If these men could be brought together, it might revive the sense of camaraderie that prevailed in the war itself. Since few of the men had ever returned to the battlefields, the Goodwins decided to organise an expedition for fourteen of them. This was a considerable undertaking, given the veterans' age and infirmities, but it proved a great success. Battlefield visits were less common then, and this one was reported in the press, after which many people contacted the Goodwins, who founded their Association in response. Numerous further visits to France and Belgium followed and this raised awareness among younger generations, who became interested both in visiting the battlefields themselves and in meeting men who had fought there a lifetime ago. The veterans were rescued from isolation and were reconnected not only with those who had shared their experiences but with the larger world.

One of those whose lives were changed by Dennis Goodwin was Henry Allingham, who would become fêted as one of Britain's last two surviving veterans. The son of a clerk in the family ironmongery business, Allingham had been born in modest circumstances in Upper Clapton, London, on 6 June 1896. He had sat on his grandfather's shoulders to watch Edward VII's coronation procession, seen W.G. Grace batting at the Oval, witnessed the first British airship over London and the gradual disappearance of horse-drawn vehicles from the city's streets. It was the sighting of an early aeroplane that made him enlist with the Royal Naval Air Service (RNAS) in June 1915. He would have joined up earlier, but his widowed mother had been horrified when he visited a recruiting office during the first week of the war. As her only child, he promised not to leave her, but felt able to volunteer when she died of cancer the following year.

As an air mechanic, he kept planes airworthy, flew patrols over the North Sea, and witnessed the Battle of Jutland. From September 1917 he served on the Western Front as a mechanic on the ground and as an observer, gunner and bomber in the air. Although never in the trenches, he was exposed to all kinds of danger, not least simply by going up in the highly unreliable early aeroplanes, and he suffered a shrapnel wound when the Germans bombed a depot. On 1 April 1918, the RNAS was merged with the Royal Flying Corps and so Allingham ended his war as a founder member of a new service, the Royal Air Force.

Like the majority of the veterans who lived into the twenty-first century, he had for the most part led a wholly unremarkable life. He had left school at the age of fifteen and found employment with a car- and coachbuilder. After the war he briefly joined a company that assembled aircraft, then returned to the car industry, where he spent the rest of his working life. He married happily and produced two daughters, one of whom married a GI and emigrated to America. His spare time was devoted to bicycling, sailing and playing golf, and he eventually retired to Eastbourne. For many years he never talked about the war, but as the old world gradually receded and those around him died, including his wife and the daughter who had remained in Britain, he ended up alone and housebound. When he was first contacted by Goodwin in around 2000, his eyesight and hearing were fading and he was 'literally waiting to die'. At first he insisted he did not want to talk about the war, but Goodwin eventually managed to convince him that 'there was a world out there that wanted to meet him and hear his stories'. Once persuaded, Allingham took to his new role with great enthusiasm, and it was precisely his ability to remember the war and remind later generations of its cost which gave him a sense of purpose and kept him going for so long.

The same could be said of many of the veterans. Historians had for some time been seeking out and interviewing survivors, recognising that unless their stories were preserved a hugely significant part of British history would be lost. Richard van Emden, who had interviewed 120 of those who fought in the Great War, worked on one of the first books and television documentaries to showcase their testimonies. *Veterans* was published in 1998 to accompany a BBC television series of the same name, and was followed in 2005 by *Britain's Last Tommies*. That same year the popular historian Max Arthur published *Last Post: The Final Word from Our First World War Soldiers*. It was in fact very far from being the final word.

Once encouraged to talk about their war, many veterans felt it their duty to tell others what it was really like to have been at the front. This was not merely so that their own war should not be forgotten by later generations or reduced to accounts of battle plans and strategies by historians. Some veterans wanted to ensure that when politicians with no direct experience of warfare talked blandly of the regrettable necessity of sending troops into action to defend our freedoms, people should realise what this meant in the front line. A reporter who sought Allingham out to ask his opinion of the invasion of Iraq in March 2003 was told that all wars were bad:

> Ask men who have been to war and they will all tell you the same. Yes, Hussein was an evil man. But the Americans should have

toppled him the first time they fought the Iraqis. I felt sorry for the soldiers who would once more be risking their lives. It was not the same as my war. We were fighting for our country and our homes and this is completely different. We had a lot more to lose if we failed.

Allingham was intent upon honouring those who fought in the First World War, and while keen to ensure younger gen-erations did not forget or underestimate its perils, he was dis-inclined to speak disparagingly of it. He did, however, conclude that in general 'War's stupid. Nobody wins. You might as well talk first, you have to talk last anyway.'

Other veterans were more forthright. William Roberts, who had been in the Royal Flying Corps, dismissed the war towards the end of his life as 'a lot of bloody political bull', while George Charles, who had served with the Durham Light Infantry, described it as 'a complete waste of lives'. 'The First World War was idiotic,' concluded Alfred Finnigan, who had served in it with the Royal Field Artillery at Passchendaele and elsewhere. 'It started out idiotic and it stayed idiotic. It was damned silly, all of it.' Harry Patch went so far as to describe himself as 'a pacifist' and dismiss the annual ceremony at the Cenotaph as 'nothing but a show of military force'. He never pretended that war was anything other than a waste of young lives and said that 'the politicians who took us to war should have been given the guns and told to settle their differences themselves, instead of organising nothing better than legalised mass murder'. His anger was shared by his fellow veteran Cecil Withers, who had lied about his age in order to join up at the age of seventeen. He first went into action at Arras on Easter Monday, 9 April 1917, two months before his nineteenth birthday, and in August was hit by shrapnel and temporarily blinded. Lying in a trench, semi-conscious and bleeding heavily from the head, he was mistaken for dead and was nearly carted off for burial. Having recuperated back in Britain, he was transferred to the Royal Fusiliers and returned to the front in January 1918, serving there until the end of the war. He could not forget his experiences and made sure no one else would, commenting towards the end of his life:

> People still talk a lot of rubbish about the war. I've always let people know what really went on […] I've let people know so that the truth could be a warning to them. When the war was going on, the horrors were kept quiet and the full display of dreadful things only came later […] These days, if any trigger-happy politician wants to start another war, it's my job to let people know what that means. Politicians today are pitiless humbugs. What do they know? Only those who were there can tell you what really happened.

It soon became clear that these voices would very shortly be stilled. By the time the paperback edition of Richard van Emden's *Britain's Last Tommies* appeared in 2006, Roberts, Charles and Withers had all died. Van Emden itemised what else we had lost: the last survivors of Gallipoli, Jutland and the first day on the Somme; the last holders of the Military Cross, the Military Medal, the Distinguished Conduct Medal and the 1914/15 Star; the last Old Contemptible, the last Kitchener Volunteer, the last cavalryman, the last artilleryman, and the last prisoner of war.

The last army officer to have served at the front, Lieutenant Norman Porteous of the 13th Royal Scots, had died in September 2003, and it was somehow appropriate that the only surviving British veterans who had seen active service were just ordinary servicemen who had obeyed orders and done what they were asked to do: Henry Allingham and Harry Patch. Van Emden worked with Patch on an autobiography published in 2007 as *The Last Fighting Tommy*, a title claiming a distinction that separated Patch from Allingham, who had of course fought with the Royal Naval Air Service. Allingham's admiring words about those who fought in the trenches were used as the book's epigraph. A year later Allingham responded with his own memoirs, *Kitchener's Last Volunteer*, co-written with Dennis Goodwin. Its subtitle suggested some friendly rivalry with Patch: *The Life of Henry Allingham, Britain's Oldest Man and the Oldest Surviving Veteran of the Great War*.

In the summer of 2008, Allingham and Patch had reached their 112th and 110th birthdays respectively. Another veteran of the Royal Navy, Claude Choules, was still alive at 107, but although he was born in Worcestershire he had spent the majority of his long life in Australia, having emigrated in 1926 and transferred permanently to the Royal Australian Navy, remaining in the service until his retirement in 1956. There was one American veteran left, 107-year-old Frank Woodruff Buckles, popularly referred to as 'the Last Doughboy', and one Italian, 109-year-old Delfino Borroni. There were in fact two Italians left when I first wrote this sentence in mid-June 2008: a week later Italy's other surviving veteran, Francesco Chiarello, was dead at the age of 109, and Borroni himself followed in October. There were no German veterans left, and the last veteran to have fought for the Central Powers, Franz Künstler of the Austro-Hungarian army, had died on 27 May. The last soldier to have fought for the Ottoman Empire, Yakup Satar, had died in March at the age of 110, while Poland's last veteran, 105-year-old Stanislaw Wychech, died at the end of June. The last surviving woman to have served in the war, as a barrack waitress for the Women's Auxiliary Air Force and Women's Royal Air Force, was Gladys Powers, who although British had for many years lived in Canada, where she had celebrated her 109th birthday in May. She died three months later. Also surviving were a number of veterans who had not seen active service, including the British William (Bill) Stone and Sydney Lucas, the Canadian John Babcock (all 107) and the Australian John Campbell Ross (109). Like Choules, Lucas had emigrated to Australia in the 1920s: both men served with the Australian forces during the Second World War.

The French, meanwhile, had buried the person they assumed to be their last veteran with due Gallic pomp among their national heroes in the Panthéon in February 2008. The Italian-born Lazare Ponticelli, who moved to France at the age of two, had fought with both the French and Italian armies during the war. After demobilisation, he returned to France, where he founded an engineering company in Paris, Ponticelli Frères, which made piping and did other metalworking. He became a French citizen in 1939 and, while keeping his company going by manufacturing equipment for soldiers, he also joined the French Resistance. Although he had originally declined the offer of a state funeral, he changed his mind when the supposedly penultimate French veteran, Louis de Cazenave, died in January

2008 at the age of 110. Ponticelli himself died a mere seven weeks later on 12 March 2008, also aged 110, and on 17 March the French president, Nicolas Sarkozy, and his predecessor, Jacques Chirac, stood shoulder to shoulder before his flag-draped coffin, which had been laid in the *cour d'honneur* of the Hôtel des Invalides in Paris. Both presidents attended the funeral mass in the Cathédrale Saint-Louis (known as *l'église des soldats*) along with the French premier and most government ministers, a body of currently serving soldiers, members of Ponticelli's family and representatives of the family company, which had continued in business after Ponticelli's retirement as manager in 1960. Flags were flown at half-mast, and President Sarkozy unveiled a plaque commemorating all the veterans of the First World War. Ponticelli had also been France's oldest living man, and in the wake of his death investigations to find out who now had claim to this title unearthed a 108-year-old former farmer called Fernand Goux. M. Goux, it transpired, had also served in the last months of the First World War, having been called up in April 1918. His initial job was to supply rations to the trenches and to bring back the dead for burial, but on 3 November 1918 his regiment was sent into the front line, where he spent eight days before the Armistice was signed. Although by most reckonings Goux would count as a veteran, according to French rules he was disqualified because he had spent less than ninety days in combat: the seven months he had spent in supply, however dangerous, simply didn't count. Another French veteran, Pierre Picault, who was called up in April 1918 and served as a gunner, was already known to the French authorities but similarly excluded. This ruling saved the French government a good deal of embarrassment and, more importantly, meant that Lazare Ponticelli can rest in peace in the Panthéon as '*le dernier poilu*' (officially).

In the event, neither Goux nor Picault long outlived Ponticelli, both dying in November 2008. The French case highlights the difficulties that face governments that wish to honour their last veteran. Even those with less stringent rules are sometimes caught in the dilemma of who 'counts'. For example, the afore-mentioned Claude Choules was born in Britain and fought with the British but has lived in Australia for eighty-three of his 108 years. Is he, therefore, a British veteran or an Australian one? He has never been back to Britain since he arrived in Australia in 1926, and evidently regards himself as Australian. The British government agreed, and his name was never listed among those who 'qualified' as Britain's last veteran – though Bill Stone, whom many thought did not really qualify because he was still in training when the Armistice was signed, apparently did (officially). Someone who did not was Netherwood Hughes, a veteran who was 'discovered' only in November 2008. In fact, the World War One Veterans' Association had known about Hughes for some time but at the request of his family, who were concerned about the effect the publicity might have on Hughes's fragile health, had not made their discovery public. Born in Great Harwood, Lancashire, on 12 June 1900, Hughes 'remembered' being called up in June 1918, shortly after his eighteenth birthday, and joining the 51st Manchester Battalion as an infantryman, but at the age of 108 his memory had deteriorated. 'He remembers going to Fulwood Barracks in Preston but remembers very little other than that,' Dennis Goodwin told the

Daily Telegraph. This would not have mattered greatly had there been documentary evidence to confirm his war service. Unfortunately, no records existed, and without these the Ministry of Defence would not acknowledge his claim. 'We have no reason to suspect that Netherwood Hughes is not a veteran of World War One,' a spokesman said, 'but due to the large numbers of military service records destroyed during the Blitz in the 1940s, it has unfortunately not been possible to verify that he is.' The only evidence was an old photograph showing Hughes in uniform, but lacking any regimental badge that would confirm his claim. Hughes had no particular wish to enter what at times seemed like a contest to be Britain's last veteran, and while the World War One Veterans' Association quietly admitted him to their dwindling company, the MoD stood firm.

Hughes had been invited by Dennis Goodwin to attend a special ceremony at the Cenotaph on 11 November 2008 marking the ninetieth anniversary of the Armistice, but he had been too frail to make the journey to London from Accrington. Still officially unrecognised, he would die on 4 April 2009. Bill Stone had died three months before Hughes, on 10 January, which left only Allingham and Patch. Allingham achieved an additional distinction when, in March 2009, in addition to being the oldest man in Britain, he also, according to reliable records, became the oldest British man who had ever lived. On 19 June, a fortnight after his 113rd birthday, he became the world's oldest living man after the death in Japan of Tomoji Tanabe, who was some nine months his senior.

In many ways, Allingham maintained a much higher public profile than the more retiring Harry Patch: he was more often interviewed and more often went to talk to schoolchildren or attend public occasions connected with the war. He received numerous honours, including the *Légion d'honneur*, awarded by the French government in 1998 to all surviving British veterans; a gold medal and the freedom of St-Omer, where he had unveiled the British Air Services Memorial to the 4,700 air personnel killed in the war, in 2004; honorary membership of the Fleet Air Arm Association (the aircraft division of the Royal Navy) in 2005; and the freedom of Eastbourne, the town in which he had lived for forty-two years, in March 2006. On this last occasion he was presented with a vellum scroll, a medal on a ribbon, and the additional gift of a bottle of malt whisky, this last a nod to his much-quoted remark that he owed his long life to 'cigarettes, whisky and wild, wild women'. Increasingly frail, but apparently indomitable, he had recently been persuaded to move from his flat to a residential home only after being certified blind and suffering a couple of falls.

His 110th birthday in June that year was noted in the House of Commons, where his local MP tabled a motion offering the House's congratulations. The birthday telegram from the Queen he had now received by post for ten years was delivered in person by the Defence Secretary and the Chancellor of the Exchequer. While this birthday was celebrated in a local Eastbourne hotel, the following one took place aboard HMS *Victory*, at the invitation of the Royal Navy. In 2007 he also received Special Recognition at the *Daily Mirror*'s Pride of Britain awards, celebrating the country's 'unsung heroes', ordinary people who had done remarkable things and voted for by members of the public. The award was made for his continuing work in educating children about the First World War. His 112th birthday in June 2008 was hosted by the RAF and marked by a fly-past. He was awarded the freedom of Brighton and Hove in April 2009 and an honorary doctorate in engineering from Southampton University a month later. He was already the recipient of the President of the Institution of Mechanical Engineers' Special Award for Outstanding Contribution and Achievements on behalf of the Engineering Profession, and received a further honorary doctorate of engineering from the Warsash Maritime Academy in Southampton that May. Two months later, on 18 July 2009, Henry Allingham died in his sleep, and his passing was headline news around the world. As a result Harry Patch became Britain's Last Veteran.

No one doubts that Henry Allingham had a tough war, in which he served with great distinction, but as he himself said: 'It was the men in the trenches who won the war.' Harry Patch would make no claim to have had anything to do with winning the war, but it is the infantryman who has become the most popular representative of all those who fought in it, and it therefore seems fitting that the Last Tommy should also become the Last Veteran. Patch seems truly representative of his generation and a lost world, much in the way George Sherston, that simplified version of the author in Siegfried Sassoon's autobiographical trilogy, stands for the decent, ordinary public-school officers who led rankers like Patch into battle. Like many people born in the countryside in the Victorian era, he remained firmly attached to his local roots. For most of his life, apart from his war service, he rarely left Somerset, the county in which he was born and in which, 111 years later, he died and was buried. His voice retained a distinctive Somerset burr right to the end, even when it had been reduced to a whisper. As the then Poet Laureate, Andrew Motion, observed in 'The Five Acts of Harry Patch', the poem he wrote in March 2008 at the request of the BBC, the Last Veteran's name had a Shakespearean ring to it, one that might have placed Harry Patch among the ragtag of ordinary soldiers fighting alongside Henry V at Agincourt. The history of the Duke of Cornwall's Light Infantry, with whom Patch served, stretches back to the early eighteenth century and the many battles in which the regiment took part down the years are resonant with English history: Dettingen, Corunna, Waterloo, Sebastopol, Tel-el-Kebir. Perhaps the regiment's most celebrated action took place between 30 June and 18 November 1857 when, vastly outnumbered, it defended the Residency at Lucknow in one of the bloodiest episodes of the so-called Indian Mutiny.

Not that this roster of military glory and gallantry meant much to Patch, who was decidedly not one of those who rushed to the recruiting station as soon as war was declared in August 1914. He recalled people singing a song about his county's military keenness, written by Somerset-born Fred Weatherly, whose 'Roses of Picardy', set to music by Haydn Wood, became one of the most famous songs of the First World War. The final verse of 'Up from Somerset' runs:

> For we'm come up from Somerset,
> Where the cider apples grow,

> For we're all King's men in Somerset,
> As they were long, long ago,
> An' when you're wanting soldier boys,
> An' there's fighting for to do,
> You just send word to Somerset,
> An' we'll all be up for you!

Word may have been sent, but Patch was not inclined to respond. 'While a lot of local lads went and joined up in the local regiment, the Somerset Light Infantry,' he recalled, 'I never gave it a second thought.' Sixteen at the time, Patch 'didn't welcome the war at all, and never felt the need to get myself into khaki and go out there fighting before it was "all over by Christmas" […] I'm not saying I knew any different, but at my age I was keen to continue my apprenticeship.' He was at the time apprenticed to a plumber, and his family had a long connection with the building trade.

The son of a master stonemason, Henry John Patch was born in the village of Combe Down near Bath on 17 June 1898, and his family's roots were buried deep in the Somerset soil. His father, whose family originated in a village near Glastonbury on the other side of the county, had been born at Claverton, a mile or so from Combe Down, while his mother had been born in the neighbouring village of Monkton Combe. The Patches had thoroughly colonised this small corner of England, and by the outbreak of the war there were fourteen different Patch families in Combe Down, including those of Harry's five paternal uncles, whose names were absolutely characteristic of the time and place: Herbert, Alfred, Eli, Walter and Harry. All six brothers, including

Harry's father, William, were intimately bound up with the surrounding landscape in their working lives, as builders, masons and gardeners, or, in the case of Herb, in the employment of 'a nearby earthworks called Tucky Mill'. Harry was the youngest of three boys, the eldest of whom, George, became a carpenter and cabinetmaker, while the middle brother, William, became a bricklayer. As well as being master mason on such prestigious projects as the Empire Hotel in Bath, the boys' father invested in local properties, renting them out or building new houses on adjoining land. He was an expert gardener, whose carefully tended plot at 'Fonthill' (a semi-detached house somewhat grandiosely named after William Beckford's folly in neighbouring Wiltshire) boasted fruit trees, beehives, a small flock of chickens, pigsties and numerous beds of vegetables, which supplied the family with food the whole year round. Harry's mother had been in service, eventually taking charge of the household staff of a prosperous local doctor, but such was the success of William's enterprises that the family soon had staff of their own: a cook, a butler who waited at table, and a housemaid. This was not of course unusual at this period, when even very modest families who could afford it employed servants. The cook and housemaid lived in when the family moved to a larger house in Combe Down called Rosemount, which boasted 'a nursery, four bedrooms, a drawing room, dining room, kitchen, scullery and conservatory'. Grand as this house was by local standards, it had no gas or electricity or internal plumbing. It was heated by open fires and lit by candles and oil or paraffin lamps, and all drinking water came from a well and had to be boiled before use. There was no bathroom: family members took a weekly bath in a tin tub

239

filled by hand with water from a boiler heated by the coal range in the kitchen, and had to make do with an outside privy.

Neither did relative prosperity mean that the Patch boys were automatically sent away to smart boarding schools such as nearby Monkton Combe, where their father had worked on the chapel. Harry's oldest brother attended a private school at the cost of 2*d* a week, but Harry himself, by his own reckoning, 'wasn't worth the expense', and went instead to the local Church of England primary school from the age of five. Some two hundred pupils were divided into four classes and received a basic education as well as lessons in handicrafts for the boys and housekeeping for the girls. Although in history classes Harry learned about some of the wars and battles in which his future regiment had been involved, stories of British heroism did not inspire him to want to join the army: 'I was content with my life.' He was more interested in local history and archaeology than in distant battlefields, in the lives of ordinary people such as himself, traces of which from earlier ages could be found not only in nearby Bath but in his immediate surroundings. He enjoyed exploring Combe Down's abandoned open-cast quarries and underground mines, which had supposedly supplied stone for the Romans and still bore the tool-marks of more recent workings. Combe Down had not only provided building materials for Georgian Bath and Bristol: in the nineteenth century blocks of limestone were hewn out of underground workings and shipped to London on the Kennet and Avon Canal in order to provide facings for such famous buildings as Buckingham Palace, Apsley House and All Souls, Langham Place.

Harry's childhood was typical of its period, blessed with a freedom that now seems unimaginable. Unsupervised, Harry and his friends roamed the countryside, exploring mines in which people had been killed by tunnel collapses, messing about on the recently closed Somerset Canal, taking out boats on the river and deliberately steering them over weirs. In winter they skated on the Kennet and Avon Canal or tobogganed down a steep run that ended on a railway line, which meant keeping a wary eye on the signals. Moorhen nests were raided for their eggs and local birds, dogs and cats became the targets of boys bearing catapults. For their elders, social life was built around the church and the many pubs that were a legacy of the area's mining industry, and poaching in order to supplement the family diet was widespread. The outside world barely impinged upon this rural community: the only newspaper Harry's father read was the *Bath and Wells Chronicle*, and such national phenomena or tragedies as the Women's Suffrage Movement or the sinking of the *Titanic* had little impact.

Harry knew that he was destined to leave school at fourteen, and when a new headmaster introduced evening classes, open to everyone, he joined these, reckoning that geometry and algebra might come in useful when he sought work. Towards the end of 1912, he began a five-year apprenticeship with Jacob Long & Sons, one of the area's leading builders, in order to learn the plumbing trade. The outbreak of war two years later had little immediate effect on Harry, even though his brother William had joined the regular army the previous year – much to the dismay of their mother, who held the popular view of the time that only 'scruffs and villains' took the king's shilling – and was immediately posted to France. As more and more men enlisted, however, Harry's employers lost staff. This meant that apprentices such as himself were soon taking on jobs normally given to fully qualified men. Harry took advantage of this to further his career and enrolled in evening classes in order to prepare for the London Guild of Registered Plumbers exam, which he sat and passed at the end of 1915.

In January 1916 the government passed the Military Service Act, which meant that all men between the ages of eighteen and forty-one who had not volunteered would be called up to serve in the already severely depleted British army unless they were medically unfit or were in reserved occupations. The Act came into force in March, and Harry Patch turned eighteen in June. His eldest brother, George, suffered from asthma and was ineligible for military service, but for Harry 'there was no getting out of it'. His lack of enthusiasm had been reinforced when his other brother, William, had returned to Combe Down a few months later after being wounded in the legs at Ypres, bringing with him tales of the mud and filth in the trenches, the prevalence of lice, and the dangers of shrapnel to which his injuries bore tangible witness. Harry's papers arrived in October and, with five other men from the village, he collected his uniform from a local barracks and took the train for Exmouth to attend a basic training course.

The commandeered house in which he was billeted was spartan and the drill and physical training he underwent during the unusually cold winter arduous. For reasons he never discovered he was awarded a lance corporal's stripe, but this was taken away from him after he got into a fight when a fellow soldier stole his boots. Further training, including gas and bayonet drill, took place when he was posted to Sutton Veny in Wiltshire at the beginning of 1917. The men slept in huts and learned to handle rifles, taking part in target practice on Salisbury Plain. Patch proved a good shot and won the crossed-rifles badge of a marksman, which meant he could go to war as a sniper or as part of a Lewis-gun team. Disliking the notion of lining up individuals in his sights and shooting them in cold blood, Patch opted for the Lewis gun, a portable lightweight machine gun then widely in use on the Western Front. The Lewis gun had been designed by an American army colonel of that name in 1911 and was distinguished from other machine guns of the period, in which bullets were fed into the weapon from an ammunition belt, by a revolving drum magazine containing forty-seven bullets which was mounted on top of the gun. 'Lightweight' in this context meant a weapon officially weighing 28 pounds. Even so, the effort of carrying it into position through the mud of the front line was considerable, and resulted in Patch mistakenly recalling that the gun weighed 38 pounds – which may have been what it felt like. The US army failed to adopt the new weapon, so Lewis moved to Europe to find a new market. He set up a company in Belgium, then worked in Britain with the Birmingham Small Arms Company (BSA), which manufactured firearms, shells and military vehicles for the British army and bought a licence to make the Lewis gun in 1914. The weapon came into general use at the front in October 1915, and its effectiveness may be judged by freely circulated stories that any prisoners taken by the Germans found to be wearing the Lewis-gun badge on their sleeves were more likely to be shot than ordinary infantrymen. A well-practised Lewis-gun team could fire up to 500 rounds per minute.

Patch embarked for France at Folkestone in Kent in June

1917, a week before his nineteenth birthday. The naive enthusiasm of 1914 had long since evaporated, most particularly in the wake of the dreadful events on the Somme in July 1916. 'We all knew what we were going to,' Patch recalled; 'there were no illusions any more, no excited chatter or joviality.' It was not until they reached Boulogne and settled into camp that they learned which regiments they had been assigned to. Volunteers early in the war may have been able to choose which regiment they joined, but conscripts in 1917 went where they were most needed, to regiments that had suffered most casualties or were experiencing other manpower shortages. Boys who had grown up together, and as young men endured the long months of training at the same camp, were now parted. While Patch's close Combe Down friend Charlie Wherrett was drafted to the Somerset Light Infantry and sent to Egypt, Patch himself was sent to the 7th Battalion of the Duke of Cornwall's Light Infantry. He was immediately made part of a Lewis-gun team, taking the place of a man who had been sent home on compassionate leave. As No. 2 on the team of five, it was his job to carry spare parts, including a spare barrel, so that if the gun jammed or was damaged it could more or less be rebuilt on-site. Since the spare parts weighed almost as much as the gun itself, it would be difficult for the No. 2 also to carry a standard-issue rifle, and so Patch was given a Webley service pistol of the sort officers usually carried in exchange for his Lee Enfield. No. 1 carried the gun itself, while Nos 3, 4 and 5 carried between them 200 rounds of ammunition. The team spent a couple of days behind the lines doing target practice and getting used to taking apart and putting together the gun, then moved to the front, passing one of the most famous sites of the war, the ruined Cloth Hall at Ypres. A testament to the town's medieval wealth and splendour resulting from the Flemish cloth trade, this huge thirteenth-century building had been virtually razed by German shelling. Frequently depicted on postcards of the era, it had so much become a symbol of the devastation caused by the war that Churchill suggested it should not be restored but remain in its shattered state as a memorial to the sacrifices made between 1914 and 1918.

The individual ranker in the First World War – such as the military Everyman officially listed as 29295 Pte. H.J. Patch, C Company, 7th DCLI – took his place within the fighting force at the bottom of a large and complex chain of command. An army, commanded by a general, would consist of some 200,000 men, and each army was divided into ever smaller but still huge units: corps of around 50,000 men commanded by a lieutenant-general; divisions of about 12,000 under a major-general; brigades of 4,000 commanded by a brigadier; and regiments of 2,000 under the command of a colonel. It was only at the regimental level that where one belonged in the force became meaningful, since each regiment had a name and a history, rather than being an apparently amorphous unit designated merely by a number. The strength of a force obviously fluctuated depending on casualties and recruitment, particularly in a war in which massive losses could be suffered on a single day. In principle, however, individual regiments consisted of two battalions of around a thousand men each commanded by a major. It was the next unit that began to have real significance for the ranker: a battalion's four companies, each consisting of 250 men led by a captain, who would probably know at least by name every man under his command.

Companies were further subdivided into platoons, fighting units of around sixty men, commanded by a junior and often very young officer, the second lieutenant or 'subaltern'. As a training manual published in 1917 put it: 'The Platoon Commander should be the proudest man in the Army. He is the Commander of *the* unit in the attack. He is the only Commander who can intimately know the character and capabilities of each man under him.' Within each platoon were sections of fourteen men under a lance corporal, the rank Patch attained before his fight back in England; but gun teams were special. At this period companies tended to be allotted four Lewis guns each. Although members of a company, gun crews such as Patch's were excused the boring everyday duties to which most rankers were subjected and were expected instead to spend their time keeping their weapons in good working order. Furthermore, although overseen by NCOs, they operated as an individual unit under the command of the team's own No. 1, in Patch's case a man called Bob Haynes. Patch always knew, and later could only remember, the three other members of the team by their nicknames. No. 3 was known as Maudy ('There was an actress of that name. He had a good sense of humour,' Patch recalled), while Nos 4 and 5 were known as Jack and Jill. Female nicknames were not uncommon, and in no way significant, in the trenches. Gun teams had to rely upon each other even more than members of the same platoon or section would, jointly committed to keeping their precious weapon clean and oiled and fully functional. Doing so in the front line was not easy, since around Ypres in 1917 even the summer months were characterised by a great deal of rain, from which the guns had to be protected as a main priority, often with the rain capes officially meant for their operators. Indeed, the rain started on 30 July and continued throughout August, which was unseasonably cold. This rainfall, the heaviest for thirty summers, increased the already quagmire-like nature of the area in which the soldiers were operating, an area that reminded Patch of the Somerset Levels, the partly submerged and flood-prone region in the centre of his home county. More water meant more mud, the chief enemy of machine guns, which, unless kept scrupulously clean, could easily jam and so perhaps be put out of action at a crucial moment in an attack.

The fact that a gun team was a small individual unit, set slightly apart from their infantrymen comrades in the same company, meant that the bonds between its members became particularly strong. Even more than a platoon, they relied upon each other for their own collective safety, and could not really function except as a group of five. 'We were just that little body alone, and we shared everything,' Patch recalled. As did infantrymen, the gun crew distributed among themselves the contents of any parcels received from home: tobacco, cigarettes, chocolate, cakes – even new socks. But it was more than that.

> You could talk to them about everything and anything. I mean, those boys were with you night and day, you shared everything with them and you talked about everything. We each knew where the others came from, and what their lives had been, even where they were educated. You were one of them; we belonged to each other, if you understand. It is a difficult thing to describe, the friendship between us. I never met any of their people or any of their parents but I knew all about them and they knew all about

me. There was nothing that cropped up – doesn't matter what it was – that you couldn't discuss with them in one way or another. If you had anything pinched, you could talk to them, and if you scrounged something, you shared it with them. You could confide everything in them. When they got letters from home, any trouble, they would discuss it with you.

This camaraderie, a common feature of the war, helped men endure conditions at the front, which were often extremely primitive. During the four months, from June to September, that he spent there, Patch never had a bath or a change of clothes, and body-lice were a constant irritant. 'Each louse – he had his own particular bite,' he recalled, 'and he'd drive you mad. We used to turn our vests inside out to get a little relief, and tomorrow you'd be just as lousy as you were today.' Attempts to get rid of these pests by the use of such patent remedies at Keating's Powder or Harrison's Pomade, or by such crude expedients as running a candle-flame along the seams of filthy uniforms, had only limited success. When Patch was finally given a communal bath in water containing some sort of insecticide, he reckoned that the dead lice could have been 'shovelled' out. All water had to be carried up the line, mostly in old petrol cans which tainted it, and latrines were often little more than a plank placed across a shallow trench. Rats were everywhere, grown fat on corpses, gnawing their way through equipment, devouring rations, and running across the faces of sleeping soldiers. 'It doesn't matter how much training you've had,' Patch recalled, 'you can't prepare for the reality, the noise, the filth, the uncertainty and the calls for stretcher-bearers.' Conditions were also very frightening, with Germans shelling the trenches and aircraft circling overhead – hence the calls for stretcher-bearers, or sometimes just for shovels in order to scoop into empty sandbags the remains of what had a few moments before been one of your fellow soldiers, perhaps even a close friend. 'Anyone who tells you that in the trenches they weren't scared, he's a damned liar,' Patch said towards the end of his life; 'you were scared all the time.'

It was always said that the trenches of the Western Front stretched 'from Switzerland to the Sea', and indeed the front line ran for some 457 miles north-west from the French–Swiss border through France and Belgium right up to the North Sea coast near the border with Holland. Front-line trenches in fact consisted of three roughly parallel lines. The first of these was the fire trench, from which men went over the top or kept watch on the enemy in the trenches opposite. Behind this was the support trench, which contained the company headquarters, a first-aid post overseen by a medical officer, kitchens and stores, and dugouts for officers. This was where troops alternating with those in the fire trench waited until called forward. Farther back still was the reserve trench for further reinforcements. These three lines were connected to each other by zigzagging communication trenches, and all were vulnerable to shellfire. Because of the waterlogged terrain, trenches in the sector where Patch served were comparatively shallow, and it had been necessary to build substantial breastworks for the protection of the troops in addition to the usual parapet of sandbags (usually filled with earth rather than sand) at ground level in front of the trench and the matching parados at the rear. The bottom of the trench was covered with wooden duckboards, intended to keep the soldiers' feet out of the mud and the water that accumulated there. These were not always effective: Patch recalled 'watching the water flow beneath the duckboards' and having to use (and so waste) boxes of ammunition to stand on in places where the mud had become too deep.

Fire trenches were not built in one straight line but consisted of alternating firebays and traverses. The firebays, where men regularly 'stood to', peering out across rolls of defensive barbed wire into no man's land from raised platforms known as firesteps, projected forward; traverses, where men 'stood down' after being on duty and, if lucky, ate or napped in 'funk-holes' scooped out of the sides of the trench, projected backwards. One obvious advantage of this crenellated arrangement was that it prevented any enemy troops who managed to overrun a trench from being able to enfilade, or fire along it for any distance. Another was that it contained bomb blasts or the effects of grenades lobbed into a single bay of the trench. Even so, being in any part of the front line tested even the strongest man's nerves. 'The shelling was ferocious at times,' Patch remembered; 'you'd feel the vibration of the ground, you couldn't help but tremble, mild shellshock.' Shells were what men feared most. They might talk about a bullet having someone's name on it, and the dangers from enemy snipers when standing to were very real; but shells were horribly random and could land anywhere in the front line. If you suffered a direct hit you might quite literally be blown to pieces, but in some ways immediate extinction seemed preferable to the terrible injuries caused by shrapnel, which could damage or remove limbs, destroy faces, emasculate and eviscerate. Many such wounds proved fatal, and death could be painfully protracted. Those who survived were often left with permanent injuries that might get them out of the war but would leave them permanently disfigured or disabled. 'You couldn't deal with the fear and apprehension we had about being hit by shrapnel,' Patch recalled. 'It was there and it always would be. I know the first time I went into the line we were scared; we were all scared. We lived hour by hour, we never knew the future. You saw the sun rise, hopefully you'd see it set. If you saw it set, you hoped you'd see it rise. Some men would, some wouldn't.'

As was customary, Patch's battalion served three days in the front line, then made its way back along the narrow communication trenches as the relieving battalion came in. These regularly congested trenches proved tempting targets for the Germans, and changeovers could be quite as dangerous as being in the front line, as Patch would later discover to his cost. The battalion was being removed only as far as the support trench, where the men waited in case they were needed to bolster the front line if it came under attack. After four days in support, they came out of the line and caught up on some much-needed sleep in tented billets, where the daily allowance of water drawn from a well was one bucket per seven men. With this they had to fill the drinking-water bottles they carried with them, shave and wash their faces. Being out of the line did not mean men could enjoy day-long relaxation, since there were numerous jobs that needed doing, from repairing tracks to carrying food or duckboards up the line.

There was, however, one place in this sector where men could take their rest uninterrupted. Talbot House, universally known as 'Toc H' (signallers' code for its initials), was a clubhouse in rue de l'Hôpital in Poperinghe, a small town close to the front line. Damaged by shellfire during the summer of 1915, the house had been leased to the British army by its Belgian owner, and in December that year, at the instigation of a British army chaplain called Philip 'Tubby' Clayton, had been refurbished and opened as somewhere for all serving men to relax. It was named in memory of Lieutenant Gilbert Talbot, the son of the Bishop of Winchester, who had been killed in action in July of that year. In spite of the involvement of the Church, the refuge Toc H provided was not specifically religious – though an upper room built for the drying of hops was converted into a chapel for those who wanted to visit one or take what in all too many cases turned out to be a last communion. A motto above the house's front door, adapted from the one over the entrance to hell in Dante's 'Inferno', stated the main principle of its foundation: 'All rank abandon, ye who enter here'. Conceived as a wholesome alternative to the bars, cafés and brothels of Poperinghe, it was comfortably furnished and boasted a library from which books could be borrowed, a piano for sing-songs, and various kinds of board games. Patch remembers getting a cup of tea and food there too. He also recalled receiving Holy Communion from Clayton himself, along with the four other members of the gun team.

The men of the Duke of Cornwall's Light Infantry returned to the front line in July 1917 to take part in the Third Battle of Ypres. Popularly known as Passchendaele, which subsequently became a byword for pointless slaughter, it was the last major battle of attrition to take place on the Western Front. The initial attack opened at 3.50 a.m. on 31 July and, in heavy rainfall and atrocious conditions, the offensive continued sporadically until 6 November, when the village of Passchendaele was finally captured. It was not General Haig's finest hour, as we have seen, and the numerous assaults, often carried out against all advice on the ground, eventually resulted in British casualties of some 310,000 men. In preparation for the first attack, British guns launched a massive bombardment on 22 July, during which around 4,250,000 shells were fired at the German front line. Although some gains were made along the 11-mile front as British troops advanced in the early hours of 31 July in what became known as the Battle of Pilckem Ridge, attempts to follow up these small successes were hampered not only by the incessant rain but by the damage the bombardment had done to the drainage systems, which meant that the terrain was more water-logged than ever. Tanks were rendered more or less useless and troops quickly became bogged down in the Flanders mud. The Allies gained at best some 2,000 yards of ground at the cost of some 32,000 men killed, wounded or missing.

General Gough, whose Fifth Army formed the bulk of the attacking forces, informed Haig that it was impossible in such conditions to renew the attack and that any attempt to do so would be both very costly and tactically worthless; but his opinion was disregarded. So, on 16 August, a second offensive was launched, an offensive in which Harry Patch first went into battle. This action was subsequently named the Battle of Langemarck after the village that was its chief objective. Moving up to the front line in preparation for this attack took a long time: starting the night before, C Company began arriving in position at 4.15 a.m. The company was to take part in the second wave of the attack, shortly after the first troops went into battle at 4.45, and assembled in front of the Steenbeek, a flooded stream lined with smashed and denuded trees. Using unstable pontoon bridges, they crossed the water in single file and reassembled on the other side, ready for the signal to advance. There was no top to go over: the troops were going into the attack from open ground cratered with shell holes, their starting place surreally marked by white tape laid in the mud. Any notion of advancing in a calm and orderly line, as British troops had done so disastrously on the Somme on 1 July 1916, had to be abandoned, and once the whistle had blown men were obliged to make their way as best they could over the shell-ruptured terrain. A creeping barrage, in which guns put down a heavy curtain of shellfire ahead of the advancing troops, supposedly destroying everything before them, was in progress when Patch, hung about with spare parts for his Lewis gun, set off towards the German-held objective, a line drawn on a map marking a boundary some 1,500 yards from their starting point.

It was during his unsteady progress through this hellish landscape, obscured by smoke, briefly illuminated by shellfire, littered with the wounded and dying of both sides, that Patch came across a young soldier from A Company, which had led the attack. Of all the terrible sights that he encountered, it was this which would remain with him throughout his extraordinarily long life. The soldier, Patch recalled, 'was ripped open from his shoulder to his waist by shrapnel, and lying in a pool of blood'. Seeing men from his own battalion, he begged them to put him out of his misery. In Patch's terse but eloquent phrase, 'he was beyond all human help', and in fact died before anyone could draw a revolver and comply with his desperate request. 'It is an image that has haunted me all my life,' Patch wrote some ninety years later, 'seared into my mind.' Troops were not in fact supposed to give succour to, or even stop for, the wounded during an attack. Their only objective was to advance. Those hit by bullets or shrapnel, however horribly injured, were the responsibility of medical orderlies, who would do what they could *in situ*, then arrange for those with a chance of surviving their injuries to be carried back behind the lines to dressing stations or field hospitals. Evacuation of the wounded was particularly difficult at Passchendaele because of the condition of the ground: a well-known photograph shows a stretcher party of seven men sunk literally up to their knees in mud as they struggle with their alarmingly tilting burden.

The job of a Lewis-gun team was to cover the advancing infantry, putting out of action any enemy troops who had not been obliterated by the creeping barrage or killed by troops in what was sometimes hand-to-hand combat. Patch's task when the gun was in use was to change the magazine while the No. 1 adopted the firing position, usually lying on the ground. At one point during this chaotic advance a German emerged from a trench and, with his bayonet fixed, ran towards Patch, who disarmed him by drawing his service revolver and shooting him in the shoulder. Still the German came on. The gun team had made an unusually humane and highly irregular pact that they would not shoot to kill unless absolutely necessary, and Patch remembered this code as he took further aim at the advancing German. 'I couldn't kill him,' Patch recalled in old age. 'He was a man I never knew, I couldn't talk to him. I shot him above the ankle, above the knee. He went down. He said something to me in German – God knows what it was – but for him the war was over.'

When C Company reached the German trenches at around midday, they found them empty and immediately set about converting them into a new British front line. Since these trenches were a mirror image of the British ones, this meant transforming traverses into firebays and vice versa, an arduous job which was carried out under the ever-present threat of a counter-attack, which in the event never came, and to the accompaniment of the cries and groans of the wounded from both sides, who were still lying on the battlefield. The battalion was relieved at 1 a.m. on 18 August and made the long march back to camp. 'The period out of the line, after the fighting, is something of a blank to me now,' Patch confessed in his autobiography. 'I've been shown pages of the [official] War Diary, but for the most part it's hard to relate to the record.' Similarly, battle plans may have looked neat and tidy on paper, but they meant little to men stumbling under cover of dark, behind a deafening creeping barrage, with the constant threat of enemy fire and with fellow soldiers falling to left and right, over a terrain rather more complicatedly three-dimensional and battered than anything shown on a map. 'How were we to know that a pile of rubble was this village or that, or that a gentle slope was a particular ridge, let alone what was going on across the front?' Patch asked ninety years later. 'You only knew what was right next to you, and even this was often obscured by smoke or fire. Strategy we left to those higher up.' He also said that in spite of what everyone imagines, those higher up were not often discussed in the trenches. Of Haig, he wrote: 'I know people think we must have spoken about him, but I can't remember ever doing so. We were there to do a job, and we did it. We weren't there to criticize; we knew when they'd gone wrong.'

The attack on 16 August had in fact gone reasonably well as far as Patch's regiment was concerned, with the objective achieved and comparatively few casualties: forty-three men killed and 140 wounded for 1,500 yards gained. By the harsh standards of Passchendaele, this was more or less a success; but elsewhere the attack had once again been a costly failure. As Liddell Hart put it, to the right of the DCLI, 'where alone an advance might have a strategic effect, a heavy price was paid for nought'. Haig nevertheless decided to launch yet another offensive, though this was again delayed by bad weather, which had closed in once more following a brief respite immediately after the 16 August attack. The date chosen for the new offensive was 20 September.

Patch's battalion had been ordered to be ready to move to the front line, but were not immediately required. On the night of 22 September, Patch and his gun team were making their way back into reserve in single file across open ground because there were no communication trenches at this point. Although the regiment had suffered casualties the previous day as a result of being bombed by enemy aircraft, the night seemed relatively quiet. The crew were waiting briefly in a huddle while the No. 1 was 'attending to the call of nature', when there was a flash of light and Patch was thrown to the ground. He lay there, 'conscious but incapable of anything', for a couple of minutes before he realised he had been hit in the groin by shrapnel. He applied the field dressing that all soldiers carried with them and, with very little notion of how much time was passing, waited for stretcher-bearers. Taken by ambulance to a casualty clearing station, he had his wound cleaned and dressed by a doctor, but the fragment of shell remained in place. The shock and the anaesthetising effect of hot metal searing flesh were wearing off, and he began to feel acute pain.

Since Patch's injury was less serious than those suffered by many of the men at the clearing station, he was obliged to wait until the following evening before seeing another doctor. He was told that the shrapnel could be removed but was warned that no anaesthetic was available. Since the wound was hurting a great deal, Patch decided to endure two minutes of further pain as four men held him down while the fragment was cut out of him and the wound stitched. He had clearly made the right decision because this procedure brought swift relief. He declined to accept the 2-inch-long piece of jagged metal as a souvenir and was relieved to learn that his wound had been classed as 'a Blighty one', meaning he would be invalided back to Britain. A couple of hours later he was taken by train to the base camp at Rouen, where he was at last given a bath – in fact, two baths: one containing insecticide, the other clean water – and exchanged his torn, bloodied, muddy and lice-ridden uniform for a sterilised one in what was known as 'hospital blue'. These blue serge uniforms were reserved for serving men who had been injured, partly to remind them that they were still in the army even if on sick leave, but also so that when they were recuperating back in Britain they weren't mistaken by the patriotic for 'shirkers', as they might have been in civilian dress unless their wounds were visible or otherwise obvious.

That evening Patch was stretchered aboard a hospital ship, which set sail the following night, delivering its cargo of wounded to Southampton the next morning. In spite of being asked which was the nearest military hospital to his home, Patch ended up in

Liverpool, where his wound was disinfected and dressed daily and where he recovered from other, minor, injuries caused by his being flung to the ground: a sprained foot and some torn chest ligaments. Although he did not yet know it, his time in the trenches was over. He was still only nineteen.

It was while he was in hospital that Patch received a letter from his No. 1, Bob Haynes, to tell him that the three other members of the gun crew had been killed outright by the shell that had injured him when it burst above their heads: 'there was nothing left, nothing left to bury'. 'My reaction was terrible,' Patch recalled; 'it was like losing part of my life.' His physical wounds would eventually heal, but as for many of those who lost comrades in the war, the death of these three men was something from which he never really recovered. The date on which they died became his own private day of remembrance, far more important to him than 11 November.

Patch's recovery was aided by a new friendship with an entertaining fellow patient from Australia who had suffered shrapnel wounds in his legs. The two young men joked with the nurses, played practical jokes and, when sufficiently recovered, were allowed out of the hospital, sometimes to visit the local cinema, where their hospital blue entitled them to free tickets. Like many friendships forged in the war, this one proved temporary: they were sent to different convalescent camps and although they exchanged addresses and even corresponded for a while they never saw each other again. 'I never once considered going to Australia,' Patch confessed. 'My home was Somerset.' He was still, however, a long way from returning to Combe Down, apart from a brief visit just before Christmas. Instead he was posted to No. 2

Convalescent Camp at Sutton Coldfield near Birmingham. The intention was that he would eventually be passed fit and returned to the front, and there was little for him to do except wait. Rather than sitting around whiling away the time with games of cards, as other convalescents did, Patch decided to take a correspondence course in order to qualify as a sanitary engineer. He also met his future wife, Ada Billington, in the town, though he did not propose until the following December. Given the uncertainties of the time, uncertainties that made some couples snatch at happiness only to have it cruelly taken away when newly married wives were almost instantly widowed, this was no doubt sensible. Patch later discovered that in 1914 Ada had been briefly engaged to a soldier who had soon afterwards been killed in action. In spite of Patch's pleading, Ada insisted she would not marry anyone until the war ended. The couple did, however, see a lot of each other while Patch remained in Sutton Coldfield, where he was introduced to Ada's family.

In August 1918, Patch was deemed fit enough to be sent to Tidworth in Wiltshire, in order to resume training. He knew exactly what this meant, and dreaded being sent back to the front, but it turned out that he wasn't after all fully recovered. The ligaments in his chest had not healed properly, as he discovered when he first put on his heavy equipment. He was excused duty for a week, but when he went on parade again a fortnight later, the same trouble flared up. He was sent back to hospital, conveniently in Handsworth and so within easy reach of Ada. The treatment for his damaged ligament was electronic massage, which went on for several weeks, after which he was told to report for duty on the Isle of Wight. Patch believed that the chest injury may well have saved his life. Instead of being sent back to the Western Front in the summer of 1918, he was still on the Isle of Wight when the Armistice was declared on 11 November. Patch's war had ended.

Like many of those who survived the war, Harry Patch simply returned to his former life when the hostilities ceased and his long-delayed demob was granted; but what he had been through had altered his life altogether. The First World War was like an earthquake, its aftershocks going on for many years afterwards. For a long time he continued to have bad dreams about the night he was wounded and lost his friends. 'The war might have been over, but its effects were never far away,' he recalled. He returned to Combe Down 'thoroughly disillusioned': 'I could never understand why my country could call me from my peacetime job and train me to go to France and try to kill a man I never knew. Why did we fight? I asked myself that, many times. At the end of the war, the peace was settled round a table, so why the hell couldn't they do that at the start, without losing millions of men?' The dreadfully wounded soldier who had begged Patch to finish him off had cried out 'Mother!' as he died, and Patch had been convinced that this was a cry not of despair but of greeting. 'I'm positive that when he left this world, wherever he went, his mother was there,' Patch wrote towards the end of his life, 'and from that day I've always remembered that cry and that death is not the end.' Even so, he left the army with his 'faith in the Church of England shattered'. In an unsuccessful attempt to revive it he joined the church choir: 'in the end I went because I enjoyed the music and had friends there, but the belief? It didn't come. Armistice Day parade – no. Cassock and surplice – no. I felt shattered, absolutely, and I didn't discuss the war with anyone from then on, and nobody brought it up if they could help it.' This attitude persisted well beyond the immediate aftermath of the war: he refused to join veterans' associations, had no wish to revisit the battlefields, never attended a regimental reunion and avoided all war films and 'anything to do with war on television'. He did not even join the British Legion until bribed with a bottle of whisky to do so in the very last year of his life. Nor did he ever again meet the other surviving member of his gun team, although the two men 'kept in touch' until Bob Haynes died in the 1970s. At the first general election in which he was eligible to vote, Patch put his cross against the name of the Liberal candidate, a Quaker who had campaigned against conscription.

His disillusionment in the immediate aftermath of the war was not much helped by the fact that, like many returning servicemen, he was in dispute with his former employers, and was obliged to take on temporary jobs. Many returning servicemen were so desperate for work that they would travel miles or simply move to where the jobs were. At first, Patch was determined to remain in Combe Down, where his father had promised him a house on his forthcoming marriage, and he considered joining the Somerset County Police. Although taller than the average working-class British recruit (who, stunted by poor diet and an unhealthy urban environment, was 5 inches shorter than his middle-class equivalent), at 5 feet 8 inches, Patch was 1 inch shorter than the height then required for the police force and was rejected. He dug trenches for the privately owned Combe Down Water Company when the village was put on the mains, but eventually decided to move to. Gobowen, a small town in Shropshire close to the Welsh border, where he'd been offered a nine-month plumbing job on a new housing scheme. Apart from the pay, which was better than anything on offer around Bath, he was now within easy reach of his fiancée, who was living with her brother in a village called Hadley near Wellington. It was here, on 13 September 1919, that Harry Patch and Ada Billington were quietly married, and they spent their honeymoon walking in the hills around Church Stretton. Their first son, Dennis, was born in Shropshire the following June, just after Patch's job came to an end. The new family moved in with Ada's brother, and Patch joined a building firm in Ludlow. The company dealt mostly with private clients, some of them living in huge country houses, with hordes of staff. The amount of respect such people still commanded in the early 1920s was made clear to Patch when he was doing a job for Lady Mary Cambridge at Shatton Hall. Having missed his train from Whitchurch back to Shrewsbury, he was surprised when the stationmaster, hearing that he had been working for her ladyship, said he would make the next express train stop so that Patch could travel in the guard's van.

In 1921 Patch returned with his wife and baby son to Combe Down and settled into 5 Gladstone Place, one of the houses built by his father a decade earlier. His brother William was next door at No. 4, and his parents and brother George were also living in the village, where large crowds turned out on a beautiful late summer's day for the unveiling of the village war memorial. A service was held at Holy Trinity Church, after which Patch and his fellow choir members walked in their robes to Firs Field, where the new memorial in the shape of a cross was concealed beneath a Union flag. The congregation sang 'O Valiant Hearts', after which the memorial was unveiled by 'some big noise in uniform, covered in medal ribbons, or scrambled egg', as Patch dismissively put it.

Patch found full-time employment with the building firm Sculls of Bristol, which at that time was working on the Wills Memorial Tower in the city. This soaring 215-foot Gothic revival structure formed part of Bristol University's Wills Memorial Building, named for its first chancellor, a founder of the famous local W.D. & H.O. Wills tobacco company, whose products had been so highly valued at the front. The building of the tower, which was made of reinforced concrete but faced with local Bath stone, had been interrupted by the war and restarted only in 1919. It would provide Patch with four years' guaranteed work, something of a luxury for former servicemen in 1921, when they accounted for a large percentage of the one million unemployed. In an age before mechanical cranes, working on tall structures was a precarious business. Apart from the fact that the core of the tower was concrete, building methods and materials had changed little since the fourteenth century. The tower was surrounded by free-standing wooden scaffolding and everything apart from bricks, including such heavy materials as rolls of lead and bags of tools, had to be carried up ladders by hand. It was with lead that Patch worked, supplying flashing and pipes and acquiring a new skill of lead burning to make watertight seals. The tower was officially opened by George V in June 1925, but Patch was no more impressed by his king than he was by the 'big noise' who unveiled the Combe Down war memorial: 'I don't remember much,' he wrote, 'I can't say I was that interested.'

His employer encouraged him to take another exam and become a Member of the Royal Sanitary Institute: when he failed the exam, his employer offered to pay his expenses for another attempt, telling him that he could reimburse him from his wages if he passed, which he did. He was subsequently appointed manager of the Clifton branch of Sculls, going every day on the hour-long journey from Bath to Bristol by early-morning train to open the shop at 8 a.m., returning after closing-time at 5 p.m. This extension of steady employment at an increased wage was all the more welcome because his second son had been born the previous year. When the General Strike took place in May 1926 and the trains stopped running, Patch bicycled the 12 miles to work. After a while, the job changed and he resigned in order to set up his own business, taking advantage of the numerous contacts he had made while working for Sculls. Most of the work he did was local, but in order to carry tools and materials to jobs farther afield, he bought his first car, a second-hand Austin 7. Known affectionately as the Baby Austin, the vehicle had gone into production in 1923 and was the first British car mass-produced for ordinary people. By far the most popular car of the period, it transformed the lives of thousands of families and meant Patch could take his wife and children on day-trips to places such as Weston-super-Mare on the Somerset coast. He had been taught to drive by the son of a local grocer and at this period no driving test was necessary: those taking to the road merely applied to their local council for a licence.

By the 1930s, the amount of work Patch was able to procure meant that he was able to employ three other plumbers, local men he had known for a long time. Most of the work was domestic and so not as badly affected by the Depression as major building projects – though Patch learned how to lay bricks and did other odd jobs when times were thin. By the end of the decade, Patch's two sons had left school, the younger, Roy, following his father into the building trade, the elder, Dennis, training to be an accountant. His brother-in-law had emigrated to Chicago, where he ran an accountancy firm, and when Dennis said that he was going to join his uncle, Patch and Ada considered emigrating too. But all these plans were abandoned in September 1939 when Britain declared war on Germany.

At forty-one, Patch was too old to be called up once more, but conscription brought back unhappy memories of 1914. Patch himself may have been ineligible for service, but his sons were both of military age. Not wishing to be conscripted into the army, Dennis volunteered for the Royal Navy, while Roy joined the Royal Army Service Corps. Both served overseas but returned safely at the war's end. Patch's own Second World War, serving with the Auxiliary Fire Service and as a civilian garrison engineer, has already been described. The latter job meant moving to Compton Dundon, a village just to the south of Glastonbury, where he and Ada would live in a thatched cottage for the next ten years. The cottage came with an extensive garden in which, like his father before him, Patch grew vegetables and kept pigs. There was also an orchard containing rare varieties of cider apples, a Somerset speciality. Patch no more felt like celebrating the end of the Second World War than he had the first: both his nephew and his niece's fiancée had been killed. Rather than starting up his own business again, he took a job as a plumber with a company called E.R. Carter at West Hendford on the outskirts of

Yeovil, and moved to nearby Preston Grove. His holidays were almost always spent in Somerset, often in the caravan he had constructed, although he was also a frequent visitor to Weymouth in neighbouring Dorset, where his lifelong friend from Combe Down, George Atkins, now lived.

In spite of his employer's suggestion that he was fit enough to carry on working, Harry Patch retired at the statutory age of sixty-five in 1963. The sixtieth anniversary of the outbreak of the First World War the following year, and the renewed interest in the war throughout the 1960s, passed him by entirely. He had never spoken to his wife about the war, nor discussed it with any of his work colleagues, and would continue to remain silent about his experiences for the next thirty-five years. Instead he pursued his interest in more distant history, becoming something of an amateur expert on Roman Bath and the geology of Somerset, in particular the mines of Combe Down. He occasionally gave public talks on these subjects, and in his nineties, when concern was expressed about the danger of subsidence in Combe Down after a hole had opened up in Firs Field, he was called upon to lead geologists from Bath University through the tunnels he had explored as a boy seventy years earlier, tunnels that had been sealed off as a safety measure in the late 1920s.

The 1970s and early 1980s brought Patch more than his fair share of difficulties and unhappiness. Ada died after a stroke at the age of eighty-one in 1976, and George Atkins died the following year. Patch moved in with his unmarried elder son Dennis, who was living in Wells, but this proved disastrous. Dennis had been very close to his mother and, deeply affected by her death, began drinking heavily. In order to fund his alcoholism, he sold off many of his father's possessions, including his war medals. After four years of increasingly unhappy cohabitation, Patch met and married a widow called Jean, later admitting: 'To be honest, I married to get out of my son's way.' He was now eighty-two and moved with Jean into sheltered accommodation at Valley Close in Wells. They were so concerned about Dennis's health that they persuaded him to see a doctor. Dennis was admitted to hospital with advanced sclerosis of the liver and died eight days later aged only sixty-one. The complications of Patch's relationship with Dennis led to an estrangement between him and his other son, Roy, which lasted until the latter's death from cancer in 2002. Jean also developed cancer and died after four short years of marriage, spending a considerable time bedridden and nursed by her husband. Patch and his neighbours in Wells, Fred and Betty Isaacs, had become close and mutually dependent friends. Patch looked after Betty when her husband died, and the two of them did some travelling; but when in 1996 Betty became too frail for this and was advised to move into a residential home, Patch decided to go with her. He would remain at Fletcher House for the remainder of his life. After Betty died, Patch became the inseparable companion of another resident, a Londoner called Doris who although in her nineties was still sixteen years his junior.

Harry Patch never had any desire to visit the places where he had fought as a young man, but shortly after his second marriage he had been offered tickets for a tour of the Normandy beaches that had played so significant a role in the Second World War. While he found he could take a detached historical interest in old dugouts and gun emplacements, he found the huge American cemetery above Omaha Beach at Colleville-sur-Mer over-whelming. Containing 9,387 burials, this is the largest American cemetery of that war – though it is far surpassed in size by the Meuse-Argonne Cemetery containing 14,246 burials from the First World War, many of them men killed during the very last days leading up to the Armistice. Patch recognised that he may well have known some of those buried at Colleville, having spent time with them when he was overseeing the plumbing and sani-tation at their military camps in Somerset in 1944. He could not bring himself to wander among the graves as his fellow tourists were doing, but instead stood there and wept. It is evident from the vocabulary he used to describe his thoughts as he looked out across the massed gravestones and imagined those who lay beneath them that he was also reminded of the losses of his own war: 'they didn't die a normal death, they were shot, bayoneted or torn to death by shrapnel'. He regretted coming and swore he would never again venture abroad. The seventieth anniversary of the Battle of Passchendaele was widely marked in 1987, but Patch kept his counsel and took no part in the commemorations. The seventieth anniversary of the Armistice the following year also passed him by.

Patch had done his best to repress his memories of the war, but after he moved to Fletcher House a minor incident brought everything back with startling immediacy. The door to his room was opposite a linen cupboard. One night someone had gone to get some linen and turned on the fluorescent light inside the cupboard. As the tube flickered into life, flashes of light came through the glass panel above the door to Patch's room, where its occupant lay in the dark, half asleep. He was transported in an instant back to Passchendaele. 'It was the flash of a bomb,' Patch recalled. 'That flash brought it all back.' When he celebrated his 100th birthday shortly afterwards, newspapers and television companies got in touch. He had been suffering from bad dreams about the war and decided that the time had come to face his demons, so he agreed to appear on television in *Veterans*, a BBC documentary series commemorating the eightieth anniversary of the Armistice based on the research among veterans carried out by Richard van Emden. In his search for survivors, van Emden had regularly scanned the *Caring Times*, the house magazine of the care-home profession, which always noted when a resident had reached 100. He would then telephone the relevant home to ask whether the centenarian had taken part in the First World War and would be prepared to talk about his experiences. He had already persuaded 120 of them to commit their memories to tape when he first went to meet Patch on 1 July 1998. Patch later claimed that although he took part in van Emden's television documentary, he 'slept through most of it', and had no inkling that he would become a world-famous spokesman for his generation. One poignant aspect of the book that accompanied the series was photographs of the veterans as they look at the end of the twentieth century juxtaposed with ones taken during the war. This was not possible in the case of Patch. Given his view of the war and the fact that he had for so many decades attempted to erase it from his life, it is appropriate that there appeared to be no photographs of Private Harry Patch at the front, or even on his way there. The only photograph of him in uniform in his autobiography was taken at his brother George's wedding in 1918 after he had been back in England for many months recuperating from his wound. Standing at the back, he is barely discernible, a ghostly figure partly obscured by those standing in front of him.

Patch was prepared to be interviewed about the war, but in spite of repeated offers and requests had absolutely no intention of returning to the battlefields, as many of his fellow veterans had done. He relented in November 2002 when he agreed ('I don't know why') to attend a ceremony marking the seventy-fifth anniversary of the unveiling of the Menin Gate at Ypres. He was 104 and was joined by Jack Davies, 107, who had also served with the Duke of Cornwall's Light Infantry, and Arthur Halestrap, 104, who had become a regular visitor to battlefields, cemeteries and other sites in France and Belgium. Although Patch found the whole experience very emotional, he was glad that he had gone, and thereafter returned several times. Even so, he could not for a long time face going to Pilckem Ridge or Langemarck, though he visited the chapel at Toc H, where he and his gun crew had received communion in the summer of 1917. When he finally went to Langemarck to lay a wreath on the memorial to the 20th (Light) Division, to which his regiment had belonged, he found himself unable to leave the coach: 'I looked from the window and the memories flooded back and I wept, and the wreath was laid on my behalf.' Every time he went to the Ypres Salient, he insisted it would be the last. 'I don't feel the need to go,' he would say. 'I know that Arthur Halestrap always felt that it was his duty to go until the end, but I don't know, we shall have to see.'

In the autumn of 2004 he was prevailed upon to travel once more to Belgium for the BBC television documentary *The Last Tommy*. He would play a leading role in the second half of this two-part film, which opened with Patch, by now in a wheelchair, sitting among the massed gravestones at Tyne Cot Cemetery a few miles north-east of Ypres. Tyne Cot is the largest British war cemetery in the world: the stones that stretched away from Patch to the horizon mark 11,945 burials, 8,367 of them containing unidentified bodies, many of them recovered from Passchendaele. In addition the Tyne Cot Memorial to the Missing records the names of a further 34,900 men for whom there was no room on the nearby Menin Gate. 'It's painful,' Patch commented later in the film in his by now slow voice, with its deep Somerset burr. 'I've got three mates buried here somewhere. I don't know where.' Looking across the serried ranks of gravestones, he echoed what many people had thought over the years, but did so with a simple authority only his own experience and long memory could give: 'It's too many. When you look at it – why did they die? Look at them. Why? All of them dead.' He shook his head slowly. 'No.'

This was to be, Patch declared, his final pilgrimage, and it was to have a remarkable conclusion. Recalling how he had spared the life of the German who had run at him in August 1917, Patch admitted that had this incident taken place after his gun crew had been killed 'I'd have had no trouble at all in killing him'. He once again shook his head sorrowfully. He found the whole ordeal of returning to the scenes of such incidents painful: 'I've got some bitter memories, that's the trouble. I can't forget that. Eighty-seven years. That's a long time.' The programme makers not only wanted to persuade Patch to return to Pilckem Ridge, they wanted him to meet one of Germany's last surviving veterans on 22 September, the anniversary of the loss of his gun team. A year older than Patch, Charles Kuentz had also been at Passchendaele

– on the other side. He had been conscripted into the Imperial German Army in 1916 at the age of nineteen, and was as reluctant to go to war as Patch had been. His father was French and he had himself been born in Alsace-Lorraine, a disputed border territory that had been under German rule only since 1871, when France lost the Franco-Prussian War. Kuentz had always considered himself French and spoke French as his first language and so had no particular desire to 'defend the Fatherland'. He had fought the Russians in freezing conditions on the Eastern Front before being transferred to the Western Front in 1917, where he saw action at Arras and on the Somme as well as at Passchendaele. He too had suffered the loss of a close friend, killed horribly by shrapnel beside him in a trench. He had also lost a son in the Second World War: drafted into the Waffen-SS after the invasion of France, he had been killed on the beaches of Normandy in 1944. Like Patch, Kuentz had never talked about his experiences in the war until he reached the age of 100, when people began to seek him out and ask him for his reminiscences.

It was arranged for the two men to meet at Langemarck German Military Cemetery. The Germans had consolidated their First World War cemeteries in the 1930s when bodies were exhumed from smaller plots and reburied: some 10,000 bodies from eighteen different burial sites were brought to Langemarck to join the 4,000 or so already there. Further reorganisation took place after the Second World War when Langemarck became one of three 'collecting cemeteries' for the German dead of the First World War. Bodies were exhumed from other Belgian sites – Zonnebeke, Poelkapelle, Passchendaele, Moorslede, Westroosbeke and Zillebeke – and reburied at Langemarck, bringing the total identified dead to 19,378. In addition, unidentified remains were removed from all over the Western Front and buried in the *Kameraden Grab*, a mass 'Comrades' Grave', bringing the total· number of burials to a staggering 44,234. Because of its complicated history of reburials, and because the Belgian authorities were less inclined to make land available for the dead of those who had invaded their country than for their allies, Langemarck does not mark each individual burial with a headstone as is the custom in British war cemeteries. Instead, burial plots containing up to eight bodies are marked by flat stones listing names where known, among which stand sombre groups of squat black basalt crosses. It was in this setting that two centenarians, who more than an average lifetime ago had faced each other as enemies, came together in an act of reconciliation. As at the famous 'Christmas Truce' of 1914, when in defiance of the authorities British and German troops had emerged briefly from their trenches to fraternise, the two men exchanged gifts representative of their own localities: Kuentz brought a tin of Alsatian biscuits, Patch a bottle of Somerset cider. Neither man spoke the other's language, but they shook hands and both expressed their thoughts through an interpreter. Asked whether he would hold it against Kuentz if it was discovered that it had been he who had fired the shell that killed the three members of the Lewis-gun team, Patch replied: 'No. Not today.' He repeated what had by now become one of his most often-voiced messages to later generations: 'The most important thing is don't go to war. Settle it over the table. That's how the first two wars were settled – by negotiation over a table. Why should they do it after so many lives have been lost?' '*Exactement*,' commented Kuentz's wife, who had accompanied him. '*Aujourd-hui nous sommes tous les amis*,' Kuentz himself added. Together he and Patch laid a wreath of poppies on a German grave. Patch leaned out of his wheel chair to pick up an acorn from the ground, which he presented to Kuentz, who shortly afterwards remarked in an interview: 'It means an awful lot to me. These small gestures are the things that encourage friendship between peoples, so that we will never again fight wars against each other. We shot at each other from this place, but now we are friends. What a miracle. I never believed that I would experience this at the age of 107.' Patch himself commented characteristically: 'Charles was conscripted just like myself and fought for the Kaiser as I had fought for the King, relations of course, cousins, so it was a family affair. It shows you how stupid war is.' The two men had lunch and in the evening sat side by side to witness the act of remembrance that takes place at 8 p.m. every day of the year at the Menin Gate, when the busy road running beneath Sir Reginald Blomfield's huge memorial is closed to traffic by the police and the Last Post is played by members of the town's fire brigade. The last surviving German veteran of the First World War, Charles Kuentz died a few months later on 7 April 2005.

At the end of his trip to Ypres, Patch finally agreed to return to Pilckem Ridge, where he laid a small wreath at the 20th (Light) Division's memorial bearing the inscription: 'In remembrance of my friends in the Duke of Cornwall's Light Infantry who were lost in 1917. They have never been forgotten.' It was this inability to forget the fates of three men which explained both Patch's refusal to mention the war for eighty years and his later willingness to speak out against it. Always standing at an angle to other veterans, he even dismissed Remembrance Sunday celebrations as 'simply a military show', and had not joined his four fellow veterans – Henry Allingham (108), Fred Lloyd (106), John Oborne (104) and William Stone (103) – laying wreaths at the Cenotaph on the 90th anniversary of the outbreak of war the previous month. Public piety about the Fallen meant nothing to him – and little, he suggested, to the vast majority of people displaying it. 'I don't think there is any actual remembrance except for those who have lost someone they really cared for in either war,' he wrote in his autobiography. 'That day, the day I lost my pals, 22 September 1917 – that is my Remembrance Day, not Armistice Day.' In contrast with the very public occasion at the Cenotaph every November, Patch's own Remembrance Day was a strictly private occasion: 'I'm always very, very quiet on that day and I don't want anybody talking to me really.'

Like the last British veterans of the war, Charles Kuentz had seen it as a duty to talk about his own personal experiences of warfare in order to promote peace and to prevent more young men and women being sent into battle. He visited schools and gave talks, and was dismayed by the war in Iraq. One of his daughters said that once he started talking about the war, 'it was as if you had turned on a tap'. Harry Patch, although very outspoken about warfare, was more retiring than either Kuentz or his British fellow veteran Henry Allingham. *The Last Tommy* had made him a celebrity, but he never enjoyed the attention quite as much as Allingham, who was a natural and very engaging showman. He complained that the war was now 'usually all people want to talk about, and I'm tired of talking about it. I appreciate the fact that people want to write to me about that time, but it's

too much: photographs, autographs, letters asking for an interview, you get fed up. I'm not available!' Clearly one of the reasons
for writing his autobiography was to answer all the questions
researchers or the merely inquisitive wanted to put to him. He
was also determined that the war should take no more a disproportionate place in his autobiography than it did in his life, that
his life should be seen as a whole.

By the time the book was published in August 2007, the
ninetieth anniversary of Passchendaele was being marked, and the
previous month Patch had found himself at the age of 109 once
more returning to Ypres. By now, his visits to Belgium were international news, and on a report for BBC television he was filmed
at the place near Langemarck where he had gone into action for
the first time ninety years before. A contemporary panoramic
photograph of the battlefield was unrolled before him as he sat
looking over the same ground, now grassed over. He repeated
what had become his mantra, each word separated by a pause:
'War is a calculated and condoned slaughter of human beings.'
He was photographed wherever he went, including the Dochy
Farm New British Cemetery, apparently undaunted by the
CWGC's warning that there was 'wheelchair access with some
difficulty'. The cemetery, on the road from Ypres to Zonnebeke,
is named after a farm that in 1917 had been a German strong-
hold. It was created after the war had ended to gather together
bodies from the battlefields of Passchendaele, St-Julien,
Frezenberg and Boesinghe which had ended up in isolated graves,
and contains 1,439 burials, 958 of them unidentified. Here
Australians, New Zealanders, Canadians and South Africans lie
among their British allies, most of them killed after Patch had

been invalided home. He also visited Talbot House and the Menin Gate, where on 29 July, with the support of friends, including Richard van Emden, and leaning heavily on a walking frame, he spoke the familiar lines from Laurence Binyon's 'For the Fallen'. He had complained in his autobiography that at the Menin Gate ceremony people failed to preface the recitation of Binyon's lines with the words Tubby Clayton had always used: 'With proud thanksgiving let us remember our brethren who fell.' Now was his chance to remedy this oversight, with his own addition of '… on both sides of the line'. He failed to get Binyon's words exactly right, and had to be prompted, but it was a memorable performance.

Nor would it be Patch's last return to Ypres. The following year would mark the ninetieth anniversary of the Armistice and Patch would take a leading role in the commemoration. The inducement to revisit Belgium this time was that he was to unveil his own special memorial at the exact place he had crossed the Steenbeek ninety-one years earlier when going into action for the first time. He had paid for the memorial out of the royalties received for his autobiography, money that also helped fund a lifeboat in memory of his partner Doris, who had died in 2007. The stone plaque bore his regiment's badge and the inscription:

HERE, AT DAWN, ON 16 AUGUST 1917, THE 7TH BATTALION, DUKE OF CORNWALL'S LIGHT INFANTRY, 20TH (LIGHT) DIVISION, CROSSED THE STEENBEEK PRIOR TO THEIR SUCCESSFUL ASSAULT ON THE VILLAGE OF LANGEMARCK.

THIS STONE IS ERECTED TO THE MEMORY OF FALLEN COMRADES, AND TO HONOUR THE COURAGE, SACRIFICE AND

PASSING OF THE GREAT WAR GENERATION. IT IS THE GIFT OF FORMER PRIVATE AND LEWIS GUNNER HARRY PATCH, NO. 29295, C COMPANY, 7TH D.C.L.I., THE LAST SURVIVING VETERAN TO HAVE SERVED IN THE TRENCHES OF THE WESTERN FRONT.

SEPTEMBER 2008

A group of young soldiers from Patch's old regiment had travelled from where they were stationed in Germany to attend the ceremony, at which Richard van Emden read from Patch's autobiography and there were addresses by the military historian Peter Barton and the Mayor of Langemarck. After the sounding of the Last Post, Patch removed the British and Belgian flags covering the memorial and laid a small bouquet of flowers. Attached was a simple message: 'IN REMEMBRANCE', under which Patch had signed his name. The war, meanwhile, was still giving up its dead: the day before, the remains of three recently discovered British soldiers had been buried at Cement House Cemetery, a few hundred yards farther along the road.

It would be the last ever visit to the Western Front by someone who had actually fought there, and it was recorded for a BBC television documentary. As had by now become customary, Patch visited Talbot House and attended the ceremony at the Menin Gate, once again reading Binyon's lines, during which many of those in the large crowd were moved to tears. He then laid a wreath at the monument bearing a label reading 'Remembering Both Sides of the Line'. In pursuit of this equal remembrance, he once again visited Langemarck Cemetery to place a small wooden cross bearing the words 'Comrades All. H.P.' on the grave of a

279

German soldier. He collected two acorns from beside the grave, taking them back with him to Fletcher House to plant. During this trip he also signed copies of his book and a map of the battlefield to be presented to the Commonwealth War Graves Commission. He had become reconciled to his celebrity and even took pleasure from it, particularly at Ypres, where he was a much-loved and admired figure, applauded wherever he appeared. He had to be protected from well-wishers who crowded round wanting to greet him or simply touch him, the last surviving person who had fought to drive the Germans out of Belgium. In recognition of all this he was that year appointed Knight of the Order of Leopold, the country's highest honour, by the Belgian king, Albert II. The medal was presented to Patch by the Belgian ambassador at his residence in London on 22 September 2008, Patch's own Remembrance Day.

He was equally popular back in Britain and, like Allingham, had been awarded numerous honours over the years, including the freedom of the city of Wells and an honorary degree from the University of Bristol. The Wills Memorial Building, on which he had worked over eighty years before, had undergone major restoration, and Patch was invited to reopen it at a ceremony in 2008. Other honours were highly individual. In 2004 the Gaymer Cider Company of Shepton Mallet in Somerset had produced a special batch of a 'premium quality sweet cider' named 'Patch's Pride'. Patch had been involved in the development of the drink, tasting several different versions until he was satisfied. The 106 bottles, one for every year of his life, were not for public sale but made for Patch and his friends, with several bottles being sent to the Duke of Cornwall Light Infantry's regimental museum at Bodmin. Those unable to buy a bottle of 'Patch's Pride' could nevertheless place a bet on 'Harry Patch', a bay gelding named in the veteran's honour by the trainer Michael Jarvis. On the Friday before Remembrance Sunday in 2009 the two-year-old was the 4–1 favourite in the 1.30 at Doncaster and romped home to win the race. The *Western Daily Press* had placed a £20 bet and donated its £100 winnings to the British Legion. Perhaps the most unlikely honour paid to Patch was when in September 2007 he was invited by the men's magazine *FHM* to guest as an agony uncle. Presumably it was felt that this 'century-straddling king of the wrinklies' was well placed to advise men of a much younger generation. One reader, 'fed up with following my generational flock to places like Australia, Thailand and Ibiza', asked Patch about other holiday destinations: 'Where have you been that has stuck with you throughout the years?' Weymouth, Patch replied. As long as you were in enjoyable company, he added, 'there's no need to travel all over the planet'. He advised the questioner to go camping in the UK. Another asked whether he should allow his girlfriend to become a topless model: Patch thought not. Other questions were more serious and relevant to Patch's own experiences. A soldier who had been in Iraq for six months complained that no one seemed very interested that he'd been risking his life on their behalf. Patch admitted that returning home after a war was never easy, but said one just had to 'get on with life and look to the future'. He advised the soldier not to be resentful because those who had not been in a war simply had no idea what it was like: 'They are lucky.'

In his official capacity as Poet Laureate, Andrew Motion wrote 'The Five Acts of Harry Patch', a sequence of sonnets based on

Patch's autobiography and conversations with the veteran. At a reception at the Bishop's Palace in Wells in February 2008, Motion read the poem aloud to Patch and an audience of local dignitaries. The poem was subsequently used as the basis of a choral work by the Master of the Queen's Music, Sir Peter Maxwell-Davies, commissioned by Portsmouth Grammar School and premiered in the city's cathedral on Remembrance Sunday. Embraced by the Establishment, Patch was invited to Downing Street and was introduced to several members of the Royal Family. He may have been modest, but he was not in the least afraid to state his opinions to whoever he might be talking to. The war had left him with a lifelong hatred of injustice, and in the 1980s he had been a regular and persistent champion of local causes who 'never hesitated to write letters to the council or the local newspaper, usually firing on all cylinders when he did so'. His determination to see justice done undimmed by age, he took advantage of a visit to No. 10 to tell the Prime Minister that he fully supported the 'Shot at Dawn' campaign, which had lobbied Parliament and the Ministry of Defence to gain formal pardons for the 306 British soldiers who had been court-martialled and executed for cowardice or desertion between 1914 and 1918. The campaign had been started by relatives of the executed men when the official papers relating to their cases were declassified in 1990. The shame surrounding the deaths of these men had lasted down the years and many families had often felt stigmatised, but in November 2000 a large number of them and their supporters marched past the Cenotaph. In June the following year a Shot at Dawn Memorial was unveiled at the National Memorial Arboretum in Staffordshire. A 10-foot-high statue of a blindfolded soldier tied to a post (modelled on a real seventeen-year-old soldier shot for desertion) is surrounded by a semicircle of 306 wooden stakes recording the names of all those executed. Campaigners argued that a great many of those shot at dawn were suffering from shell shock or some other form of battle trauma which had made them no longer responsible for their actions. Although this was clearly not always the case, in August 2006 the government eventually agreed to a blanket pardon on the grounds that 'everybody involved in these terrible cases were as much victims of World War I as those who died in the battlefield'.

For the ninetieth anniversary of the Armistice, Patch was called upon to launch the British Legion's Poppy Appeal on board HMS *Somerset* in Avonmouth docks. He was joined by Simon Weston, a well-known veteran of the Falklands War, who had suffered extensive and disfiguring burns when his ship was bombed at Bluff Cove. The continuing human cost of warfare was emphasised not only by Weston's participation at the launch but by the revelation that the number of young servicemen who had applied to the Legion for help had more than doubled in the past year thanks to the continuing military campaigns in Iraq and Afghanistan. The Army Air Corps flew over the *Somerset*, dropping poppies, and more of the red flowers were fired over the ship from dockside cannons.

The Queen, as usual, led the nation in the service at the Cenotaph on Remembrance Sunday, which fell on 9 November, but Patch and his two fellow veterans, Henry Allingham and Bill Stone, were called upon to lead a special ceremony in Whitehall two days later, marking the exact moment when, ninety years before, peace had been declared. In his autobiography Patch had, with characteristic outspokenness, declined to consider Stone a true veteran, pointedly declaring that the honour of being the Last Veteran should be awarded to a person 'who had seen action on the Western Front, not to anyone who happened to be in uniform when the war ended'. He nevertheless put aside his reservations for the occasion, which was attended by the Prime Minister, the Defence Secretary, the Duchess of Gloucester, who was patron of the World War One Veterans' Association, and a crowd of thousands. Unlike the Remembrance Sunday ceremony, this one was focused specifically upon the First World War. It included readings by young actors of a letter written from the front and poems by A.E. Housman and Siegfried Sassoon, and a military band played the *Elegy for Strings* written in 1915 in memory of Rupert Brooke by his friend F.S. Kelly, who survived Gallipoli, but was killed on the Somme the following year. It was an extraordinary circumstance that the last three veterans should each have fought with a different service, the army, the air force and the navy. Now Patch, Allingham and Stone, each bearing a wreath for his own force, were wheeled one at a time to the foot of the Cenotaph, assisted by three representatives of the present armed forces, all of them decorated: Lance Corporal Johnson Beharry, who'd been awarded the VC in Iraq; Flight Lieutenant Michelle Goodman, the first ever woman to be awarded the Distinguished Flying Cross, also in Iraq; and Marine Mkhuseli Jones, who had been awarded the Military Cross in Afghanistan. The laying of the wreaths was followed by the Silence, after which the Bishop to the Forces, who had led the brief religious service, intoned 'For the Fallen', prefacing it with Tubby Clayton's words about remembering 'our brethren who fell', but omitting Patch's customary addition of 'on both sides of the line'. Keen as he was to avoid the 'show business' of Remembrance Sunday, Patch declared himself very happy to participate in this additional event. 'It is not just an honour for me but for an entire generation,' he said, adding (to make up for the Bishop's omission): 'It is important to remember the dead from both sides of the conflict.' The ceremony was followed by a reception at Downing Street, while at Tate Britain three black-and-white portraits of Patch, Allingham and Stone taken by the veteran war photographer Don McCullin and commissioned by the Ministry of Defence went on display. Patch also made an appearance to a standing ovation at the Festival of Remembrance at the Albert Hall: even the Queen stood with the rest of the audience as he came onstage.

On 9 March 2009 the French ambassador visited Fletcher House in order to enrol Patch as an Officer of the *Légion d'honneur*. The same honour was bestowed on Allingham, upgrading Britain's last two surviving veterans from their previous honour as Chevaliers of the order. 'I greatly appreciate the way your people respect the memory of those who fell, irrespective of the uniform they wore,' Patch told the ambassador. 'I will wear this medal with great pride and when I eventually rejoin my mates it will be displayed in my regimental museum as a permanent reminder of the kindness of the people of France.' On 17 June 2009 Patch celebrated his 111th birthday with a party in the garden of Fletcher House. 'Happy Birthday' was played by pipers and he received a pile of handmade birthday cards from local schoolchildren. The following day a portrait of Patch went on display at the National Portrait Gallery as part of the annual

BP Portrait Award exhibition. Dan Llywelyn Hall's painting, depicting a relaxed-looking veteran, his collar undone and striped tie loose, his jacket hung with medals, was used on the poster advertising the exhibition all over London. It was, in its way, Harry Patch's last public appearance. At 9 a.m. on 25 July, only a week after the death of Henry Allingham, the man who finally and briefly became Britain's Last Veteran died at Fletcher House. He had been the oldest man in Europe and the third-oldest man in the world, but had remained alert and articulate until the end, still planning a fortnight before his death to make one more visit to Belgium.

It might have been very different. It was an extraordinary stroke of good fortune that Britain's last veterans, though of course physically frail, were otherwise not in the least incapacitated. At their very advanced ages they might well have been bedridden, senile or comatose. The Last Veteran himself could have been lying in a hospital wholly unaware of his status. Instead, it would be hard to imagine a more outspoken and eloquent representative of his generation. His words may have become fewer, spoken with increasing pauses between them and in a hoarse whisper, but they always remained pungent and to the point. The Prime Minister and the Prince of Wales paid tribute on television, and the following day news of Patch's death made the front pages of most of the British newspapers – although at the morning service in Wells Cathedral 'Harry Patch, local veteran' took his place inconspicuously on a list read out by the canon of people in the diocese who had died that week. This was just as Patch would have liked it, as he would no doubt have been touched to have known that candles were lit in the windows of Ypres, the town that had adopted him as its own. Further tributes to both Patch and Allingham came from the National Poet of Wales, Gillian Clark, the recently appointed Poet Laureate, Carol Ann Duffy, and the band Radiohead. The BBC had commissioned Clark and Duffy to write poems marking the passing of Britain's last veterans: Clark's 'The Plumber' was specifically about Patch, whereas Duffy's 'Last Post' was a more generalised salute to those who had just been 'released from History'. Duffy read her poem on the *Today* programme on the morning of Allingham's funeral, and six days later Radiohead's 'Harry Patch (In Memory Of)' was played in a similar slot. The Radiohead song, which had in fact been written in advance of Patch's death and used his own words from a BBC radio interview as lyrics, was subsequently released as an Internet download costing £1, which went to the British Legion.

When asked what he thought about the idea that the Last Veteran should be given a state funeral, Patch had replied characteristically: 'Overall, the idea was all right, I suppose, wanting to honour the generation who fought, but I wasn't interested. I want to be buried in Monkton Combe alongside my family in the churchyard.' His wish for 'a simple, private funeral' would be observed, but in order to obtain this privacy it was necessary also to organise a large public event so that the nation could pay its respects. The press, naturally enough, spoke of a 'Hero's farewell for Harry Patch', but this was not what he wanted. 'He could have dealt with it by ignoring the whole thing completely,' said his friend and spokesman Jim Ross, 'but in fact he decided to use this to represent his generation with a message which he thought they would have wanted broadcast, and that message was one of peace and reconciliation.' The event would be held in Wells Cathedral and 1,050 tickets made available to the public by personal application at the Cathedral offices. Some four hundred people had already formed a queue when the office opened at 9.30 a.m. a week before the funeral. Some had camped out overnight on the Cathedral Green to ensure they got tickets.

Patch's public funeral was meticulously planned to convey his message to future generations. Henry Allingham had always been more conventional than Patch, and his funeral was held at St Nicholas's Church in Brighton on 30 July with full military honours, his coffin carried by members of the RAF and Royal Navy, representing the two forces with which his war service had been associated. Patch's funeral, by contrast, bore out the beliefs he had stuck to throughout his life – in particular his belief that all those who fought in the war were victims, irrespective of the uniforms they wore. His coffin, therefore, would be borne into Wells Cathedral by six members of the 1st Battalion The Rifles, successors to his own regiment, but flanked by two infantrymen from France, two from Belgium and two from Germany. All of them, at Patch's request, were young, roughly the age he had been when he fought in Belgium. Ross told the press: 'It's certainly not a military funeral, certainly not a state funeral. It's the funeral of a private man who had a message, and that message was that we should settle disputes by discussion and compromise, not by war.' Even ceremonial weapons would be banned inside the Cathedral.

The choristers of Wells Cathedral had been recalled from their summer holidays to perform at the service, which took place at noon on Thursday, 6 August, and was televised live. It was two days after the ninety-fifth anniversary of the outbreak of the war that had interrupted, shaped and eventually come to define Harry Patch's life. The Cathedral bells tolled 111 times, and the normally busy High Street, through which the cortège would pass, was closed to all traffic. In light rain, the coffin, draped with a Union flag and adorned with a single simple wreath of red roses, was driven to the Cathedral the short distance from Fletcher House through streets lined with people seven deep. Members of the Royal British Legion dipped their flags as their recent and oldest member passed; police on duty saluted; the public took photographs and applauded. When the hearse arrived at the Cathedral, Patch's great-nephew, David Tucker, placed a box containing his uncle's medals on the coffin in preparation for them to be formally handed over to the regimental museum during the service. Every one of the Cathedral's 1,400 seats was occupied, with Patch's friends and relatives and ticket-holding members of the public joined by the Duchess of Cornwall, representing the Royal Family; the Duchess of Gloucester, patron of the World War One Veterans' Association; the Veterans Minister, Kevan Jones, representing the government; and General Sir Richard Dannatt, the soon-to-retire Chief of the General Staff, representing the British army. On the Cathedral Green provision had been made for some four thousand people who had been unable to obtain tickets to watch the service on giant screens. Umbrellas mushroomed there on this characteristically damp English summer morning.

The service was conducted by the Dean of Wells Cathedral, who in his opening address described Harry Patch as 'an ambassador for peace and reconciliation'. This theme was reflected by the choice of people who took a leading part in the service. The first reading was taken from *The Last Fighting Tommy*, the scene in which Patch witnessed the death of the young infantryman, and concluded that death is not the end. It was read by the Belgian chargé d'affaires. The second reading, from Corinthians, was read by her German opposite number, while the French chargé d'affaires formally presented the box containing Patch's medals to the president of the Duke of Cornwall's Light Infantry Museum.

The eulogy was given by Jim Ross, whose principal theme was that Harry Patch was an ordinary man, made extraordinary by circumstances. He recalled that Patch had told him about his war experiences the first time they had met, but never mentioned them again in eleven years of friendship because there were always other things to talk about. Patch was someone who, though he may have been haunted by the past, was determined to live in the present. The hymns were traditional, but the Cathedral's leading chorister sang Pete Seeger's 1960s anti-war anthem 'Where Have All the Flowers Gone?' to a simple piano accompaniment. The prayers, led by the Precentor of Wells, remembered not only those who had died in Harry Patch's war, but those who were currently fighting and dying in Afghanistan. Several newspapers the following day would draw comparisons between Patch's funeral and another one taking place the same day: that of an eighteen-year-old soldier from the 2nd Battalion The Rifles, killed by a Taliban bomb.

Two buglers sounded the Last Post as the coffin was carried out of the Cathedral, marking the beginning of a minute's silence. The sky had darkened and there was a heavy downpour – appropriately, given the weather always associated with Passchendaele in the summer of 1917. Another of Patch's close friends read the familiar lines from Laurence Binyon's 'For the Fallen', lines that would never now be spoken by someone who had not only served alongside the Fallen but had seen many of them fall. To the strains of Elgar's 'Nimrod', a hearse then drove Britain's Last Veteran out of the Cathedral Green and took the road to Monkton Combe church for a private burial attended by those who had known him personally. 'No one else – no press, no media, no public – just a quiet funeral for Harry with all of his friends,' as Jim Ross put it.

Back on the Cathedral Green, almost everyone, it seemed, had something to say about Britain's Last Veteran, from the head of the British army to the young representatives of the armies of Belgium, France and Germany who had acted as an honour guard. There was a general feeling that in some way Harry Patch belonged to us all, that he was not only a hugely significant part of British history, but also part of the very fabric of the nation. Those who had met him recalled his charm, his sense of humour, his outspokenness, his modesty, his essential decency. Even so, the private man was already fading. People were also speaking of him as someone who symbolised 'all that's best about the British army – determination, devotion to duty, but humanity as well', and claiming that present-day soldiers were 'in a direct line' from Patch because 'he felt such a strong duty to join up, to go and defend the nation'. This was to assert his symbolic role at the expense of the biographical facts. 'I didn't want to join up,' Patch wrote in his autobiography. 'I didn't want to go and fight anyone, but it was a case of having to. When it came, army life didn't appeal to me at all and when I found out how rough-and-tumble it could be, I liked it even less. I had no inclination to fight anybody. I wasn't at all patriotic. I went and did what was asked of me and no more.' It was a reluctant conscript, not an eager volunteer, who with enormous grace and patience, and at no small emotional cost to himself, had become the last representative of his generation. As the hearse made its way to Monkton Combe, Harry Patch was leaving behind this public role, which had reached its climax in a great cathedral, in order to return quietly to a place where he truly belonged, lying among his unremarkable family in an English country churchyard.

At some point, no doubt, people will be interviewing the last British veterans of the Second World War, old soldiers who are already in their eighties or beyond. Then there will be the last veterans of the Korean War, the Falklands War, the Gulf Wars, of Iraq and Afghanistan; but it is doubtful that any of these people will achieve quite the iconic status Harry Patch did. It is partly a matter of scale, of course. While in terms of global carnage the Second World War was quite a match for the First, it never achieved the same resonance and did not leave the country with such an overwhelming sense of national loss. Subsequent wars in which the British have been involved have been comparatively small-scale, confined to individual regions geographically remote from Britain and involving limited forces. More importantly, these forces have been largely made up of professional soldiers, whereas the First World War was fought overwhelmingly by civilian volunteers or conscripts, people like us.

At the same time, the generation of 1914–18 seem infinitely remote. Whether going over the top or simply making their way through a crowded street, the small black-and-white figures brought to flickering life by early newsreel and documentary footage seem not only to belong to another life, but to another world – and, in a way, they do. The faces of those who stood in long enthusiastic lines outside the recruiting stations were described by Philip Larkin in his celebrated poem 'MCMXIV' as 'archaic', but part of what now seems the almost culpable naivety among those who imagined the war would be one great adventure came about as a result of their living in the particular world they were about to lose. It was a world in which people believed in what to many of us seem absurd and outmoded clichés: they really did believe in King and Country; they believed that Britannia ruled the waves; they believed that the sun would never set on the British Empire. 'Never such innocence again,' Larkin observed poignantly; but one might also add: never such confidence, either. This, too, is our loss. As we have seen, the Edwardian era was not quite the eternal summer it has become in myth, and there were all manner of signs that everything was not as sunny in Britain and her dominions as people liked to think. But while there was widespread poverty and signs of civil unrest for those who cared to look, there was also optimism and a genuine belief in progress, a trust in the beneficial nature of technical and other advances. On the whole, people were not only proud to be British but were prepared to demonstrate their love of country by donning a uniform and taking up arms. While today's tabloid newspapers and their readers cheer on 'our lads abroad', wherever that happens to be, the flag they are rallying around is hoisted safely in Britain. Whatever enthusiasm there may have been among the populace for Mrs Thatcher's Falklands adventure in 1982, there was a conspicuous lack of civilian volunteers for service in the South Atlantic in defence of one of Britain's smaller and more remote overseas territories. The public demonstrations that attended Britain's decision to send troops to Iraq to depose Saddam Hussein would have seemed as extraordinary from the viewpoint of 1914 as the enthusiasm for a war with the Kaiser seems to us from the viewpoint of today. But it as well to remember that in all sorts of other, more important and enduring ways, the generation of 1914 was little different from us. They ran riot as children, argued with their parents, scrapped with their friends and siblings, fell in and out of love, got drunk, knew happiness and despair, and – overwhelmingly – experienced grief. Those veterans who survived into the twenty-first century provided a link between the present day and a period that already seems beyond our reach. They were both the men in hats jerkily dodging the horse-drawn trams in those early black-and-white films and the men we could still see in full colour recalling that period in numerous television documentaries about the war. As Air Vice-Marshal Peter Dye commented when Henry Allingham unveiled the British Air Services Memorial at St-Omer, a frail 108-year-old was able to 'bridge the gap between the cold stone and sharp bronze letters of the memorial and the flesh and blood of the young men it commemorates'.

The First World War generation has now passed irrecoverably into history, the final loss after all those that went before them. It has been said that the last veterans 'breathed life into the pages of history'. If so, that breath is now stilled. 'It's really impossible to talk about the Great War and talk about the millions of people who were killed or wounded,' observed the teacher whose pupils made cards for Harry Patch's final birthday; 'but if you talk about one person they really understand, they really make connections.' Those connections are now broken, and future histories of the war will be written without the living testimony of those who took part in it. The young poet Charles Hamilton Sorley, killed at Loos in 1915, wrote of the 'millions of the mouthless dead', but until now those dead have always had a spokesman. Now that the Last Post has sounded for the Last Veteran, there is no one left to say 'I know what it was like. I was there.'

BIBLIOGRAPHY

This is a bibliography of items which have proved particularly useful in researching and writing this book. Books are listed in their first editions; where other editions have been used for the purposes of quotation, the publisher (if different) and date follow in square brackets.

Allingham, Henry and Dennis Goodwin, *Kitchener's Last Volunteer*, Mainstream, 2008

Arthur, Max, *Forgotten Voices of the Great War*, Ebury Press, 2002

——, *Last Post*, Weidenfeld & Nicolson, 2005

Ashley, Peter, *Lest We Forget*, English Heritage, 2004

Babbington, Anthony, *For the Sake of Example: Capital Courts Martial 1914–18*, Leo Cooper, 1983

Barham, Peter, *Forgotten Lunatics of the Great War*, Yale University Press, 2004

Bartholomew, Michael, *In Search of H.V. Morton*, Methuen, 2006

Blunden, Edmund (ed. Martin Taylor), *Overtones of War*, Duckworth, 1996

Blythe, Ronald, *The Age of Illusion*, Hamish Hamilton, 1963

——, *The View in Winter*, Allen Lane, 1975

Bond, Brian, *The Unquiet Western Front*, Cambridge University Press, 2002

—— (ed.), *The First World War and Military History*, Clarendon Press, 1991

Brophy, John and Eric Partridge, *The Long Trail*, André Deutsch, 1965

Brown, Antony, *Red for Remembrance*, William Heinemann, 1971

Cecil, Hugh and Peter Liddle (eds), *At the Eleventh Hour*, Leo Cooper, 1998

Chapman, Guy, *A Passionate Prodigality*, Ivor Nicholson & Watson, 1933 [MacGibbon & Kee, 1965]

Churchill, Winston, *The World in Crisis 1911–1918*, Odhams, 1939

Clark, Alan, *The Donkeys*, Hutchinson, 1961 [Pimlico, 1991]

Commonwealth War Graves Commission, *The Commission's Horticulture*, 1998

Coombs, Rose E.B., *Before Endeavours Fade* (rev. edn), Battle of Britain International, 2006

Das, Satanu, *Touch and Intimacy in First World War Literature*, Cambridge University Press, 2005

Ellis, John, *Eye-Deep in Hell*, Croom Helm, 1976

Falls, Cyril, *War Books: An Annotated Bibliography*, Peter Davies, 1930

Ferguson, Niall, *The Pity of War 1914–1918*, Allen Lane, 1998

Gibson, James (ed.), *Let the Poet Choose*, Harrap, 1973

Gibson, T.A. Edwin and G. Kingsley Ward, *Courage Remembered*, HMSO, 1989

Graves, Charles, *The Home Guard of Britain*, Hutchinson, 1943

Graves, Robert, *Goodbye to All That*, Jonathan Cape, 1929 [Penguin, 1960]

—— (ed. Paul O'Prey), *In Broken Images: Selected Letters of Robert Graves 1914–1946*, Hutchinson, 1982

Gregory, Adrian, *The Silence of Memory*, Berg, 1994

Bibliography

Hannington, Wal, *Unemployed Struggles 1919–1936*, Lawrence & Wishart, 1936 [1977]

Hanson, Neil, *The Unknown Soldier*, Doubleday, 2005

Hiscock, Eric, *The Bells of Hell Go Ting-a-Ling-a-Ling*, Arlington Books, 1976

Holmes, Richard, *Tommy*, HarperCollins, 2004

Howard, Michael, *The First World War*, Oxford University Press, 2002

Hussey, Christopher, *The Life of Sir Edwin Lutyens*, Country Life, 1953

King, Alex, *Memorials of the Great War in Britain*, Berg, 1998

Lewis, Cecil, *Sagittarius Rising*, Peter Davies, 1936 [Penguin, 1977]

Liddell Hart, B.H., *History of the First World War*, Faber, 1934 [Pan, 1972]

Littlewood, Joan, *Joan's Book*, Methuen, 1994

Lloyd, David, *Battlefield Tourism*, Berg, 1998

Lloyd George, David, *War Memoirs of David Lloyd George*, Odhams Press, 1933–36

Longworth, Philip, *The Unending Vigil*, Constable, 1967

MacArthur, Brian, *For King and Country*, Little, Brown, 2008

Macdonald, Lyn, *1914–1918: Voices and Images of the Great War*, Michael Joseph, 1988

Mackenzie, S.P., *The Home Guard: A Military and Political History*, Oxford University Press, 1995

Madge, Charles and Tom Harrisson, *Britain by Mass Observation*, Penguin, 1939

McCann, Graham, *Dad's Army*, Fourth Estate, 2001

Michelin Guides, *The Somme: Volume 1*, Michelin & Cie, 1919

Middlebrooke, Martin, *The First Day on the Somme*, Allen Lane, 1971

Morton, H.V., *The Heart of London*, Methuen, 1925 [illustrated edn, 1938]

——, *The Spell of London*, Methuen, 1926

——, *In Search of England*, Methuen, 1927

Moult, Thomas (ed.), *The Cenotaph*, Jonathan Cape, 1923

Noakes, Vivien (ed.), *Voices of Silence*, Sutton, 2006

Omissi, David, *Indian Voices of the Great War*, Macmillan Press, 1999

Owen, Harold, *Journey from Obscurity*, vol. III: *War*, Oxford University Press, 1965

Owen, Wilfred (ed. Martin Taylor), *Poems by Wilfred Owen*, Imperial War Museum, 1990

Paris, Michael (ed.), *The First World War and Popular Cinema*, Rutgers University Press, 2000

Parker, Peter, *The Old Lie: The Great War and the Public School Ethos*, Constable, 1987

——, *Ackerley*, Constable, 1989

Patch, Harry and Richard van Emden, *The Last Fighting Tommy*, Bloomsbury, 2007

Percy, Clayre and Jane Ridley (eds), *The Letters of Edwin Lutyens to His Wife Lady Emily*, Collins, 1985

Pope, Stephen and Elizabeth-Anne Wheal, *Dictionary of the First World War*, Macmillan, 1995

Porter, Roy (ed.), *Myths of the English*, Polity Press, 1992

Read, Herbert, *The Contrary Experience*, Secker & Warburg, 1963 [1973]

Reed, Paul, *Walking the Somme*, Leo Cooper, 1997

Sassoon, Siegfried, *The Heart's Journey*, William Heinemann, 1928

——, *Collected Poems 1908–1956*, Faber, 1961

——, *Diaries 1915–1918*, Faber, 1983

Sayers, Dorothy L., *The Unpleasantness at the Bellona Club*, Gollancz, 1928 [rep. 1937]

Sheffield, Gary, *The Forgotten Victory*, Headline, 2001

Sorley, C.H., *Marlborough and Other Poems* (rev. edn), Cambridge University Press, 1919

Stamp, Gavin, *Silent Cities*, RIBA, 1977

——, *The Memorial to the Missing of the Somme*, Profile, 2006

Stone, Norman, *World War One: A Short History*, Allen Lane, 2007

Summerfield, Penny and Corinna Peniston-Bird, *Contesting Home Defence*, Manchester University Press, 2007

Summers, Juliet, *Remembered: The History of the Commonwealth War Graves Commission*, Merrell, 2007

Taylor, A.J.P., *The First World War: An Illustrated History*, Hamish Hamilton, 1963

Theatre Workshop, *Oh What a Lovely War!*, Methuen, 1965

Van Emden, Richard, *Britain's Last Tommies*, Leo Cooper, 2005 [Abacus, 2006]

Van Emden, Richard and Stephen Humphries, *Veterans: The Last Survivors of the Great War*, Leo Cooper, 1998 [Pen & Sword, 2005]

War Office, The, *Instructions for the Training of Platoons for Offensive Action*, 1917

Ware, Fabian, *The Immortal Heritage*, Cambridge University Press, 1937

Whaley, Joachim (ed.), *Mirrors of Mortality*, Europa Publications, 1981

Winter, Denis, *Death's Men*, Allen Lane, 1978

Winter, J.K., *The Great War and the British People*, Palgrave Macmillan, 1986

Woolf, Virginia, *The Diary of Virginia Woolf*, vol. 1: *1915–1919*, Hogarth Press, 1977

Wootton, Graham, *The Official History of the British Legion*, Macdonald & Evans, 1956

The following websites have also proved invaluable:

Aftermath: www.aftermathww1.com

BBC History World Wars: www.bbc.co.uk/history/worldwars/wwone

BBC News Channel: http://news.bbc.co.uk

BBC Ninety Years of Remembrance: www.bbc.co.uk/remembrance
British Light Infantry Regiments: www.lightinfantry.org.uk
Combe Down Heritage Society: www.combedownheritage.org.uk
The Commonwealth War Graves Commission: www.cwgc.org
Firstworldwar.com: www.firstworldwar.com
The First World War Poetry Digital Archive: www.oucs.ox.ac.uk/ww1lit
The Great War 1914–1918: www.greatwar.co.uk
The Imperial War Museum: www.iwm.org.uk
Libcom.org: http://libcom.org/history
The Long, Long Trail: www.1914-1918.net
The Ministry of Defence: www.mod.uk
The National Archives: www.nationalarchives.gov.uk
The Oxford Dictionary of National Biography: www.oxforddnb.com
The Peace Pledge Union: www.ppu.org.uk
Roll of Honour: www.roll-of-honour.com
The Royal British Legion: www.britishlegion.org.uk
Veterans UK: www.veterans-uk.com
War Grave & Battlefields Heritage: www.wargravesheritage.org.uk
The War Memorials Trust: www.warmemorials.org
The Western Front Association: www.westernfrontassociation.com
World War One Battlefields: www.ww1battlefields.co.uk

In addition, both The Great War 1914–1918 (above) and The Accrington Pals (www.pals.org.uk/wwilinks.htm) have useful links to other First World War websites.

Television
The Last Tommy, directed by Harvey Lilley (BBC, 2005)
Private Harry Patch, directed by Jenny Walmsley and Rob Wicks (BBC, 2008)

SOURCE NOTES

References to quoted material are listed by page number and in order, identified by a brief phrase or the subject matter or author. Published sources are referred to by the author's surname, and all books cited are listed in the Bibliography.

Prologue
> p.2 'At precisely –' Arthur, *Forgotten Voices*, p.311
> Allingham – *Observer* magazine, 9.11.08
> Stokes – Macdonald, p.307
> p.3 Chapman – Chapman, pp.272–3
> Worsley – Macdonald, p.314
> 'until Germany's –' Cecil and Liddle, p.55
> Marshall – Arthur, *Last Post*, p.49
> p.4 Wilson – *The Last Tommy*, BBC TV
> Lewis – Lewis, pp.207, 107
> Watson – Arthur, *Last Post*, p.196
> p.5 Graves – *In Broken Images*, p.98; *Goodbye*, p.228
> Sassoon – *Diaries 1915–1918*, p.282
> p.7 Collins – van Emden and Humphries, *Veterans*, p.219
> Owen – H. Owen, p.201
> p.8 'You were so dazed –' Arthur, *Forgotten Voices*, p.311
> 'My first thought –' van Emden and Humphries, *Veterans*, p.221
> Halestrap – van Emden, p.350
> p.12 Ackerley – Parker, *Ackerley*, pp.406–7
> p.13 Duncan Smith – Hansard, 18.4.06: Column 54WH

p.14 Duncan Smith – ibid.: Column 56WH
      Touhig – ibid.: Column 59HW
p.15 Browne – Defence News website: www.mod.uk/Defence
      Internet/DefenceNews/HistoryAndHonour/NationToCommemorate
      PassingOfFirstWorldWarGeneration.htm
      'among the most' – tomb of the Unknown Warrior in Westminster Abbey
p.17 population losses – Stamp, *Silent Cities*, p.3
p.19 Branagh – *Daily Telegraph*, 30.8.06
p.20 Sheffield – Sheffield, p.xx
p.22 schoolchild – BBC Television news, 18.4.07: http://news.bbc.co.uk/1/
      hi/uk/6569687.stm
      Patch – Patch and van Emden, p.90
      Patch – *Daily Telegraph*, 30.7.07

Chapter 1
p.30 Lloyd George – www.conservativemanifesto.com/1918
p.31 Haig – Cecil and Liddle, p.65
      manifesto – www.libdemmanifesto.com/1918
p.32 Patch – Patch and van Emden, p.129
p.33 Patch – ibid., p.134
      Patch – ibid., p.135
p.36 Bowie – van Emden and Humphries, *Veterans*, p.218
p.37 Patch – Patch and van Emden, p.138
p.39 Chapman – Chapman, pp.280–81
      Frankau – Noakes, p.371
      postcard – ibid., p.370
p.42 Hannington – Hannington, pp.12–13
      Federation – *The Times*, 29.5.19
p.43 resolution – ibid., 27.5.19
      police and protesters – ibid.
      Woolf – Woolf, p.292
p.45 Lutyens – Hussey, p.392
      East Enders – minutes of the Peace Celebrations Committee meeting,
      18.6.19, quoted in 'The Story of the Cenotaph', *TLS*, 12.11.76
p.46 Haig – MacArthur, p.411
p.47 columns of dead – Ware, p.27
p.50 King's message – e.g. *The Times*, 7.11.19

p.51 'pulse' – *The Times Armistice Day Supplement*, 12.11.20, quoted David Cannadine, 'Death and Grief in Modern Britain', in Whaley, pp.223–4
p.59 Elkington – quoted in Lewis Foreman's sleeve note for the CD *The Spirit of England* (Epoch CDLX 7172)
p.61 Cenotaph arrangements – plan reproduced on the Western Front Association's website article on the Unknown Warrior
p.63 'Wonderful –' Morton, *The Spell of London*, pp.17–18
p.64 Machen – *Evening News*, 11.11.20, reproduced in Moult, pp.15–16
p.65 Levy and Ryle – quoted Blythe, p.12
     Boxing Day – *The Times*, 28.12.20
p.66 Cenotaph 1921 – ibid., 12.11.21
     Poplar delegation – ibid.

Chapter 2
p.68 Lutyens – Percy and Ridley, p.350
p.70 'until such time' – Ware, p.78
     204,650 – ibid., p.37
p.71 'The concept' – CWGC sheet
p.72 Michelin – p.15
p.73 Mametz casualties – Holmes, p.151
     sales figures – Lloyd, p.103
p.74 Sassoon – *The Times*, 31.7.17
     Louth – van Emden and Humphries, *Veterans*, p.218
p.74 Patch – Patch and van Emden, p.199
p.75 gardening veterans – Summers, pp.32–3
     Osborne – D. Winter, pp.262–3
p.76 Hannington – Hannington, pp.16–17
p.77 *The Times* – 19.10.20
     Hannington – Hannington, pp.16–17
     Cannadine – *The Times*, 20.10.20
p.78 Hannington – Hannington, p.17
p.79 *Yorkshire Post* – Gregory, p.57
     Dundee Advertiser – ibid.
     veteran's wife – ibid., pp.58–9
p.80 unemployed figures – Wootton, p.46
     Daily Express – Hannington, p.76
     'big procession' – ibid., p.75

p.81   unemployed march – ibid., p.78

p.82   Hannington – ibid., p.13

p.84   NUX – Wootton, p.18
        'Warriors *Gulled*' – ibid., p.25

p.85   British Legion 'principles' – quoted Wootton, p.300

p.86   National Constructive Programme – in Wootton, pp.301–2

p.88   Lewis – Lewis, p.97

p.90   'Do you support' – Wootton, p.320

p.91   'to institute' – ibid., p.301
        Haig – *Daily Express*, 6.11.25, quoted Gregory, p.71

p.93   *Daily Mail* – quoted ibid., p.69

p.94   Redwood – http://www.johnredwoodsdiary.com/2007/10/21

p.95   *The Times* – 10.11.23

p.97   Morton on Cenotaph – p.26

p.99   Bartholomew – p.41
        'I believed' – Morton, *In Search of England*, pp.1–2

p.100   'I took' – ibid., pp.2–3
        'lies not' – ibid., p.15

p.101   'This village' – ibid., p.2

p.102   *Wonderful Britain* – King, p.23

p.106   'He throttled' – *The Times*, 13.11.22
        'It was probably' – ibid., 12.11.26

p.107   Wimsey's war – Sayers, p.7
        Wimsey and Fentiman – ibid., p.15

p.108   'My dear sir' – ibid., p.140
        'to get through' – ibid., p.54

p.109   'Were people' – ibid., p.147
        Murbles – ibid., p.165

p.110   Patch – Patch and van Emden, p.203

p.113   'In all' – Churchill, p.1077
        Boraston and Haig – ibid., p.1078
        Haig's tally – ibid., pp.1086–7

p.114   'Nevertheless' – ibid., p.1091

p.115   'Some may say' – Liddell Hart, original Preface
        'may at least' – ibid.

p.116   'the process' – ibid., p.33
        French – ibid., p.33

p.116 Haig's caution – ibid., p.34
p.117 'the ill-fated' – ibid., p.193
Kitchener – ibid., p.195
'was working up' – ibid., p.203
p.118 'the historian's task – ibid., original Preface
'so fruitless' – ibid., p.327
'lofty optimism' – ibid., p.335
Patch – *Daily Telegraph*, 12.7.07
p.119 Index – Lloyd George, pp.3473–8
p.121 Haig's diaries – ibid., pp.3374–5
p.122 'During the critical' – ibid., p.3378
p.123 sales figures – Bond, *The First World War*, p.7
p.124 'These books' – Falls, p.ix
'One may say' – ibid., pp.ix–x
p.125 'The general conditions' – ibid., p.xi
'to prove' – ibid., p.x
'Every sector' – ibid., p.xi
p.126 Read – Read, p.61
p.127 Owen – W. Owen, p.vii
Blunden's contents – ibid., Appendix A
Sassoon – *The Heart's Journey*, p.31
p.128 poppies – *The Times*, 12.11.37
p.129 disabled figure – Ferguson, p.437
tomb – Madge and Harrisson, p.290; *The Times*, 19.11.38
Mass Observation survey – Madge and Harrisson, p.200
p.130 Cenotaph disturbance – *The Times*, 12.11.37
p.131 disability pensions – Barham, p.4
Blunden – Gibson, p.31
p.132 Home Office – *The Times*, 11.10.39
poppy figures – ibid., 26.10.39; Wootton, p.317
Archbishop – ibid., 11.10.39
p.133 'The Faith of Armistice Day' – ibid., 11.11.39
p.134 Armistice Day 1940 – ibid., 12.11.40

Interlude
p.137 'ex-servicemen capable' – Summerfield and Peniston-Bird, p.8
Churchill – ibid.

p.138 volunteer figures – ibid., p.27
       firearms – C. Graves, p.248
       'The rally' – ibid., p.14
p.139 War Office – Mackenzie, p.41
       government memorandum – ibid., p.42
       Churchill – ibid., p.50
p.141 'capable' – C. Graves, p.11
       'generous age-limit' – ibid., p.38
p.142 Taylor – ibid., p.38
       Eden – ibid., p.38
p.143 veteran percentages – Mackenzie, p.37
p.145 'for those of us' – Patch and van Emden, p.163
p.146 'knew about water' – ibid., p.163
p.147 'Did the bombs' – ibid., p.175
       'money for old rope' – ibid., p.176
p.149 Finnigan – Arthur, *Last Post*, p.104
p.150 Churchill – Mackenzie, p.134

Chapter 3
p.153 *The Times* – 10.11.45
p.154 VE and VJ Days – ibid.
p.155 'as one war' – ibid., 5.11.45
p.158 Fisher – ibid., 8.10.46
       'Some of the world's' – ibid., 20.6.46
p.159 Remembrance Sunday 1946 – ibid., 11.11.46
p.162 correspondent – ibid., 8.10.53
       Time magazine – 22.11.37
       Kent British Legion – *The Times*, 15.10.53
p.163 Carpenter – ibid., 11.11.63
       Collins – ibid.
       'interference' and Potter – ibid., 13.11.63
p.164 Stacey – ibid., 9.11.64
       Poppy Day returns – ibid., 30.11.64
p.165 'Remembrancetide' – ibid., 13.11.65
       'Since the passing' – *Theology* LXVIII (1965), p.527
p.166 Church withdrawal and calvaries – ibid., p.529
       'practical suggestions' – ibid., pp.529–30

Source Notes

p.167 churchmen's committee – *The Times*, 22.8.68
p.168 'Having spent' – Brown, p.76
p.174 *Economist* – quoted on Clark jacket
       'This is the story' – Clark, p.11
p.175 'A resolute thrust' – ibid., p.16
       'considerations' – ibid., p.87
       'ignoring' – ibid., p.105
       'The battle' – ibid., p.96
p.176 'starved' – ibid., p.39
       'In the warmth' – ibid., p.42
       'owed more' – ibid., p.22
       epigraph – ibid., p.115
p.177 Aubers Ridge – ibid., pp.119–21
p.178 operational centre – ibid., p.121
       motoring Haig – ibid., pp.121–2
       Gough – ibid., p.123
p.179 'It had been disastrous' – ibid., p.126
       'that acknowledged master' – ibid., p.12
       Howard – *Listener*, 3.8.61
p.181 warzone captions – Taylor, illustrations 148, 61
p.182 personality captions – Taylor, illustrations 24, 81, 107, 82, 63, 120
       Loos – Taylor, p.75
p.183 Verdun – ibid., p.94
       Somme – ibid., p.105
       Passchendaele – ibid., pp.144–5
p.184 Gallipoli – ibid., pp.62, 64
p.185 Sheffield – p.xvii
       Taylor – p.179
       preface – Taylor, p.9
p.186 'pierrot show' – Theatre Workshop, p.10
       play scene – ibid., pp.98–9
p.187 Littlewood – Littlewood, p.693
       Terraine – *Spectator*, 26.4.63
p.188 Barnett and Bond – Bond, p.66
       'a distinguished general' – ibid., p.65
       Liddell Hart – ibid., p.66
p.189 Liddell Hart – *The Times*, 19.9.64

p.190 Sassoon – *Collected Poems*, p.85
p.196 Haig's horse – Bond, p.60
p.199 Kee – *Spectator*, 1.6.62
       Howard – *TLS*, 13.11.69
p.204 Liddle archive – http://yourarchives.nationalarchives.gov.uk/index.
       php?title=Peter_H._Liddle's_1914-18_Personal _Experience_Archives
p.205 'I failed' – Middlebrooke, p.352
       Death's Men – D. Winter, p.16
p.206 du Picq – ibid., p.13

Chapter 4
p.213 London Transport Museum see e.g. *Metro*, 6.8.08
       'influenced culture' – National Curriculum Programme of Study for
       English
       case study – http://www.qca.org.uk/14-19/6th-form-schools/index_
       1256.htm
p.216 Western Front Association – WFA website home page
p.218 Beckett – *Guardian* review, 17.5.08
p.221 Patch on 11 November – Patch and van Emden, p.203
p.224 Goodwin – Allingham and Goodwin, p.154
p.226 'literally waiting' – ibid., p.156
       'there was a world' – ibid., p.157
p.227 'Ask men' – ibid., p.160
p.228 'War's stupid' – BBC News Channel, 4.8.04,
       http://news.bbc.co.uk/1/hi/uk/3534068.stm
       Roberts and Charles – Arthur, *Last Post*, pp.144, 191
       Finnigan – ibid., p.105
       Patch – Patch and van Emden, pp.203, 188–9
       Withers – Arthur, *Last Post*, p.88
p.233 Hughes – *Daily Telegraph*, 20.11.08
p.236 Allingham – quoted in epigraph to Patch and van Emden
p.238 'While a lot' – Patch and van Emden, p.55
p.239 Tucky Mill – ibid., p.18
       Rosemount – ibid., p.23
p.240 'wasn't worth' – ibid., p.28
       'I was content' – ibid., p.30
p.241 'scruffs' – ibid., p.53

p.242 'there was no' – ibid., p.62
p.243 gun weight – ibid., p.73
p.244 'We all knew' – ibid., p.69
p.246 'The Platoon Commander' – War Office manual
      gun team names – *Daily Telegraph*, 12.7.07
p.247 'We were just' – Patch and van Emden, pp.111–12
p.248 'Each louse' – *Private Harry Patch*, BBC TV
      'shovelled' – Patch and van Emden, p.112
      'It doesn't matter' – ibid., p.74
p.249 'Anyone who tells' – ibid., p.105
p.250 'watching the water' – ibid., p.74
      'The shelling' – ibid., p.106
p.251 'You couldn't deal' – ibid.
p.254 wounded soldier – ibid., p.94
p.255 'I couldn't kill' – *The Last Tommy*, BBC TV
p.256 'The period' – Patch and van Emden, p.103
      Haig – ibid., p.102
p.257 wounding – ibid., p.109
p.259 'there was nothing' – ibid., p.203
      'My reaction' – ibid., p.111
      'I never once' – ibid., p.116
p.261 'The war might' – ibid., p.147
      'thoroughly disillusioned' – ibid., p.137
      'I'm positive' – ibid., p.94
      'faith in the Church' – ibid., p.137
p.262 'anything to do' – ibid., p.196
      'kept in touch' – ibid., p.203
p.264 'some big noise' – ibid., p.149
      'I don't remember' – ibid., p.154
p.268 'To be honest' – ibid., pp.193–4
p.269 'they didn't die' – ibid., p.195
p.270 flash – *The Last Tommy*, BBC TV
      'slept through' – Patch and van Emden, p.197
p.271 'I don't know why' – ibid., p.200
      'I looked' – ibid.
      'I don't feel' – ibid., p.201
p.272 Patch and Kuentz – *The Last Tommy*, BBC TV

p.275 'It means' – interview with Tony Patterson for Western Front
Association: http://www.westernfrontassociation.com/great-war-people/
48-brothers-arms/675-charles-kuentz.html
'Charles was' – Patch and van Emden, p.201

p.276 'simply a military show' – van Emden, p.356
remembrance – Patch and van Emden, p.203
Kuentz – Patterson interview, *supra*
'usually all people' – Patch and van Emden, p.199

p.277 'wheelchair access' – CWGC Debt of Honour website

p.278 Clayton's words – Patch and van Emden, p.202

p.281 *FHM* – www.fhm.com/news/harry-patch-111-year-old-fhm-columnist-
has-died-20090727

p.282 'never hesitated' – Patch and van Emden, p.216

p.283 'everybody involved' – BBC News Channel, 16.8.06:
http://news.bbc.co.uk/1/hi/uk/4796579.stm

p.284 'who had seen action' – Patch and van Emden, p.204

p.285 *Légion d'honneur* – BBC News Channel, 9.3.09: http://news.
bbc.co.uk/1/hi/england/somerset/7931817.stm

p.287 state funeral – Patch and van Emden, p.204
'a simple, private funeral' – http://news.bbc.co.uk/1/hi/uk/8185693.stm
'He could have dealt'– ibid.

p.288 Ross – ibid.

p.289 'an ambassador' – live funeral coverage, BBC News Channel, 6.8.09

p.291 'No one else' – http://news.bbc.co.uk/1/hi/uk/8185693.stm
'all that's best' – Sir Richard Dannatt, BBC News Channel, 6.8.09
'in a direct line' – Peter Barton, ibid.
'I didn't want to' – Patch and van Emden, p.59

p.294 Dye – Allingham and Goodwin, p.222
'breathed life' – ibid., p.201
teacher – BBC Television news, 17.6.09

p.295 Sorley – Sorley, p.78

ACKNOWLEDGEMENTS

My first thanks go to Nicholas Pearson at Fourth Estate, who in April 2006 suggested I should write this book. At the time there were several British veterans of the First World War alive, and the logistics of writing a book that placed the last of them at its centre were always going to be complicated. Nicholas and my agent, David Miller, discussed with me at length what sort of book it should be, sorted out a publication plan, and then left me to get on with writing it without making too many anxious enquiries as to its progress. Both they and Mark Richards at Fourth Estate, who also saw the book through the press in double-quick time, read the book in draft and in its near-final version, and I am very grateful for their many comments and suggestions. My thanks also go to Eleanor Goymer, Julian Humphries and Rebecca McEwan at Fourth Estate; to Alex Goodwin at Rogers, Coleridge and White, who read the book in its final draft and pointed out several mistakes and weaknesses; to Ian Paten for his meticulous and speedy copy-editing; and to Ben Murphy for his comprehensive index.

I took a decision right from the start that I would not attempt to meet or interview any of the veterans. This was partly because my principal concern was with the notion of a Last Veteran rather than with individuals, but also because I saw no point in bothering the survivors in their extreme old age with questions they had already answered in countless books, television programmes and newspaper interviews. While researching this book both Henry Allingham and Harry Patch published excellent autobiographies in collaboration with Dennis Goodwin and Richard van Emden respectively. I am indebted to both books, but in particular – as it turned out – to *The Last Fighting Tommy*.

As always, my first and most severe editor was Christopher Potter, whose careful reading of the book led to innumerable improvements in its structure and content. Special thanks also go to Mark Bostridge, who – enthusiastic, knowledgeable, and undaunted by torrential rain – proved the perfect companion on a trip to the Somme. Like him, other friends and colleagues alerted me to news items about First World War veterans from all around the world; supplied me with all manner of ideas and information; listened patiently while I talked about the book, and otherwise helped me during the three years it took to research and write it. In particular, I'd like to record my gratitude to: Frank Ahern and a group of Upper VIth History and English Literature pupils at Canford School, Adam Bager, Edward Behrens, Thomas Blaikie, Iain Burnside, Andreas Campomar, Miranda Carter, Niladri Chatterjee and a group of MA students at Kalyani University, Timothy d'Arch Smith, Santanu Das, Richard Davenport-Hines, Paul Fierlinger, Chris Fletcher, David Gelber, Georgina Hammick, J. Casey Hammond, Selina Hastings, Christopher Hawtree, Alison Hennegan, Christie Hickman, Sam Leith, Candia McWilliam, Wendy Moffat, Neel Mukherjee, Gina Rozner, Bill Rutkowski, Alice Sielle, Lynne Truss, Frances Wilson.

Lines from 'For the Fallen' are reproduced by kind permission of The Society of Authors as the Literary Representative of the Estate of Laurence Binyon. Lines from Gilbert Frankau's 'Only an Officer' are reproduced by kind permission of AP Watt Ltd on behalf of Timothy d'Arch Smith. Extracts from the poems of Siegfried

Sassoon, copyright © Siegfried Sassoon, are reproduced by kind permission of the Estate of George Sassoon. Country Joe and the Fish's 'I-Feel-Like-I'm-Fixin'-To-Die Rag' copyright © Joe McDonald, 1965, renewed 1993 by Alkatraz Corner Music, BMI, used by kind permission. Every effort has been made to trace copyright holders and the publisher would be pleased to hear from any that have been overlooked so that corrections and due acknowledgement can be made in future editions.

Lastly, I could not have written this book without the efficient staff and the unmatched resources of the London Library.

INDEX

Index

Index